GOYA TO IMPRESSIONISM

Masterpieces from the
Oskar Reinhart Collection

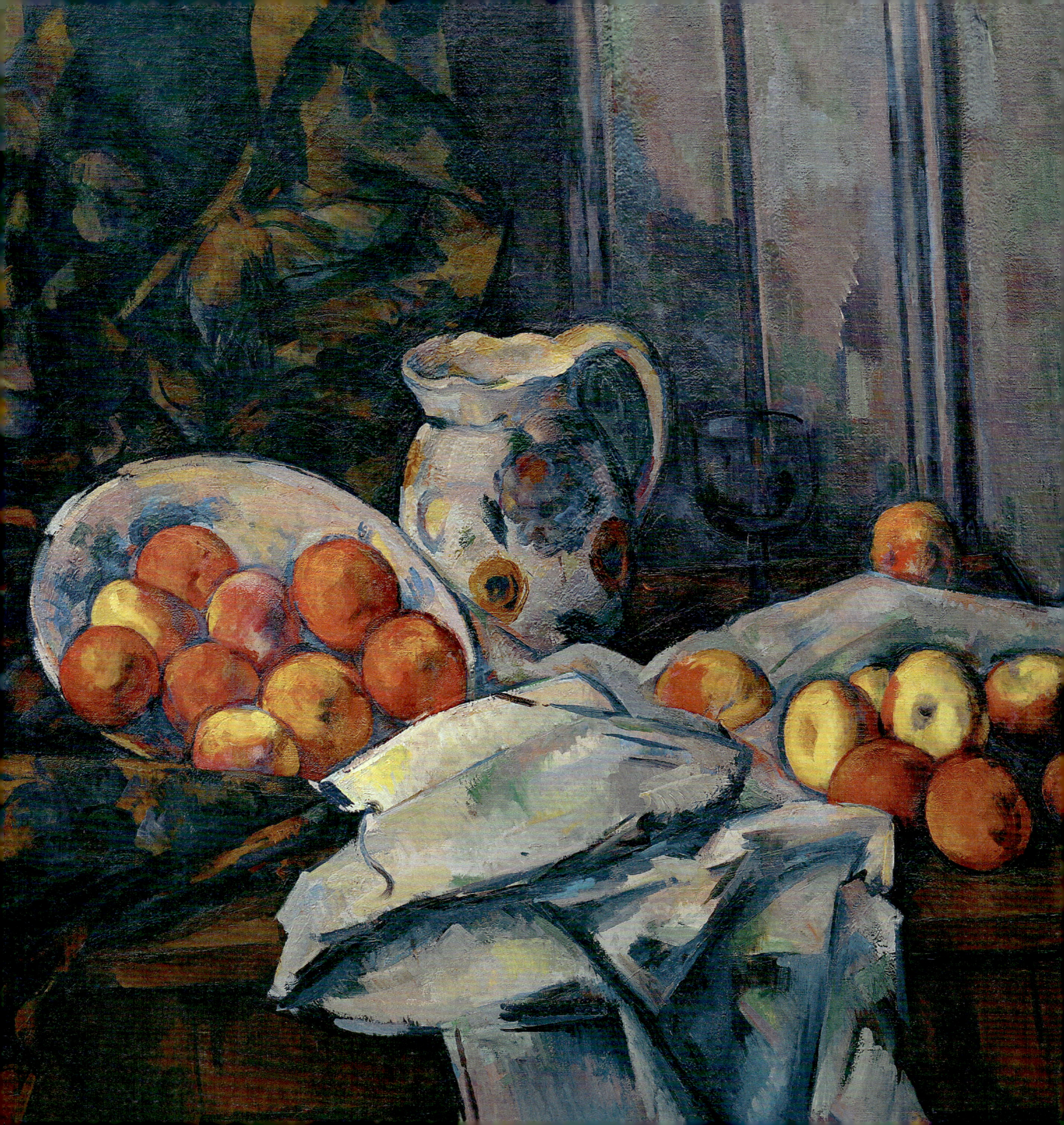

GOYA TO IMPRESSIONISM

Masterpieces from the Oskar Reinhart Collection

Edited by Ketty Gottardo

Essays by Kerstin Richter and Katja Baumhoff
Entries by Ketty Gottardo, Chloe Nahum, Karen Serres,
Rachel Sloan and Barnaby Wright

The Courtauld

in association with
Paul Holberton Publishing

First published to accompany the exhibition

GOYA TO IMPRESSIONISM
Masterpieces from the
Oskar Reinhart Collection

The Courtauld Gallery, London
14 February – 26 May 2025

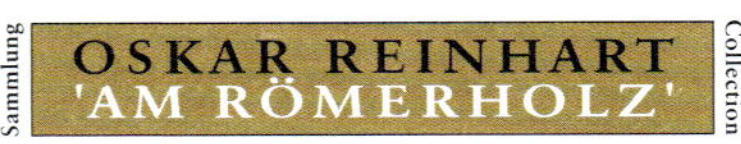

The Courtauld Gallery is supported by
Research England.

The exhibition is presented in the Denise Coates
Exhibition Galleries.

This exhibition has been made possible by the
provision of insurance through the Government
Indemnity Scheme. The Courtauld would like to
thank HM Government for providing indemnity,
and extends its thanks to the Department for
Digital Culture, Media and Sport and to Arts
Council England for administering the scheme.

Kerstin Richter is Director of the Oskar Reinhart
Collection 'Am Römerholz', Winterthur.

Katja Baumhoff is Deputy Director of the Oskar
Reinhart Collection 'Am Römerholz', Winterthur.

Ketty Gottardo is Martin Halusa Senior Curator
of Drawings at The Courtauld, London.

Text © authors 2025

ISBN 978-1-913645-81-6

British Library Catalogue in Publishing Data

A CIP record of this publication is available from
the British Library

Produced by Paul Holberton Publishing
paulholberton.com

Designed by Laura Parker

Distributed by Yale University Press, New Haven
and London

Printed by 4-Flying Srl trading as e-Graphic,
Verona, Italy

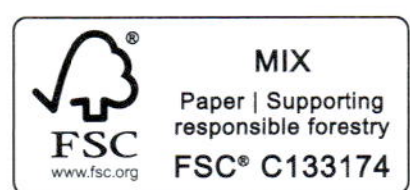

Front cover: Cat. 24 (detail)
Frontispiece: Cat. 12 (detail)
Back cover: Cat. 8 (detail)

Contents

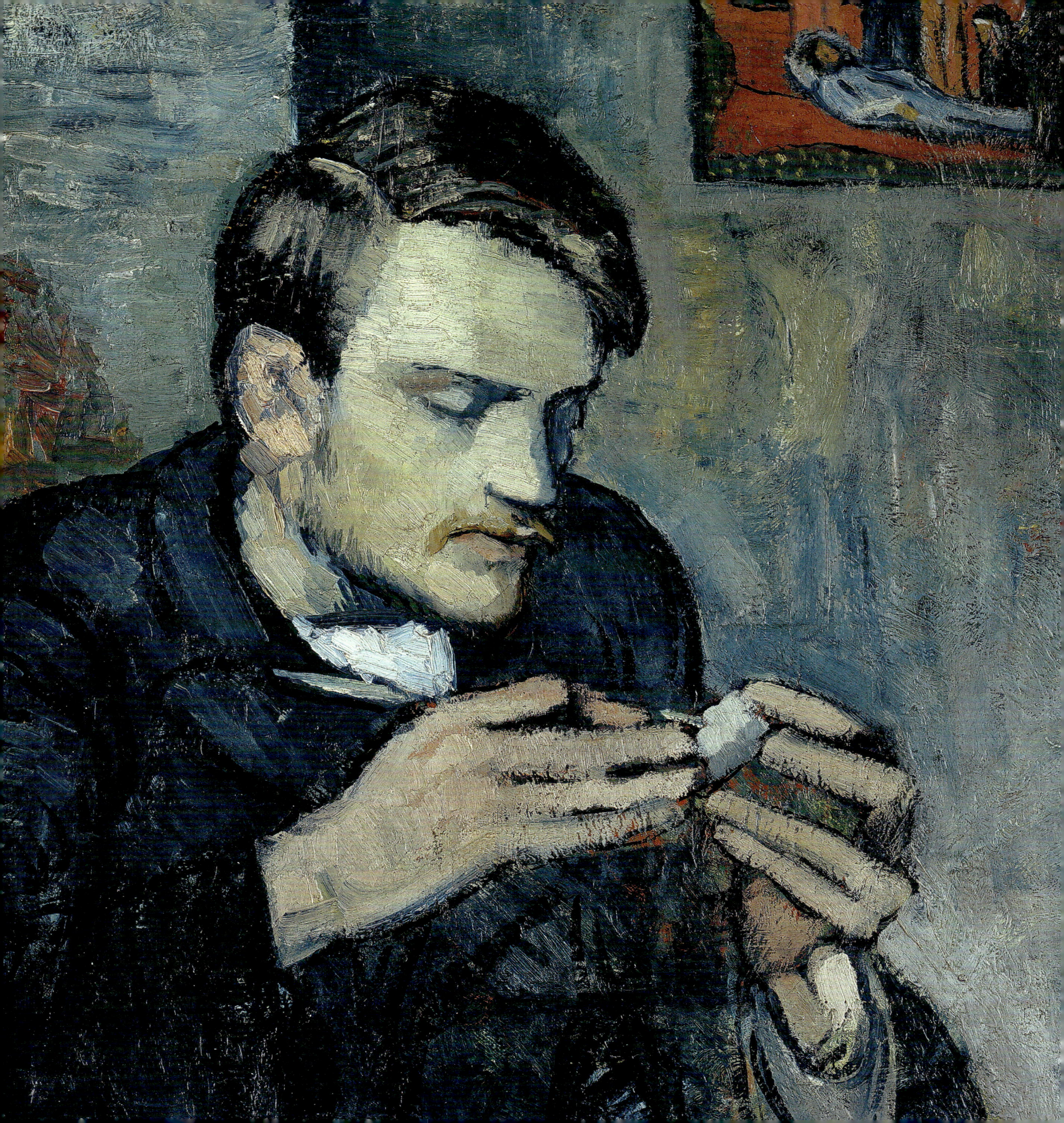

Title Partner's Message

We are pleased to sponsor *The Griffin Catalyst Exhibition: Goya to Impressionism. Masterpieces from the Oskar Reinhart Collection*, the third in The Griffin Catalyst Series of major exhibitions at the Courtauld Gallery. Griffin Catalyst, the civic engagement initiative of Citadel Founder and CEO Kenneth C. Griffin, partners with world-renowned cultural institutions to increase access to art and history that inspires and challenges visitors of all backgrounds. We congratulate our partners at The Courtauld for bringing this remarkable exhibition to life, and we hope *The Griffin Catalyst Exhibition: Goya to Impressionism. Masterpieces from the Oskar Reinhart Collection* inspires and delights. This partnership is part of Griffin Catalyst's broader mission to support vibrant communities and ensure that vital arts and cultural institutions have the resources they need to thrive.

Exhibition Supporters

The Courtauld would like to thank the following supporters for their generosity:

Title Partner

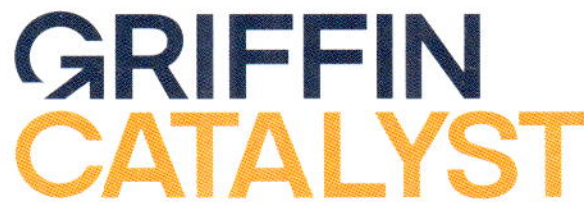

Supported by
Kenneth C. Griffin

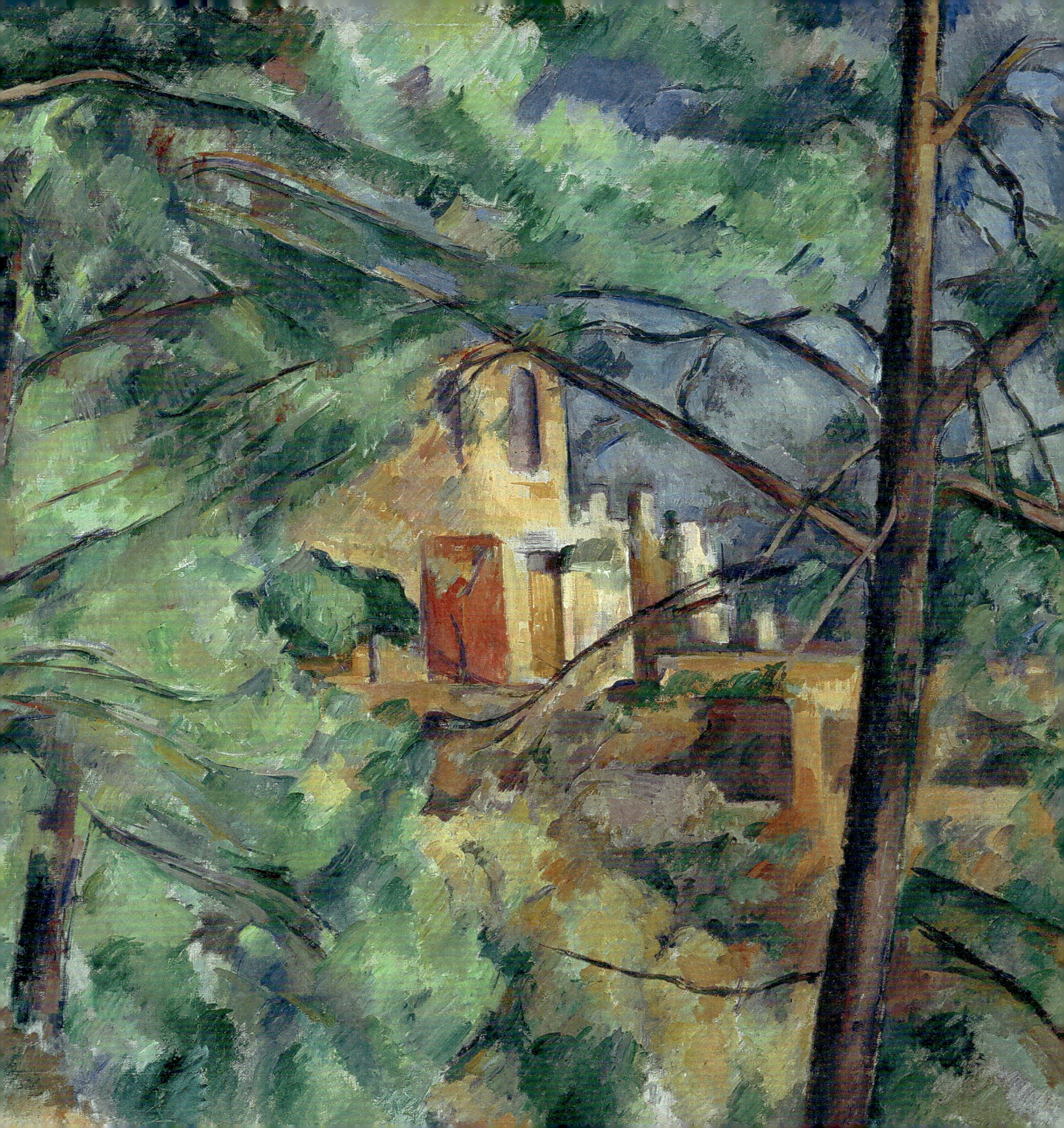

Directors' Preface

Goya to Impressionism. Masterpieces from the Oskar Reinhart Collection is an exhibition that we hope will surprise and delight, thanks to the extraordinary quality of its contents. It is also an exhibition that offers the unusual opportunity to look in two very different ways at the paintings and watercolours gathered together for this display.

First of all, this jewel of a show gives us the chance to appreciate, one by one, an astonishing group of nineteenth-century pictures by some of the greatest European – and particularly French – artists of the period. These masterpieces, lovingly assembled across the first decades of the twentieth century by the great Swiss collector Oskar Reinhart, and donated by him to the Confederation of Switzerland, have been generously lent by the museum housed in Reinhart's former home, the villa 'Am Römerholz' in Winterthur, Switzerland, during a period in which the museum is closed for refurbishment. They have never been exhibited together in the UK. Due to the lending restrictions issued by Oskar Reinhart, this exhibition is therefore a unique and unprecedented event.

These paintings offer a feast of visual pleasures, and the chance to deepen our understanding of their celebrated creators: the versatility of Renoir, for instance, as he moves deftly between the different genres of still-life, portraiture and domestic subject-painting; the lucidity of Van Gogh, as he maps the spaces of the Arles hospital in which he found himself confined after a catastrophic bout of mental illness; Manet's late fascination with the enigmatic figural juxtapositions, table-top still-lives, and decorative paraphernalia of Parisian cafes and brasseries, as captured in his *Au café* of 1878, produced just five years before his last, iconic image of another such scene, The Courtauld's own *A Bar at the Folies-Bergère*.

Thanks to its setting, *Goya to Impressionism* also encourages us to think about the pictures from Winterthur in quite another way: that is, as part of a picture collection that offers a strikingly close parallel to that built up in the 1920s by Samuel Courtauld himself, one of the founders of The Courtauld. In her essay in this catalogue, Katja Baumhoff provides an intriguing analysis of the ways in which Oskar Reinhart and Samuel Courtauld, who were born less than a decade apart, and who we know

met each other in 1932, pursued a remarkably similar pattern of acquisitions, particularly in the 1920s, and particularly in relation to their shared passion for Impressionist and Post-Impressionist art.

Visitors to *Goya to Impressionism*, rather wonderfully, have the chance to explore this connection at first-hand. Once they have enjoyed the pictures from the Reinhart Collection 'Am Römerholz' on display in The Courtauld's Denise Coates Galleries, they can stroll into the immediately adjacent LVMH Great Room, where paintings from Samuel Courtauld's own famous collection are permanently on show. Taking this walk offers the opportunity to directly compare the works of Renoir, Van Gogh, Manet, Cezanne, Sisley, Monet, Gauguin and Toulouse-Lautrec found in both collections, and to further enrich one's knowledge and appreciation of these artists' outputs. At the same time, this walk also encourages us to compare Reinhart's and Courtauld's tastes and motivations as collectors, and to think afresh about how these two individuals, one British, one Swiss, found themselves echoing each other in their ambitions as collectors and their patterns of picture-buying. As well as offering an exemplary form of Anglo-European cultural collaboration in the present day, the exhibition testifies to the fascinating parallels between two art collectors of the early twentieth century.

In offering this once in a lifetime opportunity to enjoy in London some of the most exciting paintings from the Oskar Reinhart Collection 'Am Römerholz', The Courtauld expresses its heartfelt thanks to colleagues in Winterthur. Both institutions share the hope that visitors to the exhibition will be inspired by these works and be prompted to learn more about the collection from which they derive. The Oskar Reinhart Collection 'Am Römerholz' looks forward to welcoming visitors in 2026, after the completion of the museum's refurbishment. We hope that new and returning visitors will enjoy the richness of the collection and the beauty of the museum's park setting.

PROFESSOR MARK HALLETT
Märit Rausing Director, The Courtauld Institute of Art

KERSTIN RICHTER
Director, Oskar Reinhart Collection 'Am Römerholz'

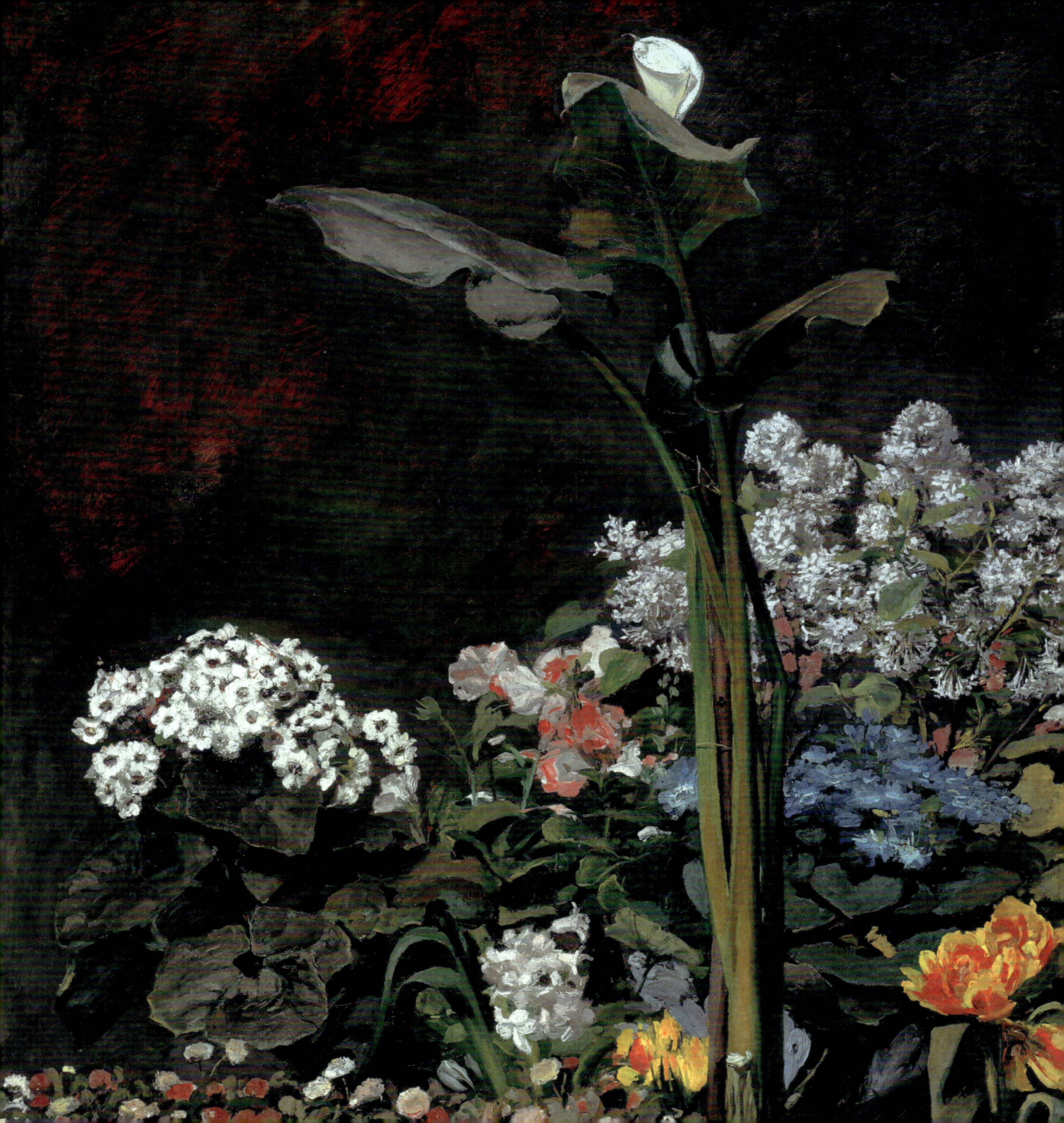

Foreword

We are honored and delighted to share with audiences in the United Kingdom this fabulous selection of masterpieces from the Oskar Reinhart Collection 'Am Römerholz', one of Switzerland's cultural jewels. The collection was formed by Oskar Reinhart (1885–1965) and is displayed in his former home, the villa 'Am Römerholz' in Winterthur, near Zurich. 'Am Römerholz' offers visitors an unforgettable experience: a collection of supreme quality presented on a personal scale in beautiful gallery spaces. The Oskar Reinhart Collection 'Am Römerholz' is a preeminently important museum of the Swiss Confederation, but in its character, as a much-loved single collection, it also manages to engage visitors on an individual level that is distinctive and memorable. Alongside great early works, such as Pieter Bruegel the Elder's *The Adoration of the Kings in the Snow* of 1563, the collection's centre of gravity is French art of the nineteenth century, especially the Impressionist and Post-Impressionist artists whose work is the focus of this exhibition.

This is the first time that such an important selection of treasures from the Oskar Reinhart Collection 'Am Römerholz' has left Switzerland, and the Courtauld Gallery may be considered a very purposeful host for this unique occasion. Oskar Reinhart and Samuel Courtauld – who met in London in 1932 – both formed the greater part of their collections in the 1920s, and the similarities in their taste is immediately apparent: the centrality of Cezanne, for example; the exceptionally important autobiographical Arles works by Van Gogh; the two celebrated and closely related *café-concert* scenes by Manet; the parallel works by Toulouse-Lautrec, Daumier and others. Both collectors more or less concluded their chronologies with single 1901 Blue-period paintings by Picasso. But there are differences too, of taste and of formation, with Reinhart perhaps leaning more to the intellectual and artistic world of Berlin, of Hugo von Tschudi and Julius Meier-Graefe, and Courtauld to Paris and the few proponents of modern French art in Britain. Both collectors saw Impressionism in terms of the continuity of the great tradition of Western painting. Most importantly, both believed profoundly in the necessity of art for society, and each formed his collection for the public good. It was this principle that led Reinhart to establish the villa 'Am Römerholz' as a museum of the Swiss Confederation, along with many other benefactions in Winterthur.

This exhibition is unprecedented and we are deeply grateful to our colleagues at 'Am Römerholz' for placing their trust in The Courtauld. I want to record my heartfelt personal thanks to Kerstin Richter, Director, and Katja Baumhoff, Deputy Director. Their warmth and generosity embodies the spirit of 'Am Römerholz'. Working with them and their colleagues has been an unalloyed pleasure. The Courtauld is also immensely grateful to Carine Bachmann, Director, Federal Office of Culture; Yves Fischer, Deputy Director, Federal Office of Culture; and Benno Widmer, Head of Department of Museums and Collections Section. Without their support this exhibition would not have been possible. Equally, we are very grateful to have had the support of the Embassy of Switzerland in the United Kingdom, and I would like to thank in particular His Excellency Markus Leitner, Alexandra Müller-Crepon and Jonas Georgsson. House of Winterthur and Switzerland Tourism contributed generously to the preparation of the exhibition.

For their support and commitment in realising this project and for providing critical expertise, I extend my warm thanks to Fabian Steiner, whose role as Registrar was essential, Sabine Gasser, Hanspeter Marty, Harry Joelson, Viola Moeckel, Michaela Ritter, as well as Bertalan Bozsanyi, Andreas Fürst, Isabelle Hagen, Martin Lanz, Nazmi Sollar, Helena Pelizzatti and Valentina Zingg.

My colleague Ketty Gottardo played an important role in first proposing this exhibition and I am most grateful to her; she is also the editor of this catalogue. In addition to insightful essays by Kerstin Richter and Katja Baumhoff, it includes contributions by Chloe Nahum, Karen Serres, Rachel Sloan and Barnaby Wright. They have all also contributed to curating the exhibition. I am grateful to Karin Kyburz, who sourced all the catalogue's images, and to Gerlind May for her translation. Amy Graves has played a central part as the exhibition's Registrar for The Courtauld. Graeme Barraclough, Matthew Thompson and Kate Edmondson have led on conservation and installation.

Thanks are also due Belinda Moore for the exhibition interpretation graphics; Zerlina Hughes and her team at ZNA for lighting; Erica Bolton, Susie Gault and the team at Bolton & Quinn; Paul Holberton, Laura Parker, Ilaria Bernocchi and Kristen Wenger at Paul Holberton Publishing; Enrico Lenti and the team at E-Graphic and Andrea Lutz, curator at the Kunst Museum Winterthur, for his help with images from that collection.

I also wish to acknowledge the contributions of Eleonore de Sibert, Chrissy Baker, Aimee Clark, Beattrys John, Camilla Knight, Stephanie Piechowiak, Margot Sprague-Davies, Savash Djemal, Matthew Hunt, Sian Morris, Jon Ping, Charlotte Yates, Rob Baker, Caitlin Brooker, Fergus Carmichael, Ashleigh Toll, Claire Forman, Anthony Tyrrell, Helen Higgins, Anne Puetz and Catherine Putz.

The position of the Senior Curator of Drawings is funded by Martin Halusa. The Courtauld wishes to express its immense gratitude to him for the ongoing support. The post of one of the exhibition's curators, Dr Barnaby Wright, is funded by Daniel Katz. The Courtauld would like to thank him warmly for his continued generosity. Last but not least, we wish to recognise the Bridget Riley Art Foundation (BRAF) for their generous support. The Bridget Riley Art Foundation Curatorial Fellowship is currently held by Dr Chloe Nahum, who has contributed to research for this exhibition and publication.

Finally, on behalf of The Courtauld I record my thanks to Griffin Catalyst, which is the Title Partner of the exhibition. Kenneth C. Griffin and Griffin Catalyst have played a key part in enabling the Courtauld Gallery's highly successful programme of exhibitions, and we are immensely grateful for Ken's generosity in helping to bring these masterpieces from the Oskar Reinhart Collection 'Am Römerholz' to London.

Kerstin Richter joins me in expressing the hope that visitors will view this exhibition as a compelling invitation to visit Winterthur and see the collection there. The museum will reopen in 2026 and looks forward to welcoming new audiences from the United Kingdom and beyond.

ERNST VEGELIN VAN CLAERBERGEN
Head of the Courtauld Gallery

Cat. 3 (detail)

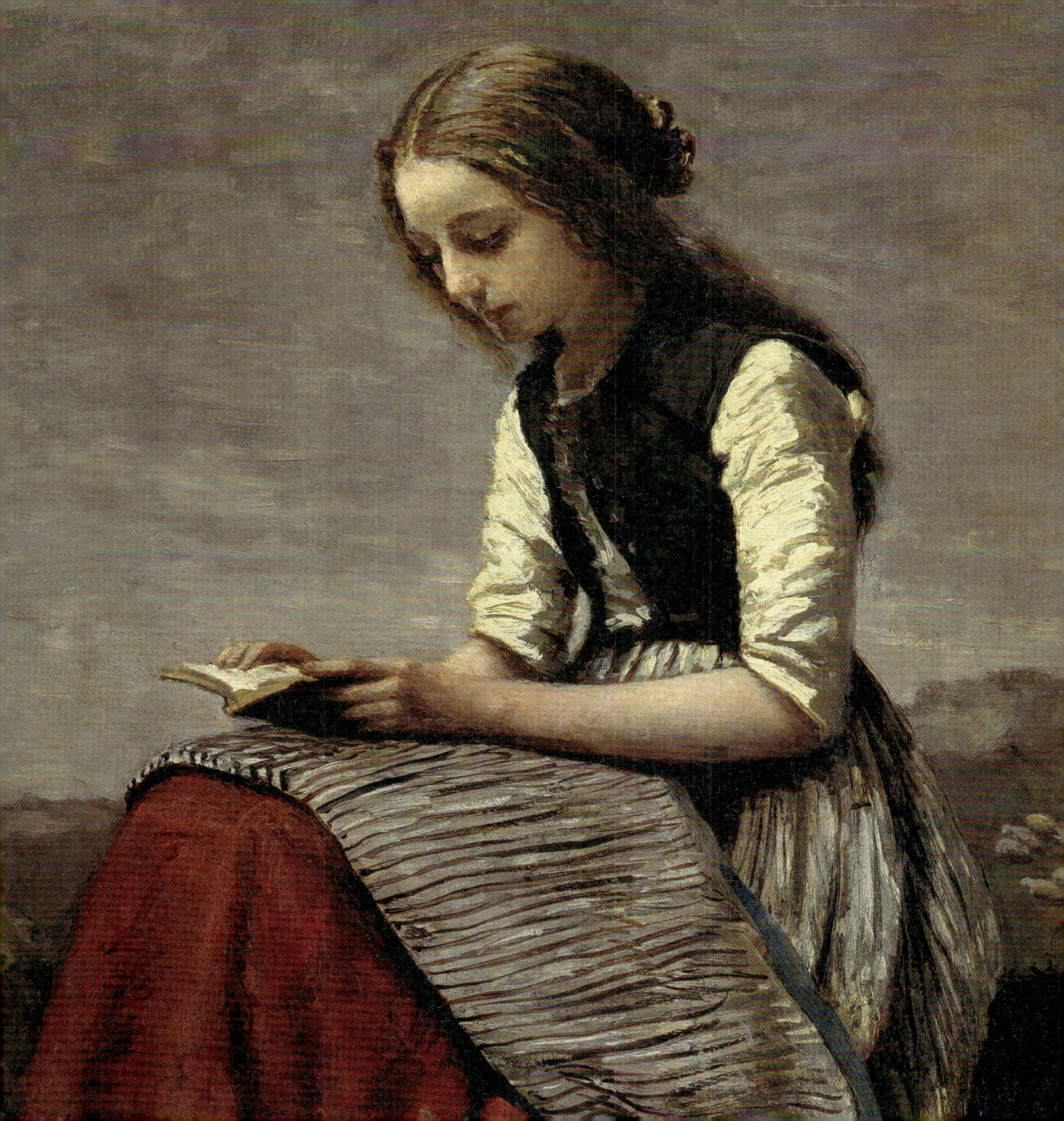

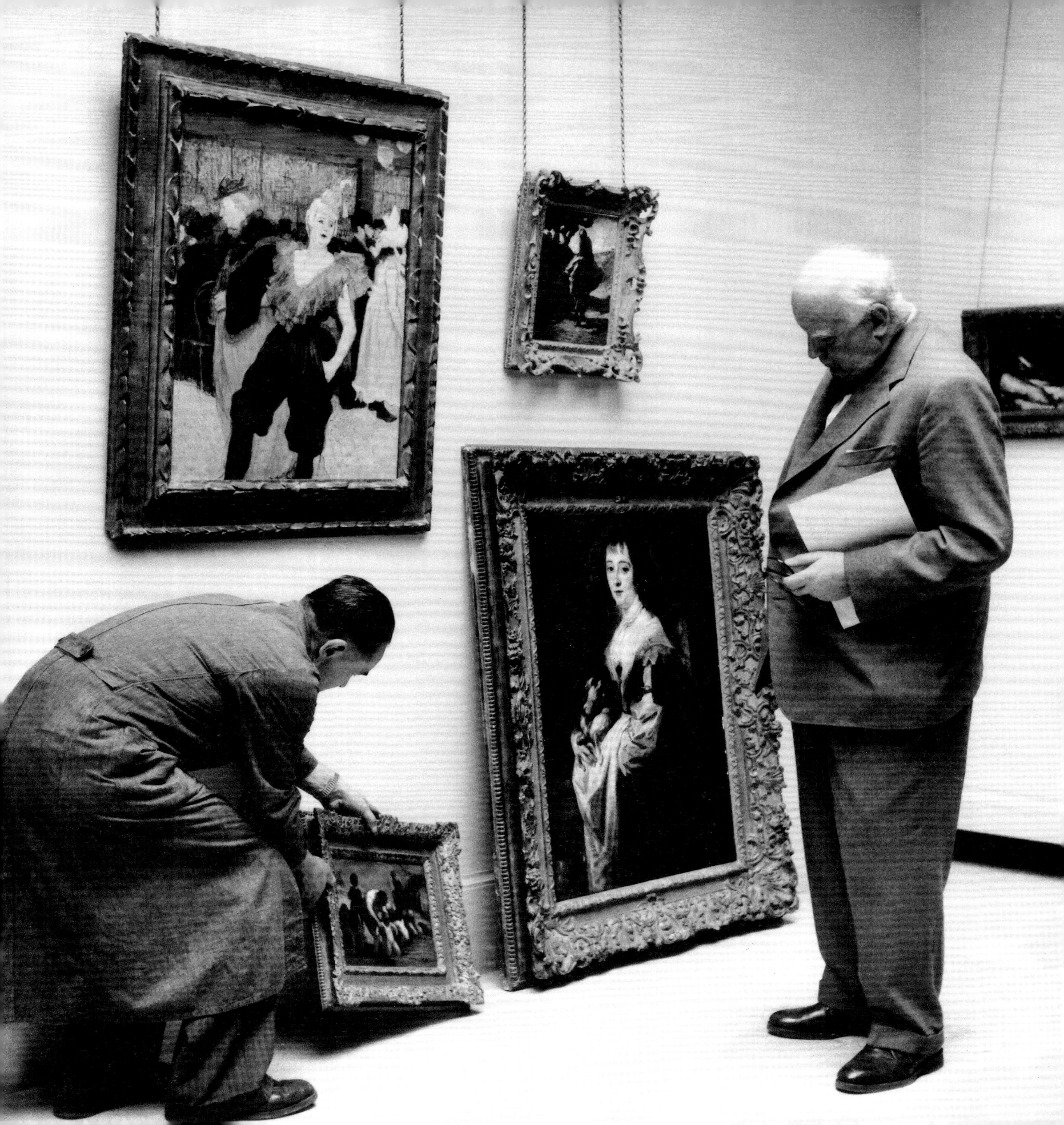

Becoming a Collector: Oskar Reinhart's Artistic Education

Kerstin Richter

Oskar Reinhart (1885–1965) was the fourth son of Theodor and Lilly Reinhart (née Volkart), one of Winterthur's leading families (fig. 2). After their marriage in 1879, Theodor took over the management of Lilly's family's firm, Volkart Brothers. The company relied mainly on the cotton and coffee trade.[1] Theodor succeeded in consolidating the main portion of the business, diversifying it through the establishment of shipping and insurance agencies and expanding its network of branches worldwide. Principally managed from the tranquil Swiss town of Winterthur, in the Canton of Zurich, Volkart Brothers grew into one of the world's leading trading companies, whose core operations remained predominantly international.

Theodor Reinhart believed in continuity, and thus raised his sons to become merchants; this meant that they should complete an apprenticeship in Volkart Brothers. The training included internships in the company's offices in various European capitals, as well as longer stays in one of the Indian branches. After completing their business management training, three of the brothers – Georg, Werner and Oskar – were appointed partners of the firm as early as 1912. The company was now entirely in the hands of two generations of Reinharts.

Theodor, who continued to be at the head of the company, was the embodiment of the typical Hanseatic merchant: social and cultural duties were a necessary part of his life. He supported younger Swiss and German visual artists, such as Carl Hofer, Robert Zünd, Hermann Haller and Ferdinand Hodler, at times through scholarships or acquisitions of their works.[2] This was not a purely private pursuit – he saw it as a public duty. In 1915 he funded an entire wing of Winterthur's new art museum and bequeathed his entire collection to be displayed there. Looking back, Oskar Reinhart later noted that 'to be able to grow up among artists and to be educated by them to look – that was the great stroke of luck of my youth'.[3]

Like his brothers, Oskar joined the company after completing his schooling in 1904. In his early youth he had written poems and novellas. He was also interested in the performing arts, and in particular in musical performance. His older brothers had broader interests in these areas – Werner, for instance, became an important patron of music, while Hans became a poet and patron of the theatre. Oskar, meanwhile, inherited Theodor's love for the visual arts, and developed this interest into a longstanding commitment to collecting. Initially, he turned his attention to the same artists his father admired. Art capitals such as Berlin and Paris held a special attraction for this inquisitive young man, in contrast to the faraway destinations of his apprenticeship, such as Thalassery and Chennai (formerly known as Tellicherry and Madras) in India. During his stays abroad in the company's European branches, therefore, Oskar took the opportunity to visit local museums and art galleries. Through his social connections he also gained access to private collections, as well as to the print rooms of public museums. Oskar kept meticulous records of these visits, noting his thoughts and impressions in his diaries and in the many letters he sent to his parents, brothers and friends.

While the commercial training was a necessary duty, Oskar's artistic interests and desire to achieve something significant in this field increasingly occupied his time. His older brother Georg, who succeeded their father within

1. Oskar Reinhart (at right) rehanging the collection, 1955. The Swiss Confederation, Federal Office of Culture, Archive of the Oskar Reinhart Collection 'Am Römerholz', Winterthur

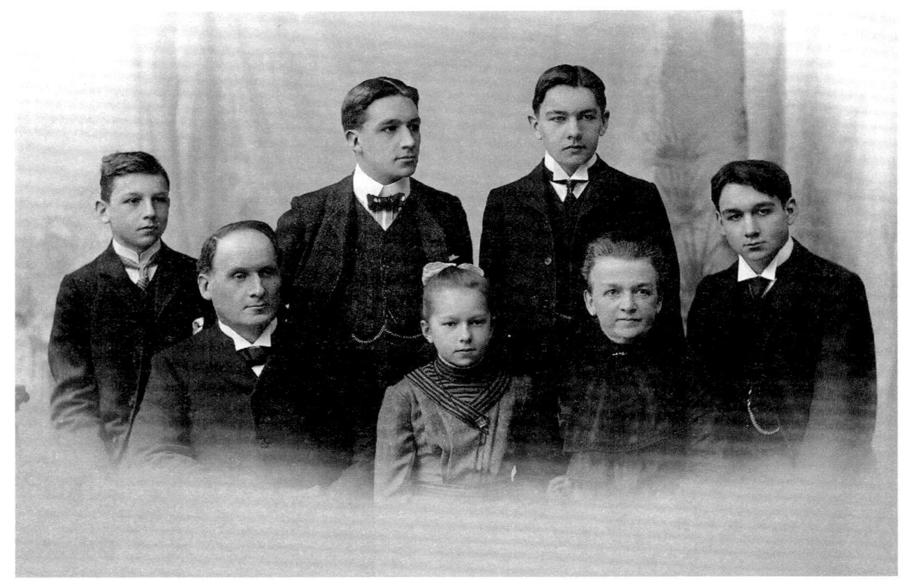

2. Theodor and Lilly Reinhart (née Volkart) with their children. At the back (from left) are the brothers Oskar, Georg, Werner and Hans, at the centre is their sister Emma, undated. The Swiss Confederation, Federal Office of Culture, Archive of the Oskar Reinhart Collection 'Am Römerholz', Winterthur

the company, also shared Oskar's interests. Georg would later assemble a magnificent collection of Asian, nineteenth-century French and, in particular, Expressionist art that, like their father, he would eventually bequeath to public institutions.[4] With Georg, but also with Werner and Hans, who collected paintings, although to a lesser extent, Oskar was able to exchange ideas and discuss the artistic qualities of the works he saw. These epistolary exchanges between the brothers reflect Oskar's growing passion for art. The letters show his passionate and, at the same time, systematic approach, charting the development and refinement of his aesthetic sense and his search for the intrinsic artistic qualities in the works that interested him. The 1906 *Deutsche Jahrhundert-Ausstellung* (German Centennial Exhibition) in Berlin, curated by Alfred Lichtwark and Hugo von Tschudi, was to have a lasting effect on Oskar Reinhart. Then, and in the years that followed, museum 'reformers' such as Lichtwark and Tschudi promoted Impressionism, in contrast to the current trends towards traditional and Romantic art, and this too influenced Oskar's own collecting ambitions.[5]

Collecting as a Life's Work

Oskar Reinhart formulated his ideas about building a collection early on, but initially, given the modest means granted by his father, he was only able to assemble a group of prints. He took as a model the acquisitions pursued by the major European print rooms, such as the British Museum, which he visited regularly during his apprenticeship years.

An approach independent of his father's taste was emerging: prints by the American artist James McNeill Whistler (1834–1903) and the Scottish Muirhead Bone (1876–1953) – the latter Reinhart's contemporary – were particularly well represented among his acquisitions, as were those by Honoré Daumier (1808–1879), and old masters such as Rembrandt (1606–1669). He initially wanted to collect broadly within the European schools. Yet, even at this early stage, Reinhart noted that he wanted to limit himself to a manageable number of prints, privileging quality over quantity. Despite repeatedly expressing his desire to limit the collection to 500/600 sheets, it ultimately comprised a much larger number. The significant increase was not least due to his commitment to the establishment of a *Kupferstichkabinett* (print room) in the Kunst Museum Winterthur, which was newly built in 1915. In his view, this should withstand comparison with other graphic collections at similar institutions.

In those same years Reinhart made his first contacts with the international art trade, as he acquired his first Impressionist painting in 1912: a small Renoir from the Galerie Durand-Ruel in Paris.[6] This was to remain the exception for several years, as his funds did not yet allow more significant purchases. Instead, he sometimes tried – but failed – to persuade his father to buy what he had 'discovered', as was the case with works by Pissarro (1830–1903) and Sisley (1839–1899) from the renowned Galerie Paul Cassirer in Berlin. Despite not having the means to buy very expensive artworks, Oskar continued to familiarise himself with the art market, as well as with the collectors, curators and directors who at the time were having a significant impact in reforming museums. He immersed himself in specialist literature and publications by renowned art theorists. In particular, Julius Meier-Graefe's groundbreaking *History of the Development of Modern Art* (*Entwicklungsgeschichte der modernen Kunst*), first published in 1904, became his main reference.[7] Following his 'guiding star', Reinhart drafted a plan for his ideal collection that he would pursue through precise acquisitions until the end of his life.

After the death of his father in 1919, Oskar Reinhart's financial resources grew significantly, allowing him to expand his ambitions for his new acquisitions programme. He began by searching the art market for specific masterpieces by selected artists – the so-called 'pillars of modern painting' according to Meier-Graefe: Édouard Manet (1832–1893), first and foremost, then Paul Cezanne (1839–1906) and Pierre-Auguste Renoir (1841–1919). In doing so, Reinhart acted independently, although influenced by other Winterthur collectors such as Hedy (née Bühler, 1873– 1952) and her husband Arthur Hahnloser (1870–1936), and Hedy's cousin Richard Bühler (1879–1967). He was not interested either in the Nabis, nor the Fauves, nor in works by his contemporaries. Despite pursuing his own path as a collector, he also exchanged ideas with others, especially his brother Georg, who had expanded his own collection of French art during the 1910s.

This new financial freedom allowed Reinhart to harbour even bigger plans, to shift from a domestic collection to a public picture gallery. This represented a further development in his aspiration to grow his profile from private collector to important public patron. In 1922 he mooted the idea of a future 'rather large-scale picture gallery' as an 'addition to the local museum'.[8] The character of this project is clearly expressed here; however, this was not intended to compete with the endeavours of the Kunst Museum Winterthur and its Kunstverein, the association of private members who supported it. Rather, Reinhart's aim was

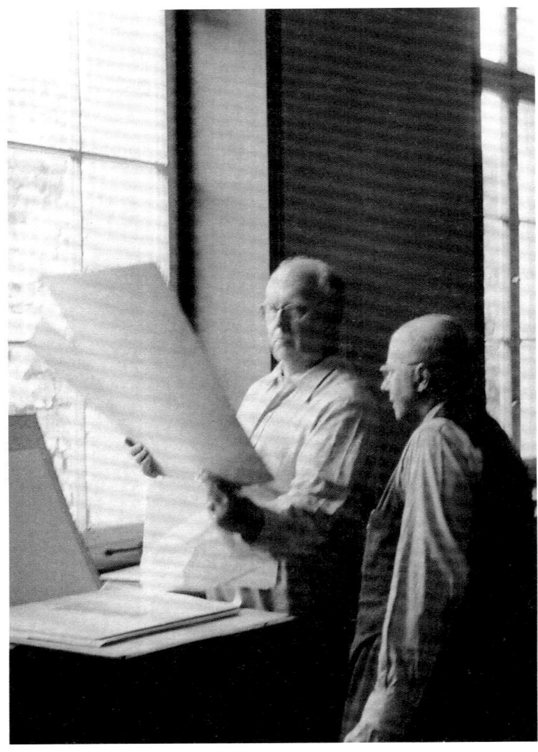

3. Oskar Reinhart (left) and the art dealer Fritz Nathan, 1942. The Swiss Confederation, Federal Office of Culture, Archive of the Oskar Reinhart Collection 'Am Römerholz', Winterthur

twofold: to build a collection that felt complete and in tune with his interests, and that was not represented in the museum of the city.

Right from the start, the idea of the greater good was profoundly entwined with his private pursuits. Reinhart himself noted that he saw his 'duty to serve others with my knowledge, my work and my possessions'.[9]

The economic upheavals in the wake of the First World War and the subsequent global economic crisis meant that circumstances changed. Fortunes were tragically reversed, and many dismantled collections came on the market. Drawing on the company's business performance, and above all on his well-honed eye for masterpieces, as well as on his contacts, Reinhart's collection grew significantly in the 1920s. He generally preferred to negotiate directly with collectors rather than art dealers, or through loyal intermediaries such as Carl Montag (1880–1956) or Fritz Nathan (1895–1972) (fig. 3).

Each new object not only had to work on its own, but also as part of the overall ensemble. It had to enrich the collection by stimulating comparisons and improving knowledge about art. To be able to make a judgement about the true artistic quality of an artwork, after initial negotiations conducted by intermediaries in which the price range would be fixed, Reinhart would usually inspect it in person. Only then was a final decision made. This approach meant an increase in travels, and time, to discuss, view and negotiate his acquisitions. This had obvious repercussions on the business activities of the company. After discussing it with his brothers, he eventually withdrew from the operative side of the business on 1 July 1924 and became a silent partner, finally able to devote himself fully to his life's interest.

A Campaign of Major Acquisitions

A year earlier, however, Oskar Reinhart had succeeded in making a spectacular acquisition that exemplifies his collecting policy. Through his network, and before other competitors, he had learned of the liquidation of the group of Impressionist works belonging to Wilhelm Hansen (1868–1936), one of Europe's most important ensembles.[10] He knew the Danish collector personally and visited him in Copenhagen; among the paintings were several that Reinhart coveted. Through an intermediary, Alfred Gold (1874–1958), who was primarily active in Scandinavia, Reinhart was able to secure the right of first choice; he travelled immediately to Copenhagen and selected twelve paintings at once – the 'Pearls of the Hansen Collection'[11] – with seven more to follow later. This acquisition was an important milestone in the establishment of a collection of international significance that, thanks to the significant number of high quality works, could pride itself in showcasing 'decisive accents and eternal values'.[12] An acquisition on such a large scale would not happen again, but this did not deter Reinhart, as his main concern remained quality over quantity. Resources, though not infinite, were available; he restricted acquisitions by sharpening the selection criteria even further, refining his collection 'like a gemstone' to make it unique.

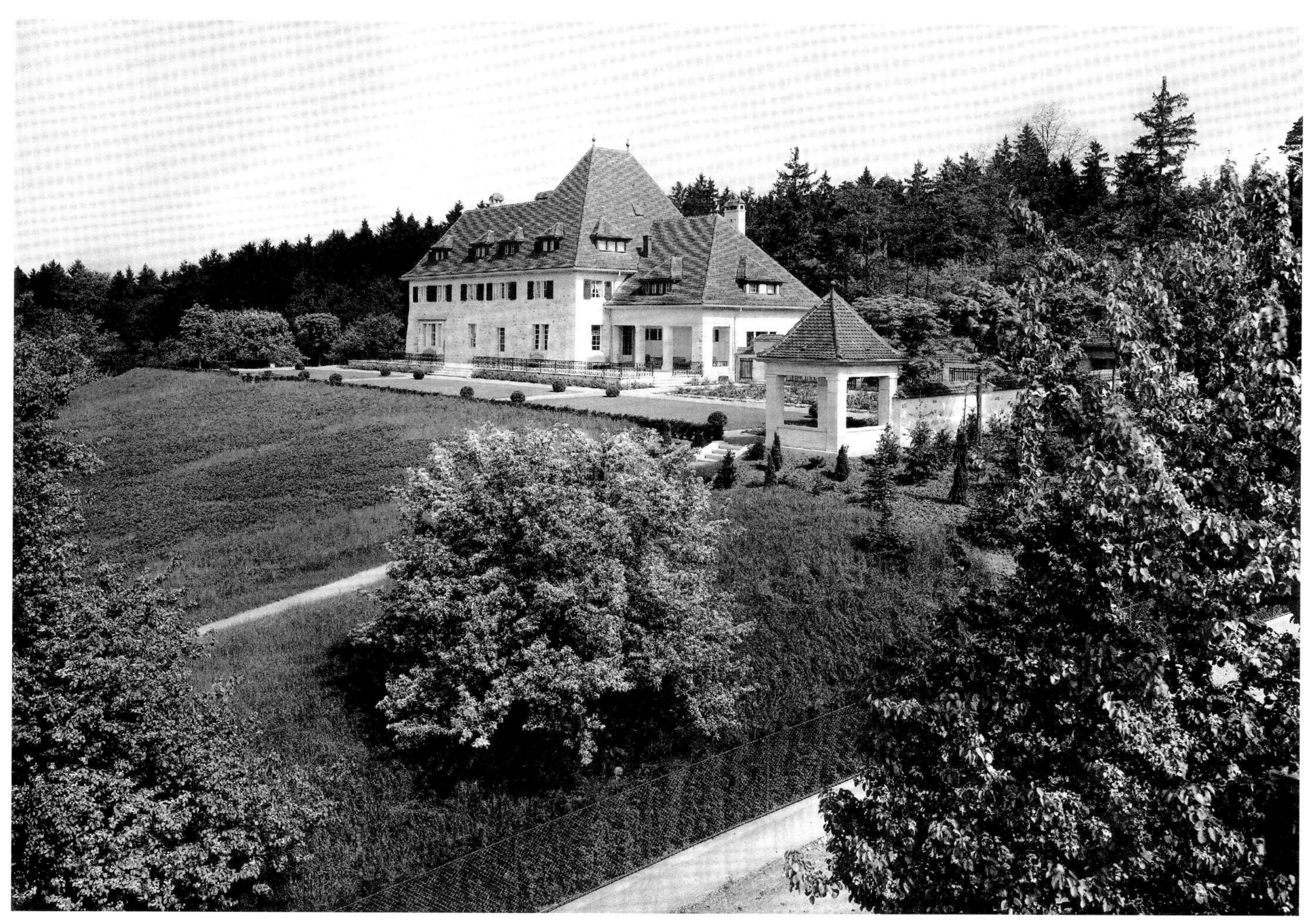

From Gallery to Museum

Oskar Reinhart still lacked something essential to realise his dream – a gallery building. After a lengthy search he acquired the villa 'Am Römerholz' (fig. 4), which became his home in 1924. For a long time he had lived with his siblings Werner and Hans in their parents' house, and in 1920 had moved to a property owned by Georg.

'Am Römerholz' was built in 1915 by the architect Maurice Turrettini (1878–1932) in an outstanding location overlooking Winterthur. Reinhart chose it for its potential to add a picture gallery to the spacious property. He tackled this project that very year and hired Turrettini to build the extension. The rather neutral rooms of the new gallery were provided with large wall surfaces and natural light (fig. 5). Reinhart had seen similar gallery spaces elsewhere, not least Wilhelm Hansen's gallery extension in Ordrupgaard near Copenhagen, an early example built in 1903. Coincidentally, this also distinguishes the

Courtauld Gallery's Great Room, where the Impressionist paintings are
currently on display, and which was the first top-lit public gallery in Europe,
designed by the architect William Chambers between 1775–1801.

In this new setting Reinhart had the opportunity and the flexibility to
change the display of his pictures time and again, creating astonishing new
associations. There were also rooms in the villa that offered the opportunity
to present works from earlier periods, from the Renaissance to the eighteenth
century, in stylish ensembles with historically appropriate furnishings. These
period rooms, such as the Louis XVI Chamber and the Renaissance Room
(fig. 6), which blend works of art with the interior, were extremely popular
at the beginning of the twentieth century.

After largely completing his collecting plans by the end of the 1920s–early
1930s, Reinhart then sought to create an outstanding third collection of art from
the German-speaking world and French-speaking Switzerland. The focus this

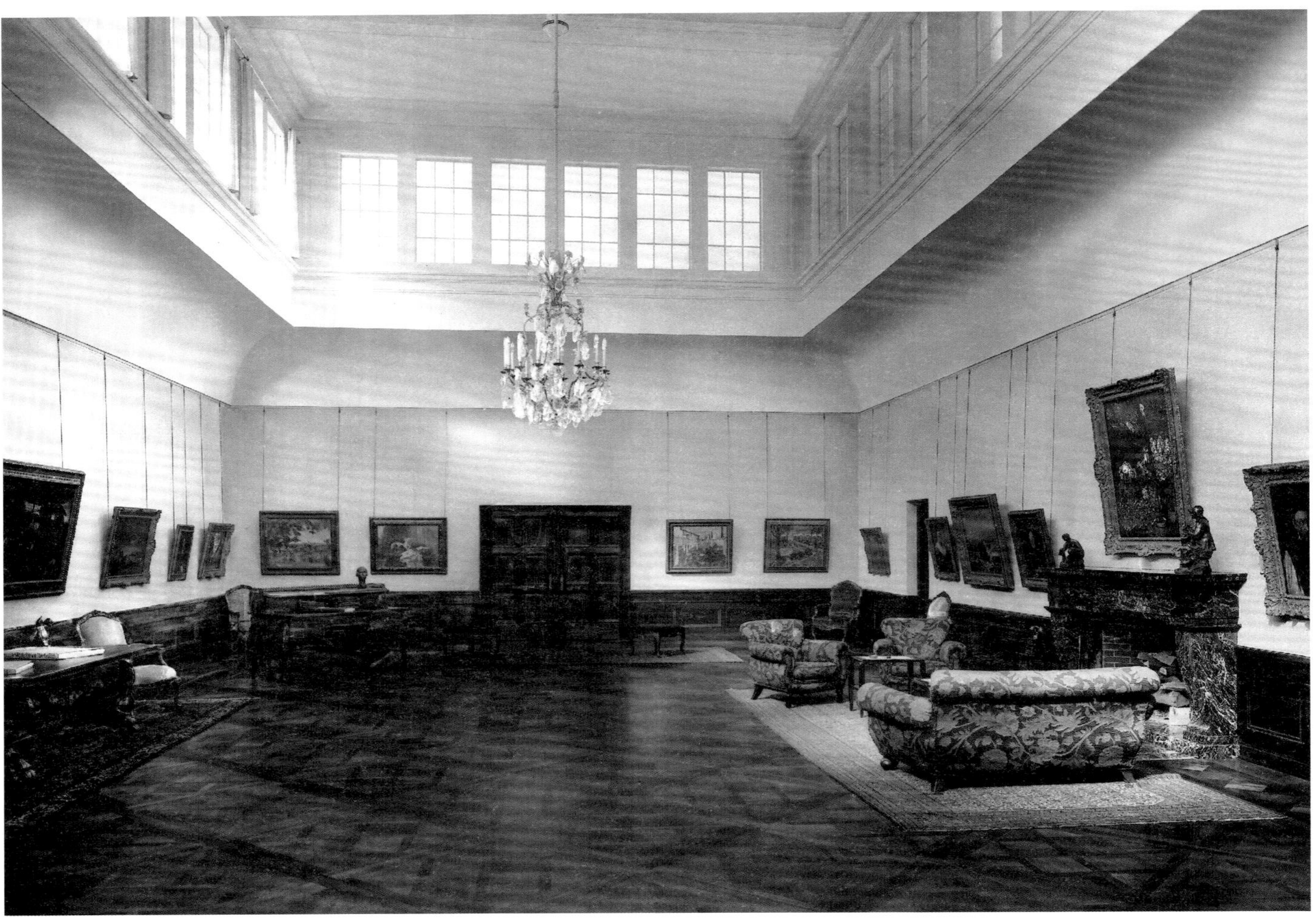

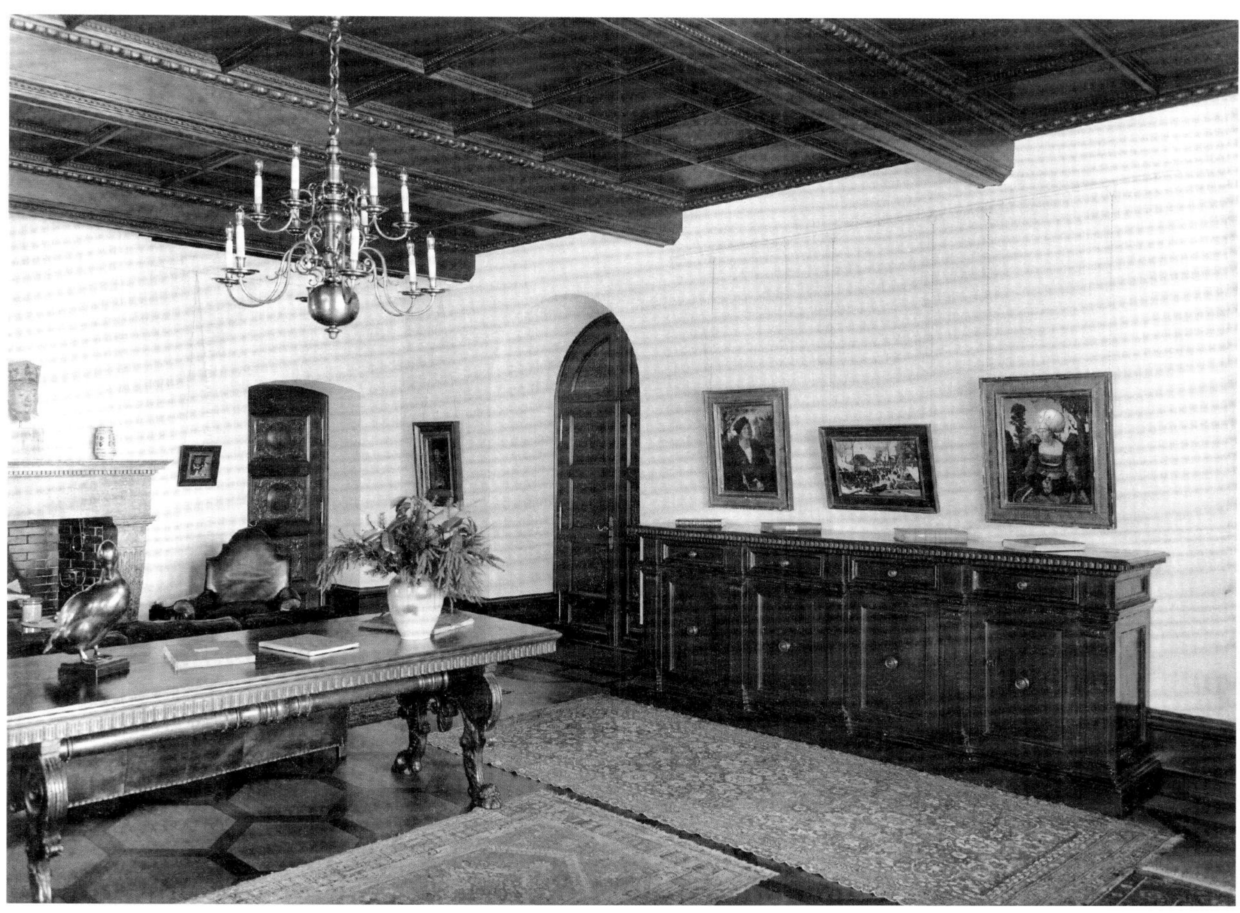

6. The Renaissance Room in the villa 'Am Römerholz', after 1930. The Swiss Confederation, Federal Office of Culture, Archive of the Oskar Reinhart Collection 'Am Römerholz', Winterthur

time would be on works of the Romantic, German Realist and Impressionist movements; among these is Caspar David Friedrich's (1774–1840) absolute masterpiece *Chalk Cliffs on Rügen* (1818; fig. 7). Here, too, can be felt the lasting effect of the 1906 *Deutsche Jahrhundert-Ausstellung*, which had strongly advocated for artists such as Hans Thoma (1839–1924), Adolph Menzel (1815–1905) and Wilhelm Leibl (1844–1900) to be considered on the same level as leading French artists such as Gustave Courbet (1819–1877). Within the new collection, Reinhart sought to form groups of works rather than searching for outstanding individual pictures. This third collection was built with a pedagogical intention to address aesthetic education and was greater in number.

As early as 1927 Reinhart saw the need to make appropriate arrangements for the future of his collections. Already in his lifetime, the villa 'Am Römerholz', although private, was opened half a day a week to interested visitors by appointment. He noted that he planned to donate the 'entire collection of paintings + other collections (sculpture, graphic arts, furniture) + the House am Römerholz to the public'.[13] This intention extended also to the third collection of

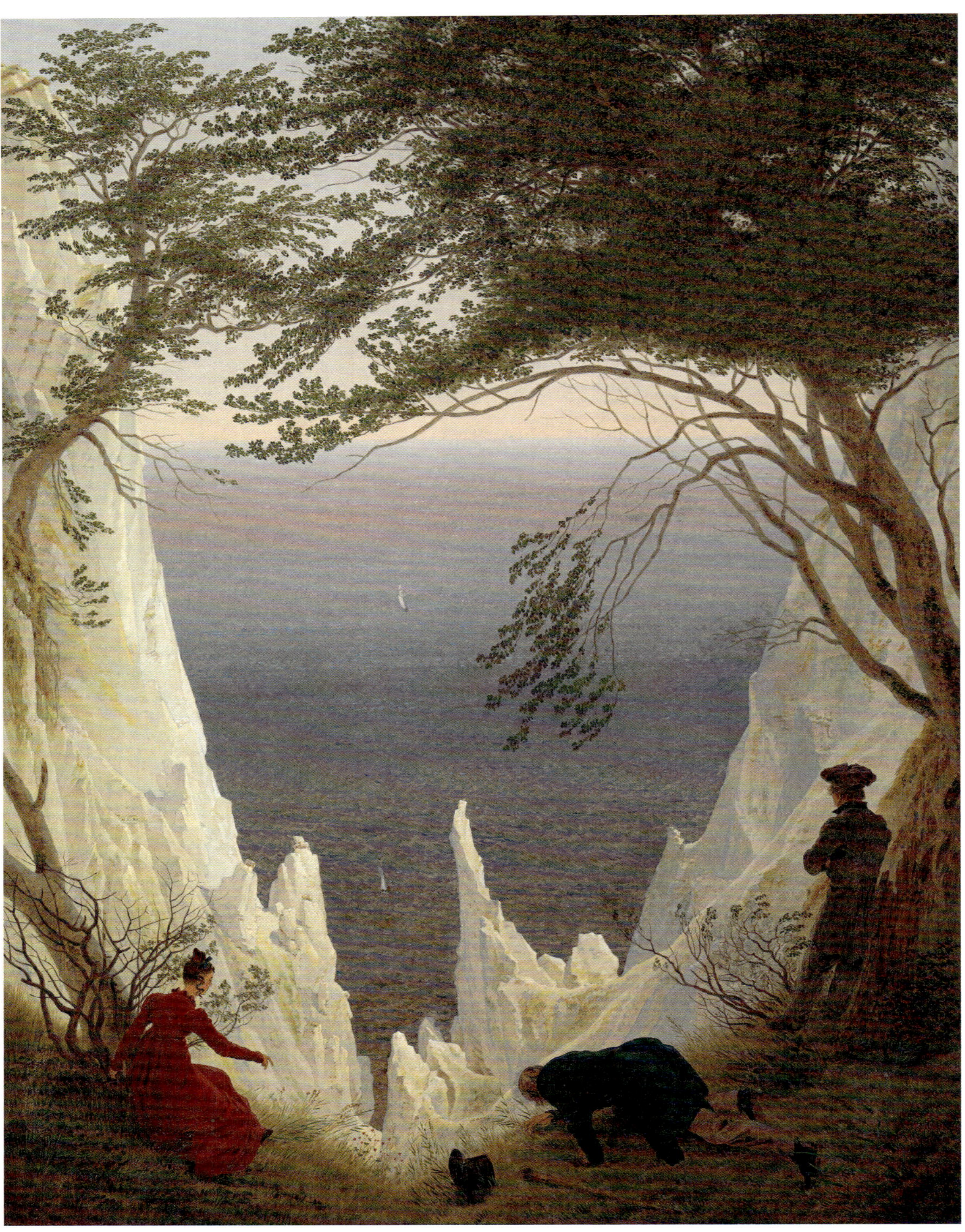

7. Caspar David Friedrich, *Chalk Cliffs on Rügen*,
1818, oil on canvas, 90.8 × 70.6 cm. Kunst Museum
Winterthur, Stiftung Oskar Reinhart, acquired by
Oskar Reinhart in 1930

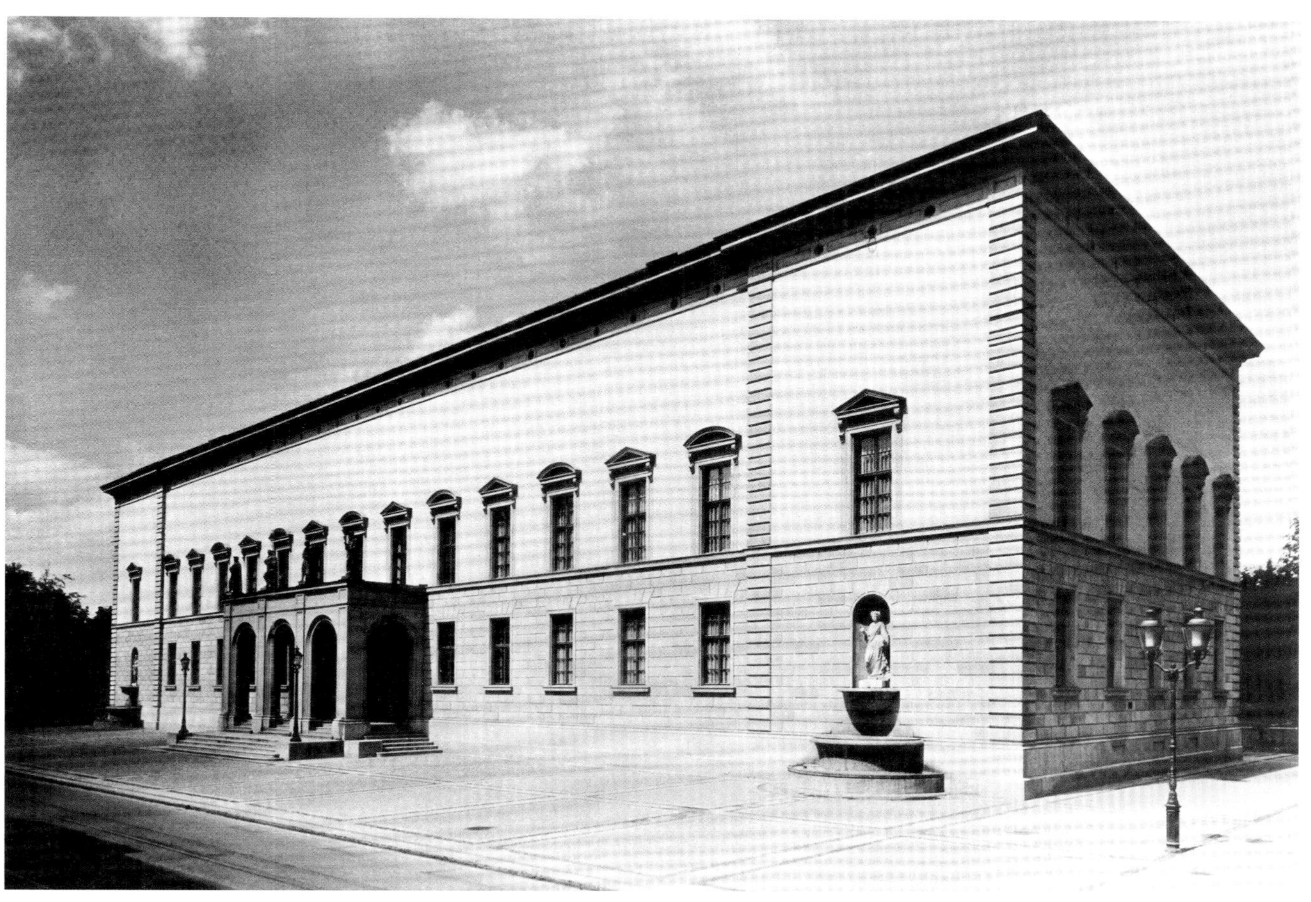

8. Stiftung Oskar Reinhart in the refurbished former boys' grammar school, today Kunst Museum Winterthur / Reinhart am Stadtgarten, c. 1960, unknown photographer. The Swiss Confederation, Federal Office of Culture, Archive of the Oskar Reinhart Collection 'Am Römerholz', Winterthur

more than 600 works of art, which he transferred to a foundation in 1940, and which opened in 1951 in the former boys' grammar school in Winterthur under the name Museum Oskar Reinhart (fig. 8); he also gifted his first graphic arts collection to the museum. Today, Reinhart's significant donation is part of the Kunst Museum Winterthur and is managed by the city's Kunstverein.

Reinhart continued to refine his two large collections until the end of his life. Manet's *Au café* (cat. 8), for instance, only found its way to Winterthur in 1953, after having been on his wish list for over thirty years. Some paintings were sold off, in keeping with the motto of the Römerholz collection: 'the smaller, the more precise and clearer the intention'.

The Profile of the Collection

Reinhart's view of art was a profoundly aesthetic one. He judged works of art primarily on their visual qualities. This judgement, which could only be made in direct contact with the works of art, determined his collecting practice throughout his life. For this reason alone, observing a picture through the trained

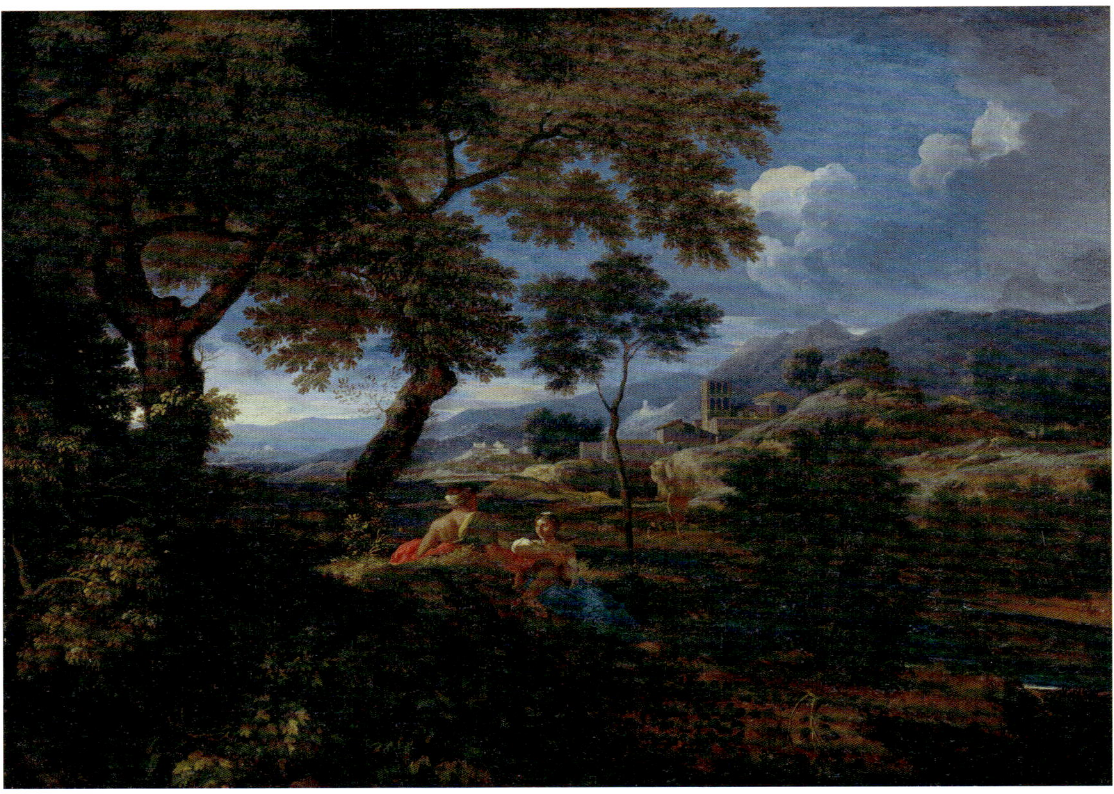

9. Jean-François Millet, *Roman Landscape*,
1665–70, oil on canvas, 94 × 130 cm. The Swiss
Confederation, Federal Office of Culture,
Oskar Reinhart Collection 'Am Römerholz',
Winterthur

and aesthetically educated eye of the connoisseur was central to him. Light, colour and movement were to be reflected in the composition and the painterly texture; the subject was secondary. For him, the historical development of art culminated in Impressionism, in his view the most important artistic movement of the nineteenth century because of its emphasis on the value of colour.

Within the collection one can also distinguish Reinhart's preference for the genres of landscape, portrait and still life, because in them the aesthetic aspect is primary and does not compete with a pictorial narrative (see his portrait, which depicts him with one of his landscape paintings in the background, figs. 9 and 10). He also favoured clearly structured compositions with solid sculptural forms over works that tend towards the dissolution of forms. This is possibly also the reason why Manet, Renoir and Cezanne are more prominent in the collection than Claude Monet (1840–1926), who pushed the limits of figuration further. Unfinished or seemingly unfinished compositions, or paintings showing areas of inferior quality also found no favour with Reinhart. An essential measure, even for the most perfect picture, was its compatibility with the quality of the whole collection.

Another significant feature of the collection is the meeting between old masters and the great protagonists of modern art. Reinhart regarded selected

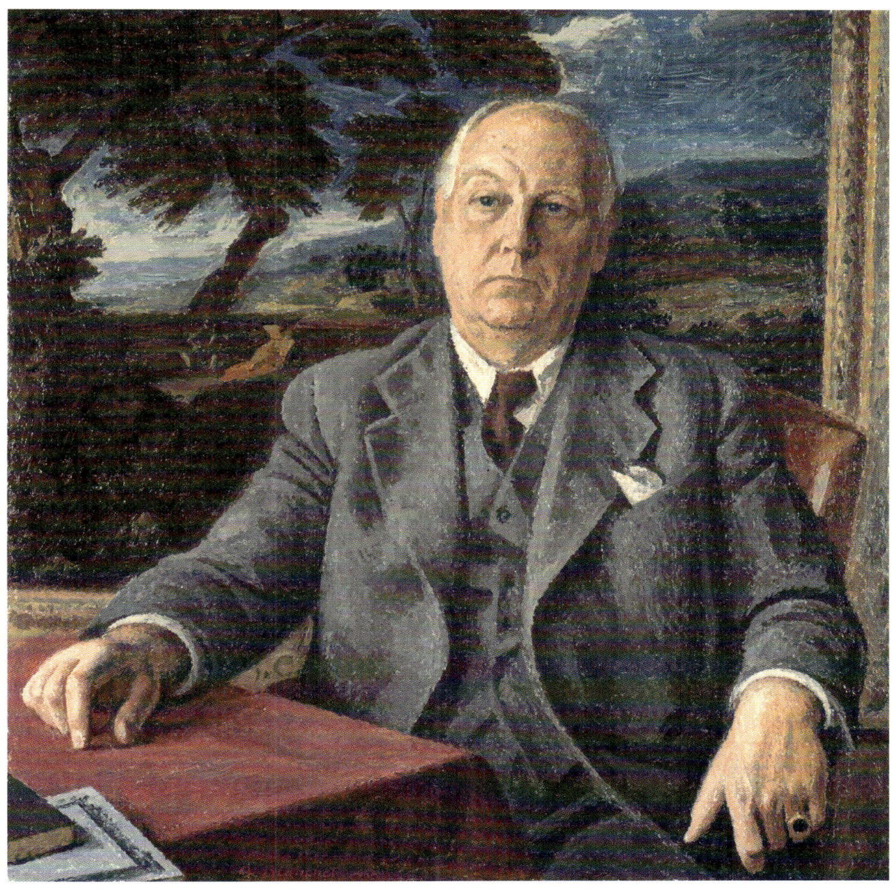

10. Alexandre Blanchet, *Portrait of Oskar Reinhart*, 1943, oil on canvas, 90 × 90 cm. Kunst Museum Winterthur, Stiftung Oskar Reinhart, acquired by Oskar Reinhart in 1943

old masters and exponents of French Classicism, such as Nicolas Poussin (1594–1665) and Claude Lorrain (c. 1604/05–1682), as ancestors of modernism; in his correspondence with Julius Meier-Graefe (1867–1935) a statement regarding the purchase of a Cezanne still life (referring to the painting illustrated on p. 81) is revealing: 'It is a wonderful piece + as classical as a Chardin' (see fig. 11).[14] Reinhart was searching in particular for works with a distinctly 'impressionistic' quality, which he saw in Frans Hals (1582/83–1666) and El Greco (1541–1614), for instance, of whom he was able to acquire some important examples.[15] Within the oeuvre of an artist, he would prefer to choose a work that showcased a painting's structure or the production process, such as the *Portrait of Baroness Pauline Jeanin* by Jean-Louis David (fig. 12). In this work, Reinhart was interested in particular in the distinctive *frottis* technique,[16] and the strong chromatic effects associated with it.

Reinhart never aimed to build a complete collection of old masters and more traditional art; as early as 1923 he noted that he wanted to 'distance himself from the old masters', as he preferred to 'admire them in public galleries' rather than having to 'chase' them.[17] His reticence towards Italian art, which he confessed he 'simply could not access', remains significant.[18] Much closer to his

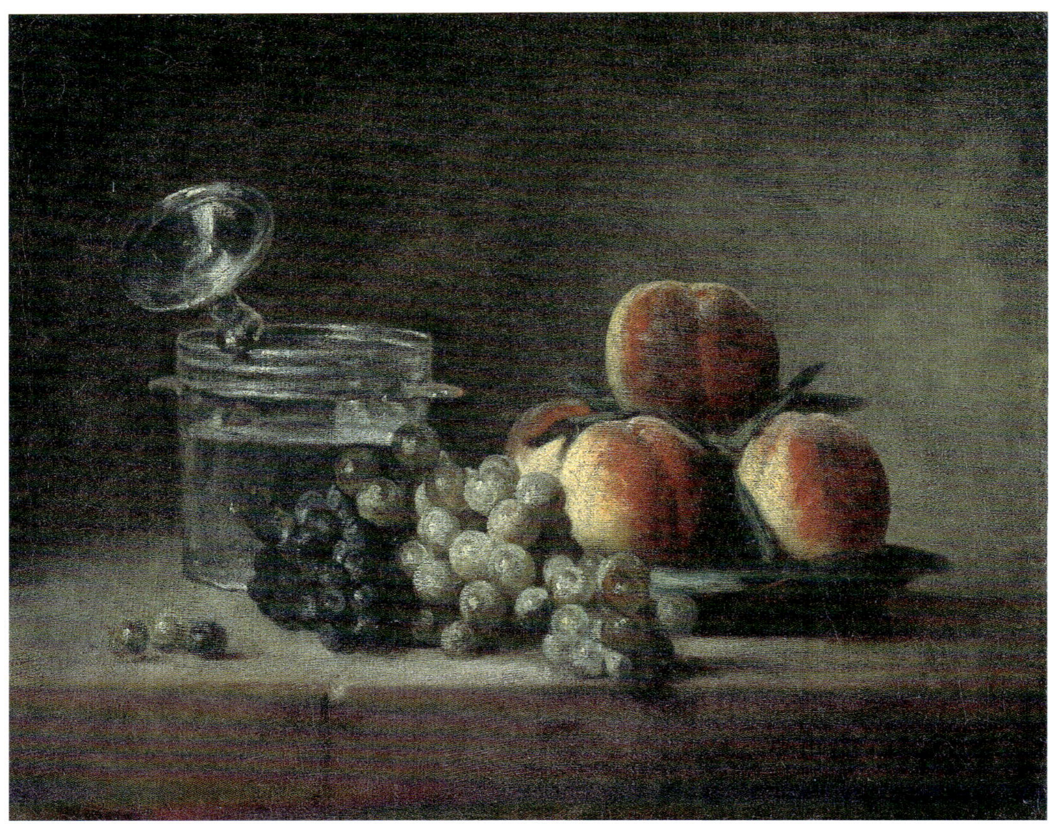

11. Jean-Siméon Chardin, *Still Life with Crystal Vessel and Fruit*, c. 1759, oil on canvas, 37 × 45.5 cm. The Swiss Confederation, Federal Office of Culture, Oskar Reinhart Collection 'Am Römerholz', Winterthur

interests, however, was the art of the Northern Renaissance. This area is well represented in the collection with outstanding examples such as the *Adoration of the Kings in the Snow* by Pieter Bruegel the Elder and the early *Marriage Diptych of Dr Johannes Cuspinian and Anna Putsch* by Lucas Cranach the Elder (figs. 13 and 14). In this light, his preference for Renaissance Netherlandish paintings by Gerard David and Geertgen tot Sint Jans and the art of the Golden Age with works by Rembrandt, and other seventeenth-century artists like Aert van der Neer and Gerard Ter Borch, among others, also has a logic.[19] In a similar way, Reinhart turned to Spanish art, and in particular to the painterly brilliance of Francisco de Goya (cat. 1), following in the footsteps of the abovementioned 'museum reformers'.

The focus of the collection, however, remained French art, from classical painters such as Poussin and Chardin (fig. 11), to the Neo-Classicism of Jacques-Louis David (fig. 12) and Jean-Auguste-Dominique Ingres (1780–1867), to the main artistic movements of the nineteenth century, the Romanticism of Eugène Delacroix and Théodore Géricault (cat. 2), the Realism of Gustave Courbet (cat. 5 and 6) and Honoré Daumier (cat. 4), and Camille Corot (cat. 3) and the younger painters of the Barbizon School, whom he inspired.

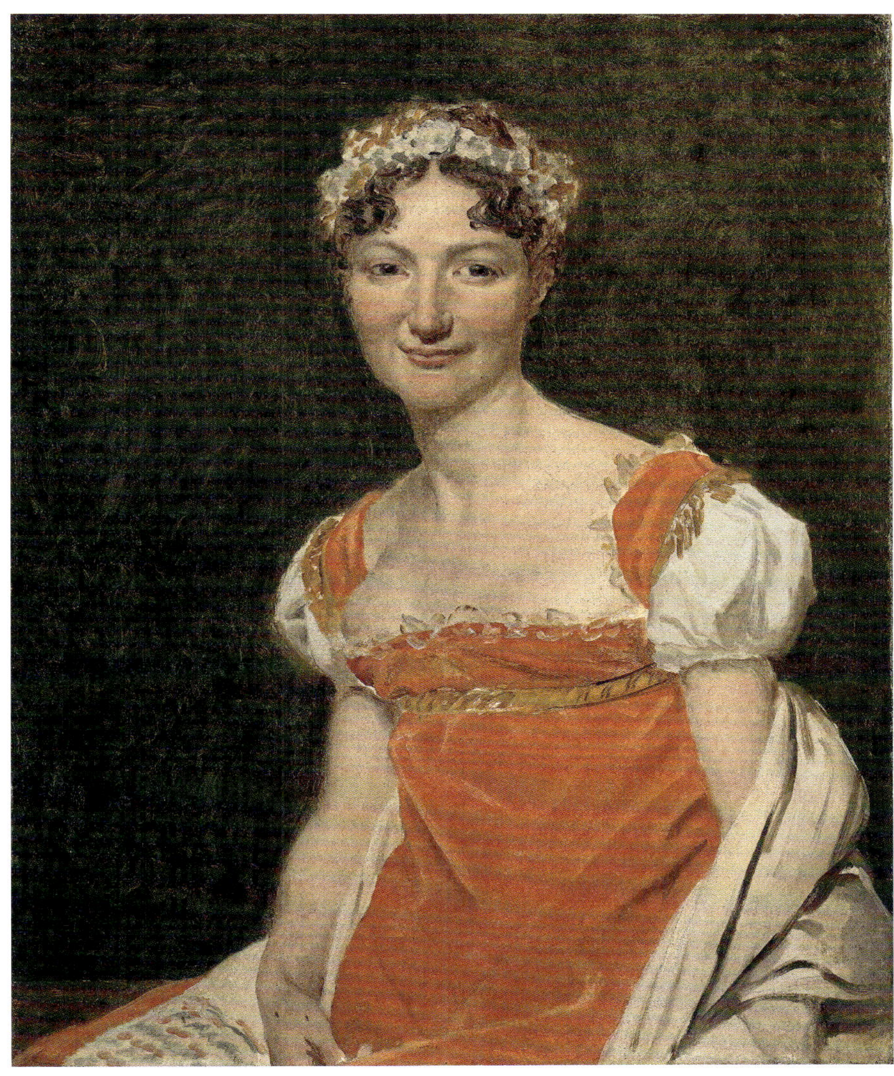

12. Jacques-Louis David, *Portrait of Baroness Pauline Jeanin*, 1812, oil on canvas, 73 × 60 cm. The Swiss Confederation, Federal Office of Culture, Oskar Reinhart Collection 'Am Römerholz', Winterthur

Coherently with this arc, the pinnacle of this artistic search would be represented by the Impressionists and Post-Impressionists, in particular by the work of Manet, Renoir, Cezanne and Van Gogh, but also Pissarro, Sisley and Gauguin (besides Camille Pissarro, all artists included in this catalogue). With an early Picasso of the blue period (cat. 25) and a few outliers such as Édouard Vuillard (1868–1940) and a classical André Derain (1880–1954), the collection of paintings comes to an end.[20] The drawings collection, though of smaller size, is similarly rigorous and structured, and largely complements the focal points of the paintings collection.[21] Only in the field of sculpture did Reinhart venture beyond his self-imposed boundaries, favouring Aristide Maillol (1861–1944) and Renoir over other artists and adding works commissioned directly from

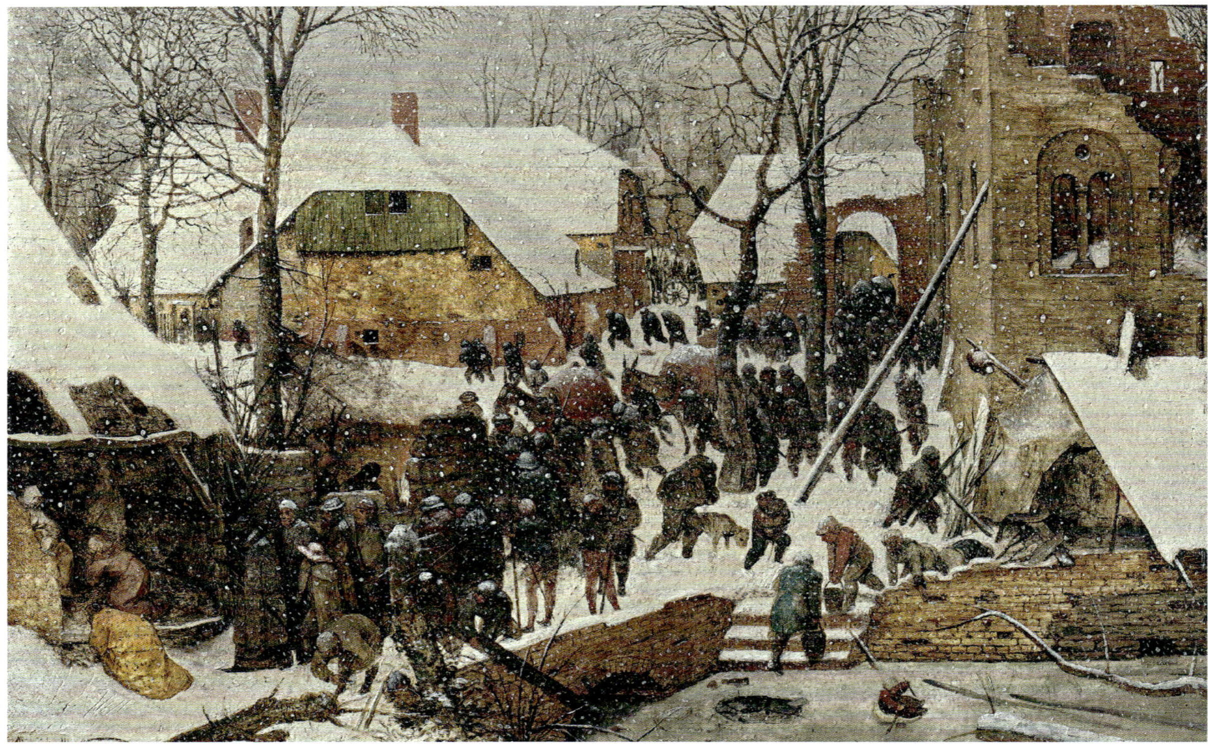

13. Pieter Bruegel the Elder, *The Adoration of the Kings in the Snow*, 1563, oil on panel, 35 × 55 cm. The Swiss Confederation, Federal Office of Culture, Oskar Reinhart Collection 'Am Römerholz', Winterthur

Swiss artists such as Hermann Haller (1880–1950). Some of the sculptures were intended for presentation outdoors, which Reinhart saw as an extension of the gallery space.

A Gift to the State

Reinhart was determined to preserve the harmonious whole of the collection, now consisting of 210 works of art. For this reason, a donation to the Swiss Confederation was agreed between him and the Federal Council as early as 1958. In addition to the works of art, the donation also included the villa with several outstanding historical pieces of furniture and chandeliers, the adjoining gallery building and a large part of the surrounding historic park. The conditions stipulated by the donor included that 'loans, sales, acquisitions and further donations' were to be avoided.[22] Although Reinhart himself had repeatedly lent pictures from his collection to special exhibitions, through this passage he wanted to protect the cohesion and the core of his collection for the future. With such a ban he was not alone among the renowned collectors of his time, as the examples of Albert C. Barnes (1872–1951) in Philadelphia or Henry Clay Frick (1849–1919) in New York show. More than fifty years later, in 2018, the general ban on lending was adapted to today's museum practice in such a way that loans became possible under certain circumstances. The aim of the amendment was to

Cat. 16 (detail)

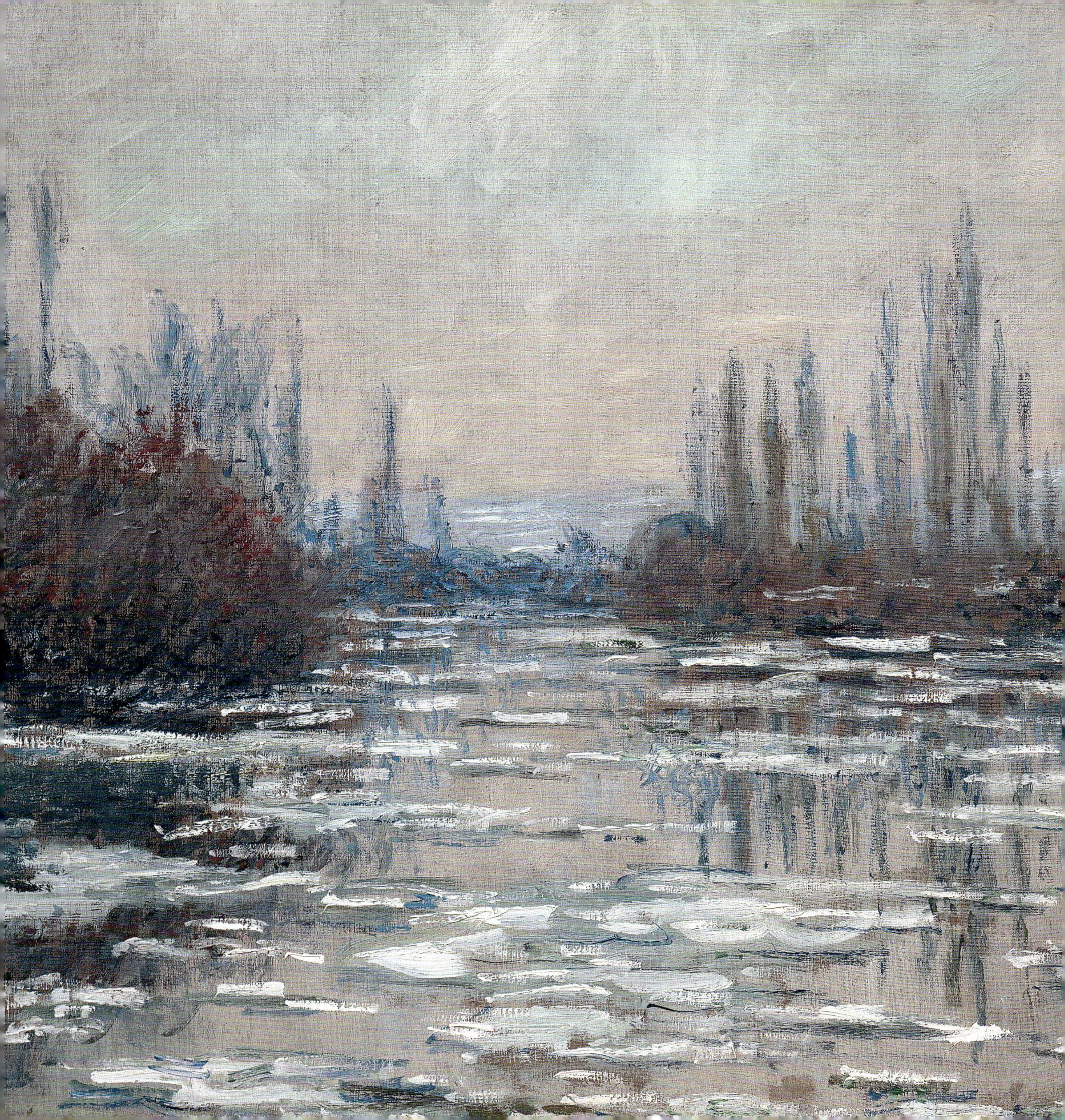

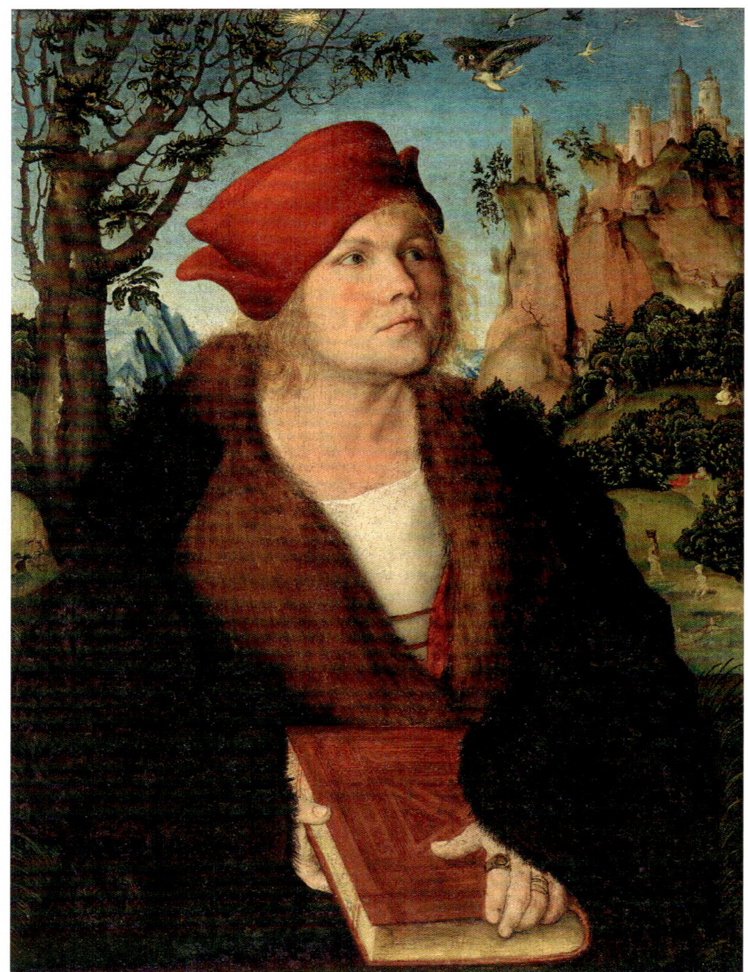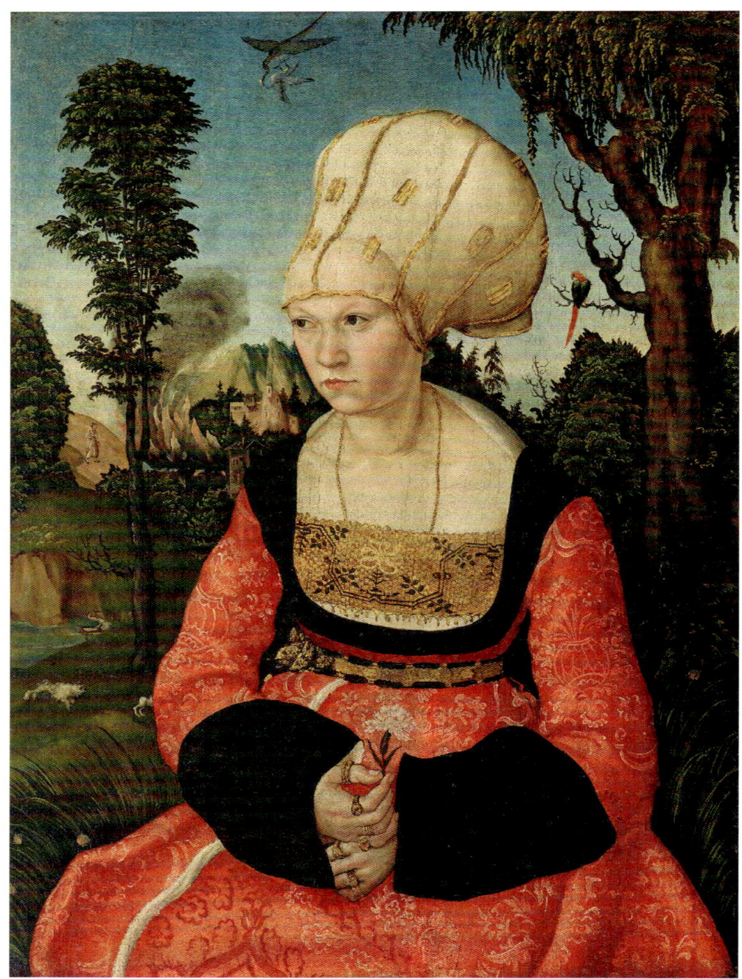

14. Lucas Cranach the Elder, *Marriage Diptych of Dr Johannes Cuspinian and Anna Putsch*, 1502, oil on panel, each 60 × 45 cm. The Swiss Confederation, Federal Office of Culture, Oskar Reinhart Collection 'Am Römerholz', Winterthur

allow further research on the works in the collection, placing them in a broader context within the framework of special collaborations.

Reinhart did not forbid changes to the display, especially since he himself enjoyed rehanging the collection in search of new visual associations (see fig. 1, p. 14). After his death in 1965 the endowment came into play, and in the years that followed the villa 'Am Römerholz' was structurally adapted to the needs of a modern public institution, finally opening its doors as a museum in 1970. Further changes provided space for an education centre, and an expanded exhibition area with a modern connected building (1997/98, and 2019/20 campaigns).

With an extensive and broad programme the museum continues to fulfil Oskar Reinhart's ideas of a comprehensive gallery of European art based on a precise aesthetic concept, and with the aim to bring art to the public. This includes educational activities such as guided tours, workshops for children and adults, concert series, academic symposia and much more. Annual special exhibitions, accompanied by publications, each focusing on works from the collection in dialogue with international loans, have been part of the museum's programme since 2005. The first, on Manet's *Au café* (cat. 8), which saw the painting reunited with its other half (fig. 32, p. 69), was followed by others on the paintings by Delacroix, Geertgen tot Sint Jans, Corot and on the collector Victor Chocquet (cat. 19). New possibilities for collaborative projects with reciprocal loans have allowed the work of the museum to be further expanded to include larger, multi-year projects, such as in 2018 and 2021 with the Kunsthistorisches Museum in Vienna on the paintings by Bruegel and Cranach, or in 2021/24 with the Musée d'Orsay in Paris on the sculptures by Maillol.

It is thanks to a partial refurbishment of the building, due to take place in 2025, that a unique opportunity has arisen to show the heart of the collection abroad – 25 of its jewels, with a focus on the nineteenth and early twentieth centuries. For the first time, the Oskar Reinhart Collection 'Am Römerholz' is presented in London, at The Courtauld. As an ensemble, it closely relates to Samuel Courtauld's own collection, and yet demonstrates the unique character of Oskar Reinhart's taste and preferences.

Notes

Translated from German by Gerlind May.
First draft copyedited by Rachel Sloan.

1   On the history of the Volkart Brothers company, and the role of Theodor Reinhart and his successors, see Volkart 1990.

2   On Theodor Reinhart's promotion of the arts, see Lukas Gloor, 'Wie der Vater, so gar nicht der Sohn. Theodor und Oskar Reinhart, Kunstsammeln auf sehr verschiedene Art', in Reinhard-Felice and Richter 2016, pp. 12–19.

3   Translated from the German, from 'Reden, gehalten bei Anlass der Eröffnung der Ausstellung Sammlung Oskar Reinhart im Kunstmuseum Bern', 16 December 1939, p. 18, Archive of the Oskar Reinhart Collection 'Am Römerholz'.

4   For example, to the Kunst Museum Winterthur and the Rietberg Museum in Zurich.

5   On Oskar Reinhart's collecting activity and the development of his collections, see Reinhard-Felice 2005, pp. 56–87; and Reinhard-Felice, 'Oskar Reinhart – kultivierter Eigensinn mit internationalem Horizont', in Reinhard-Felice et al. 2014, pp. 133–51.

6   No longer in the collection.

7   The collector used the second edition from 1915; see Reinhard-Felice et al. 2014, p. 135, ftn. 5.

8   Oskar Reinhart, *Notizblätter* (Notices) 9, 9 January 1922, Archive of the Oskar Reinhart Collection 'Am Römerholz'.

9   Oskar Reinhart, Diary, '*Was mir durch den Kopf geht*' (What goes through my head), 27 May 1919, Archive of the Oskar Reinhart Collection 'Am Römerholz'.

10   On Wilhelm Hansen's collection of French paintings and its sale in 1923, see Anne-Birgitte Fonsmark, 'Introduktion: Wilhelm Hansens samling af fransk kunst på Ordrupgaard', in Fonsmark 2011, pp. 11–23.

11   Oskar to Georg Reinhart, letter of 26 April 1923, Winterthur City Library. In the present exhibition catalogue, the works previously in the Hansen collection are cat. nos. 4, 11, 15, 20.

12   Oskar to Georg Reinhart, letter of 26 April 1923, Winterthur City Library.

13   Oskar Reinhart, Diary, '*Was mir durch den Kopf geht*' (What goes through my head), 27 March 1927, Archive of the Oskar Reinhart Collection 'Am Römerholz'.

14   Oskar Reinhart to Julius Meier-Graefe, 15 December 1921, Archive of the Oskar Reinhart Collection 'Am Römerholz'.

15   Reinhard-Felice 2005, cat. nos. 12, 30.

16   The technique consists in rubbing through some liquid paint to the priming using the fingers or a very broad brush, thus rendering the appearance of the brushstrokes very visible.

17   Oskar Reinhart, Diary, '*Was mir durch den Kopf geht*' (What goes through my head), 21 April 1923, Archive of the Oskar Reinhart Collection 'Am Römerholz'.

18   Oskar Reinhart, Travel Diary, 21 August 1938, Archive of the Oskar Reinhart Collection 'Am Römerholz'.

19   These are Reinhard-Felice 2005, cat. nos. 20–22, 36, 38.

20   Reinhard-Felice 2005, cat. nos. 160, 166.

21   The group of drawings consists of around 30 sheets; highlights include a magnificent and large drawing by Matthias Grünewald, two landscapes by Van Gogh, a group of drawings by Daumier and the two watercolours by Cezanne included in this catalogue (see Reinhard-Felice 2005, cat. nos. 5, 153–54, 88–98, 102–05).

22   Public deed on the gift upon death of Dr H.C. Oskar Reinhart and the Swiss Confederation, 26 February 1958, paragraph II, c, Archive of the Oskar Reinhart Collection 'Am Römerholz'.

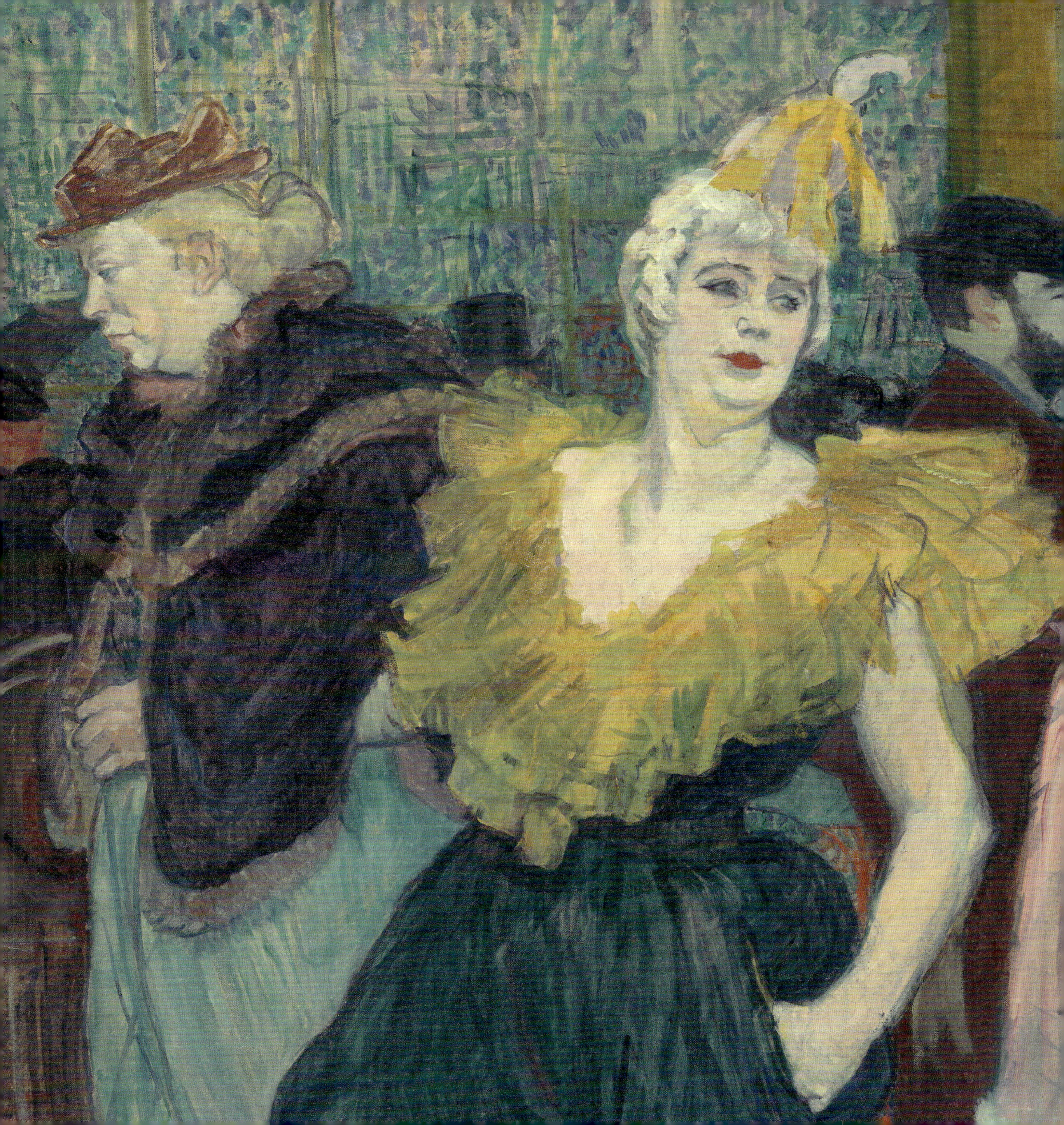

The Evolution of a Collector: Oskar Reinhart's Path to Impressionism

Katja Baumhoff

The Oskar Reinhart Collection 'Am Römerholz' stands as a testament to the transformative power of a collector's journey, a tribute to a discerning eye that embraced the revolutionary spirit of Impressionism and helped shape its enduring legacy. Oskar Reinhart's story transcends that of a mere collector of artistic treasures to become a compelling narrative of the profound impact that a passionate connoisseur can have on the art world.

Early Influences: The Importance of Tradition

Oskar Reinhart (1885–1965; fig. 15), born in Winterthur, Switzerland, grew up in a world of privilege and tradition. His family's wealth afforded him access to a world of art and culture, laying the foundations for a lifelong passion for collecting. As a young man his aesthetic sensibility was steeped in the classical tradition, and he was drawn to the timeless beauty and technical artistry of the old masters. His early artistic education was largely guided by his father, Theodor Reinhart (1849–1919), a successful businessman who had a deep appreciation for German and Swiss art, particularly for the works of Robert Zünd (1827–1909), Rudolf Koller (1828–1905), Ferdinand Hodler (1853–1918) and his contemporaries, such as Karl Hofer (1878–1955) and Hermann Haller (1880–1950).

Encountering Impressionism: A Shift in Perspective

The burgeoning art world of the early twentieth century was a whirlwind of change, marked by radical movements that challenged established norms. The rise of Impressionism at the end of the previous century, in particular, with its emphasis on capturing the fleeting effects of light and colour, its embrace of subjective experience and the representation of the modern world in a bold departure from the studio-bound practices of the academic style, produced a seismic shift in the artistic landscape.

Oskar Reinhart's path to Impressionism was a gradual one, marked by a combination of influences, personal taste and a willingness to learn. His taste for Impressionism developed alongside his broader artistic education and his encounter with influential art critics and the latest trends in the art world. Through his travels, readings and frequent visits to museums and art galleries, Reinhart gradually developed a sophisticated understanding of the movement and its importance in the history of art.

In 1906 the young Oskar travelled to Berlin, where he attended the *Deutsche Jahrhundert-Ausstellung* (German Centenary Exhibition), organized by Hugo von Tschudi, then director of the Nationalgalerie of Berlin (1896–1909) and subsequently head of the Bayerische Staatsgemäldesammlungen in Munich until his death, by Alfred Lichtwark (1852–1914), director of the Hamburg Kunsthalle, and by the influential art historian and critic Julius Meier-Graefe (1867–1935). This seminal exhibition presented on the one hand works by the recently rediscovered German Romantic artists such as Caspar David Friedrich (1774–1840), Philipp Otto Runge (1777–1810) and Carl Blechen (1798–1840), and on the other showcased the impact of French Impressionism on German

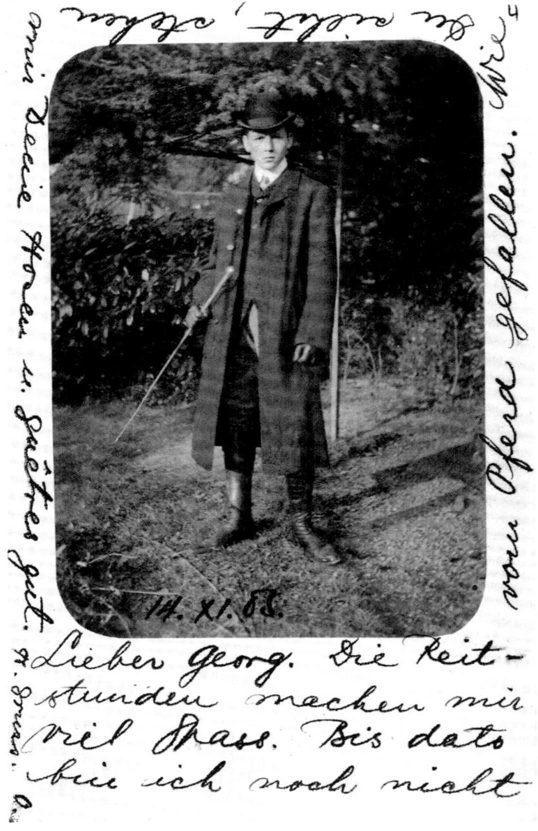

15. Oskar Reinhart in his brother Georg's riding outfit, 15 November 1903. The Swiss Confederation, Federal Office of Culture, Archive of the Oskar Reinhart Collection 'Am Römerholz', Winterthur

contemporary art. The fierce opposition with which the Prussian cultural administration, above all the Kaiser Wilhelm II (1859–1941) himself, fought against the growing presence of French modernism in Germany in the years before the First World War could not prevent its immensely growing influence. In light of the heated nationalistic climate of the time, the cultural and political significance of the exhibition's initiative to promote French modernism in Germany cannot be overstated.

The encounter with Impressionism at the *Deutsche Jahrhundert-Ausstellung* served as a catalyst in Reinhart's development of his own artistic taste, and his aesthetic sensibility began to shift. Experiencing the works of Max Liebermann (1847–1935), Adolph von Menzel (1815–1905) and the German Impressionists, alongside those of the Realist movement, including Hans Thoma (1839–1924) and Wilhelm Leibl (1844–1900), helped Reinhart develop a greater appreciation for light and colour, key elements of Impressionism. By that time he had also encountered Julius Meier-Graefe's influential *History of the Development of Modern Art* (*Entwicklungsgeschichte der modernen Kunst*, first published in 1904), which not only deepened his understanding of the movement's importance, but became his veritable 'aesthetic guidebook'.

From then on Reinhart became increasingly aware of current artistic concerns and the significance and impact of French Impressionism. An avid visitor to galleries and art exhibitions in major centres such as London, Paris and Berlin, he was increasingly drawn to the way artists like Monet, Renoir, Degas and Manet captured the ephemeral nature of light and its atmospheric effects. The vibrant colours, loose brushstrokes and unconventional compositions of the Impressionists, as well as their groundbreaking modernity, sense of immediacy and fresh perspective firmly caught his imagination.

Life of a British Gentleman: Oskar Reinhart's *Lehrjahre* in London

In 1907 Reinhart travelled to London on behalf of his family's firm, Volkart Brothers, to familiarise himself with the business world – a task he endured rather than enjoyed. He returned to London in 1911–12, staying for a longer period; this second visit was particularly influential in his development as a collector.

At the beginning of the twentieth century London was a city of many contrasts, a place where tradition met modernity. Reinhart was drawn to its vibrant social life and upper-class way of living. His diaries and letters reveal his enthusiasm for playing tennis, billiards and golf in exclusive clubs, attending horse races, football matches and regattas. He seemingly adopted the codes of English high society effortlessly, but did not try to become part of it.[1] He continued, however, to be a keen observer and to appreciate art and culture, immersing himself into English literature, attending theatre performances and the opera. He frequently visited exhibitions held at the International Society of Sculptors, Painters and Engravers, and spent long hours at the British Museum, visiting its Print Room on a regular basis; he was in close contact with Campbell Dodgson, who would become Keeper of Prints and Drawings in 1912. Drawn in particular to the British Museum's collection of Japanese woodcuts, Reinhart soon decided to purchase his first prints by Katsushika Hokusai

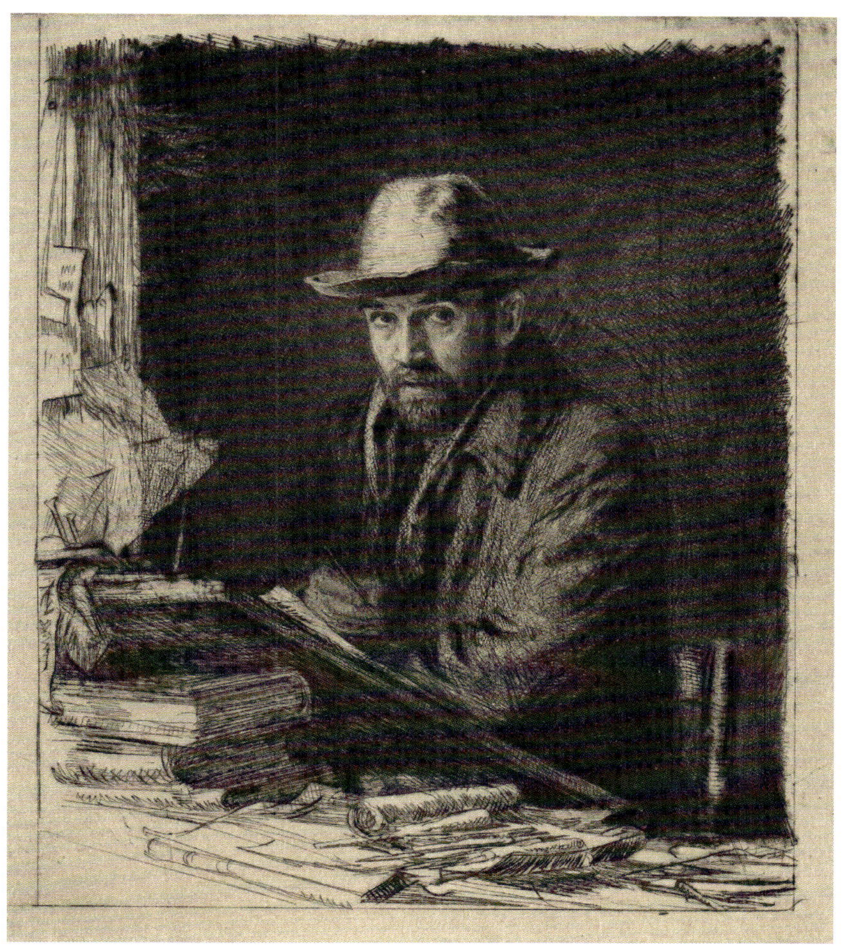

(1760–1849) and James McNeill Whistler (1834–1903), the latter a significant figure in the Etching Revival movement. These first acquisitions were soon followed by prints and drawings by contemporaneous British artists, including the Scottish Muirhead Bone (1876–1953; fig. 16), whom Reinhart met and whose work also reflected Whistler's influence.[2]

Reinhart was developing an independent artistic taste – he was willing to venture beyond the confines of his father's collection and explore new artistic avenues. Coupled with his avid reading of contemporary art journals, Reinhart's interest in modern art was thus constantly fuelled. The exposure to British art and culture, combined with his own developing aesthetic sensibilities, helped lay the groundwork for Reinhart's later collecting of French Impressionist artworks. It was a period of cultural and personal exploration, and Reinhart left London with a greater appreciation for art and a more refined sense of style.

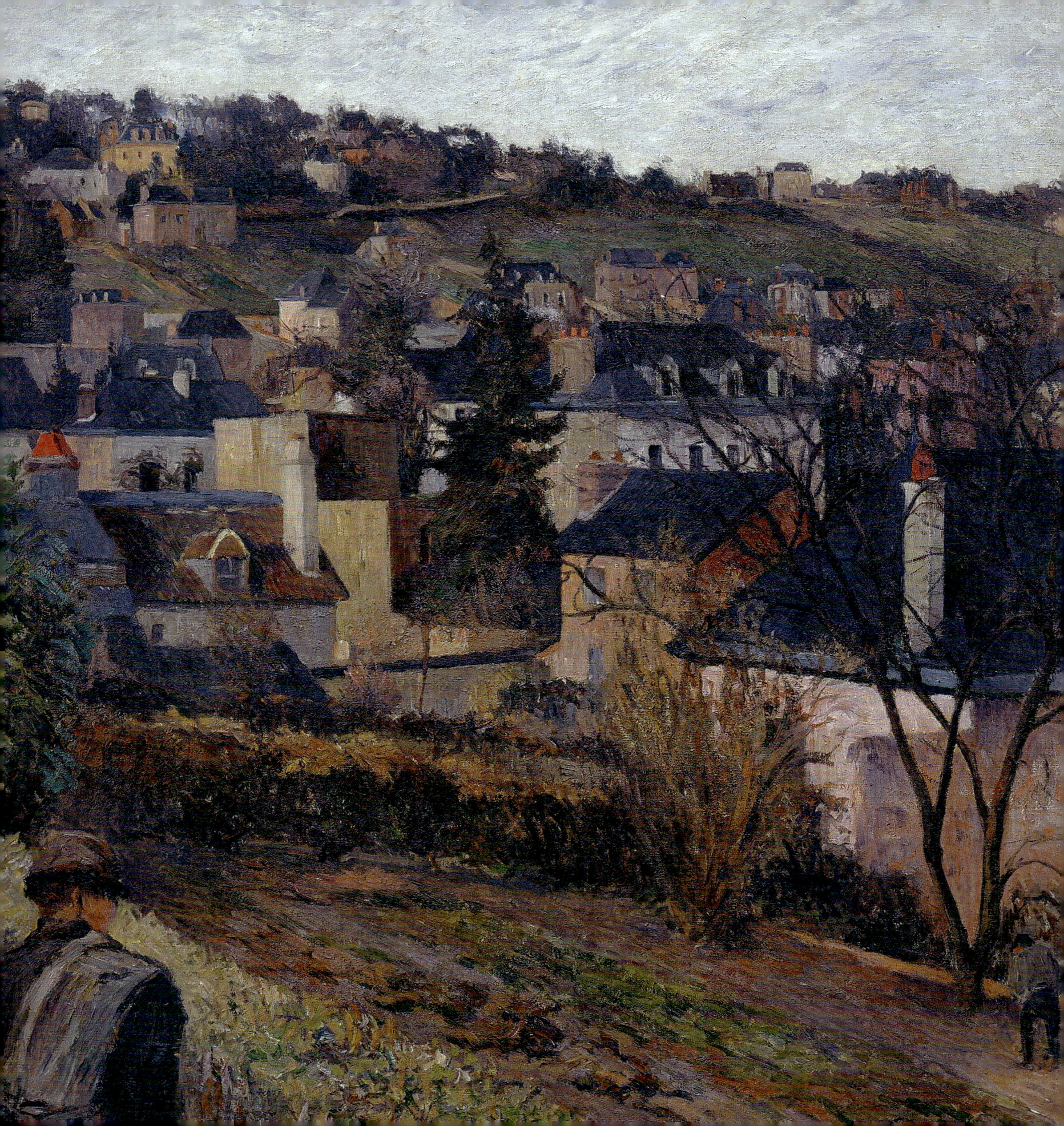

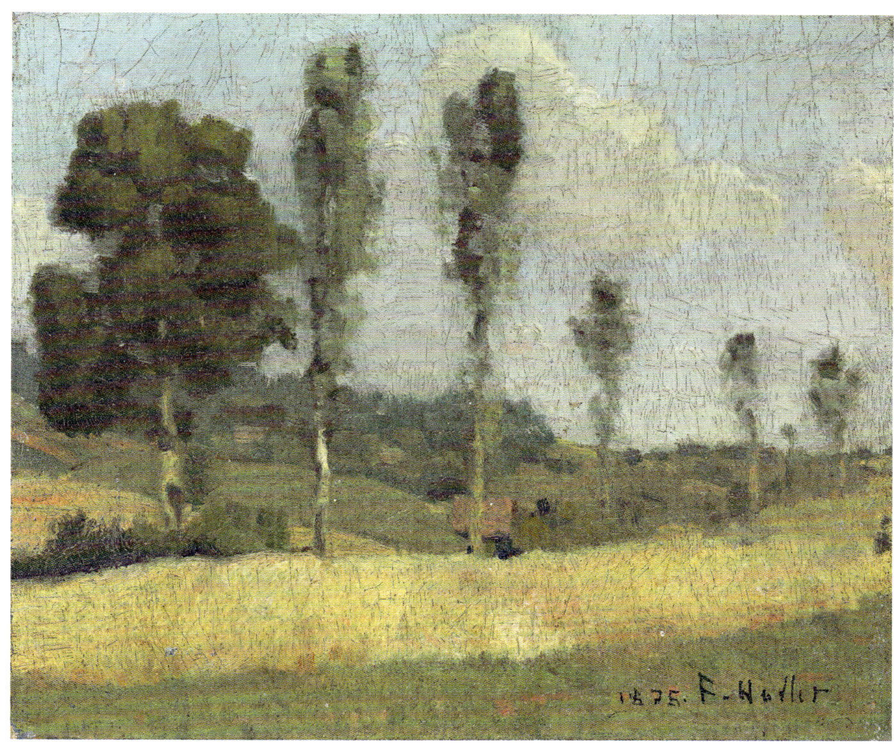

17. Ferdinand Hodler, *Landscape with Poplars*, 1875, oil on canvas, 20.5 × 24 cm. Kunst Museum Winterthur, Stiftung Oskar Reinhart, acquired by Oskar Reinhart in 1911

Julius Meier-Graefe and Paul Cassirer

In 1908 Reinhart's intellectual and aesthetic journey took a significant turn. He wrote to his father about his desire to visit Berlin again, noting that 'little by little [the city] had become the heart of intellectual life in Germany',[3] and he intended to attend university and commercial college there. He was particularly looking forward to meeting in person Julius Meier-Graefe and Paul Cassirer (1871–1926), the owner of a successful art gallery in Berlin that dealt with French and Secessionist art. Cassirer's gallery, which was a hub of innovative artistic trends, regularly published *Kunst und Künstler*, a journal Reinhart read and which featured articles by Tschudi and Meier-Graefe.

In 1911, following a trip to Munich, Reinhart purchased his very first painting: a rather small work by Ferdinand Hodler, *Landscape with Poplars*, from 1875 (fig. 17). This purchase was obviously a tribute not only to Hodler's artistry, but also to Reinhart's father, who had supported and collected Hodler extensively. By choosing a painting from Hodler's early career, however, Reinhart consciously avoided his most prominent phase, with its strong tendency towards symbolism and parallelism. Instead, *Landscape with Poplars* is rather indebted to the so-called *paysage intime* (intimate landscape) of Hodler's teacher Barthélemy Menn (1815–1893), and can be justly considered a proto-Impressionist landscape.[4]

Thus, already with his first acquisition Reinhart revealed his own developing taste. He would maintain this approach throughout his collecting life. Essentially, Reinhart did not try to acquire works spanning an artist's whole career, or an art historical movement or epoch, but each time he purposefully added individual works that responded to his perceptive eye and showcased high quality standards. In this sense, the collection is truly a private enterprise, reflecting Reinhart's taste and preferences but to the highest museum standard.

By that time Reinhart was resolute to purchase a French Impressionist painting. In 1912, during a trip to Paris, he managed to acquire a small landscape by Renoir (current whereabouts unknown) from the Galerie Durand-Ruel. This first French Impressionist painting to enter Reinhart's collection was also probably the first work of art he paid entirely out of his own pocket – albeit with a little bluff, as he initially pretended to reserve it for his father.[5]

After becoming an active shareholder of Volkart Brothers in Winterthur in 1912, Reinhart left London. This, however, did not stop him from pursuing his artistic interests, and during this time he drew up a list of desiderata: 'Rembrandt, Frans Hals (both unaffordable), Velázquez, Greco, Goya, Constable, Géricault, Delacroix, Courbet, Daumier, Corot, Daubigny, Manet, Degas, Monet, Renoir, Van Gogh, Cezanne, Sisley, Toulouse-Lautrec; Leibl, Trübner, Liebermann, Schuch, Alt, Menzel'.[6] This list could have been easily drawn up by Meier-Graefe or Tschudi, since they shared a similar view and interpretation of art history, and of Impressionism in particular. As Reinhart stated, with a definition very close to Meier-Graefe's own,[7] 'Impressionism: Painting that records only fleeting impressions, setting aside knowledge of the subject gained by other methods. Velázquez was an Impressionist and, among more recent painters, Manet, Liebermann and many others.'[8]

In 1916 Reinhart acquired *Autumn Landscape* by Pierre Bonnard, who had painted it only a year earlier.[9] The purchase was certainly influenced by his association with Winterthur collectors such as Richard Bühler[10] and Hedy and Arthur Hahnloser (see above, p. 17), who collected Bonnard and Édouard Vuillard among others – who, like Oskar and his brother Georg, were influential figures on the Winterthur's progressive art scene. In particular, the Winterthurer Kunstverein, an art association established in 1888, played a pivotal role in the promotion and appreciation of modern art in Switzerland, especially French Impressionism, during the late nineteenth and early twentieth centuries. The Kunstverein became a crucial platform for local collectors, artists and art enthusiasts, fostering an environment where modern artistic movements could flourish. The institution, which centred around the city's Kunst Museum, not only aimed to enhance Winterthur's cultural landscape, but also served as a critical space for dialogue and debate regarding modern art, including Impressionism and Post-Impressionism.

Building Up a Collection

Reinhart's collecting journey gained momentum after the First World War. The horrors of the war brought about a renewed appreciation for beauty and artistic expression when life finally returned to normal. This period saw a surge of

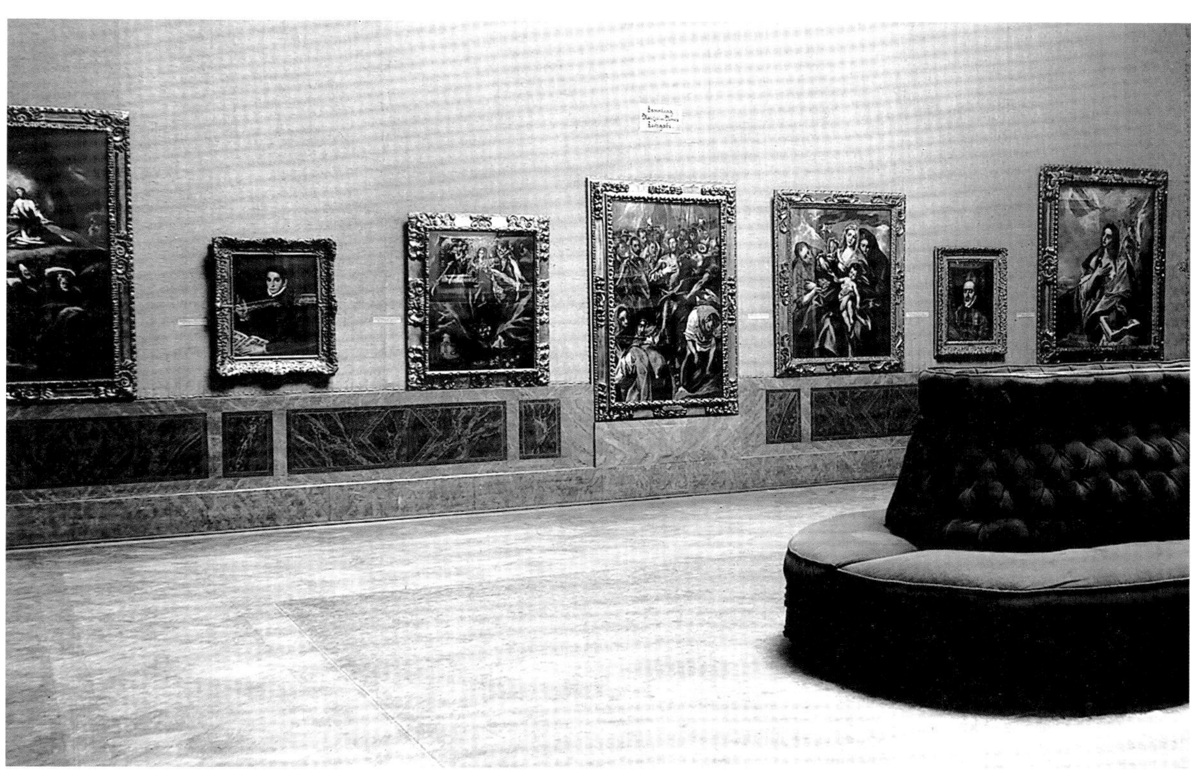

18. Hugo von Tschudi's exhibition of Marczell
von Nemes's collection at the Alte Pinakothek,
Munich, 1911. The Swiss Confederation, Federal
Office of Culture, Archive of the Oskar Reinhart
Collection 'Am Römerholz', Winterthur

*The second portrait from right, currently attributed
to El Greco, entered Oskar Reinhart's collection in
1924.*

interest for the Impressionists, whose work offered a welcome respite from the
grim realities of the post-war period. Reinhart, a man of peace and a staunch
advocate for beauty, found a profound connection with the artists whose work
celebrated the joys of modern life and the beauty of the natural world.

In 1919 Reinhart's father died, leaving him with more economic means and
free to pursue his ambitions as a collector. Through his travels and visits to art
galleries, private collections, museums and exhibitions, he found inspiration
in the artistic choices of other collectors, such as Eduard and Johanna Arnhold
in Berlin, Wilhelm and Henny Hansen in Ordrupgaard, Denmark, and the
Hungarian collector and art dealer Marczell von Nemes. Reinhart probably
saw the Nemes collection in an exhibition at the Alte Pinakothek in Munich
in 1911 (fig. 18). He would eventually internalise the basic principle of Marczell
Nemes's display strategy, juxtaposing works by the old masters with those
of nineteenth-century French artists to initiate exciting new dialogues. This
meant that it was no longer required to represent an artist's whole oeuvre
through the different phases of their career, or to feel the pressure of having to
fully represent an artistic movement. This vision offered a fresh perspective in
which 'kindred artistic spirits pursue similar concerns in painting'.[11]

The early 1920s marked a turning point in Reinhart's collecting strategy. His
acquisitions became even more focused and determined. He sought out not only

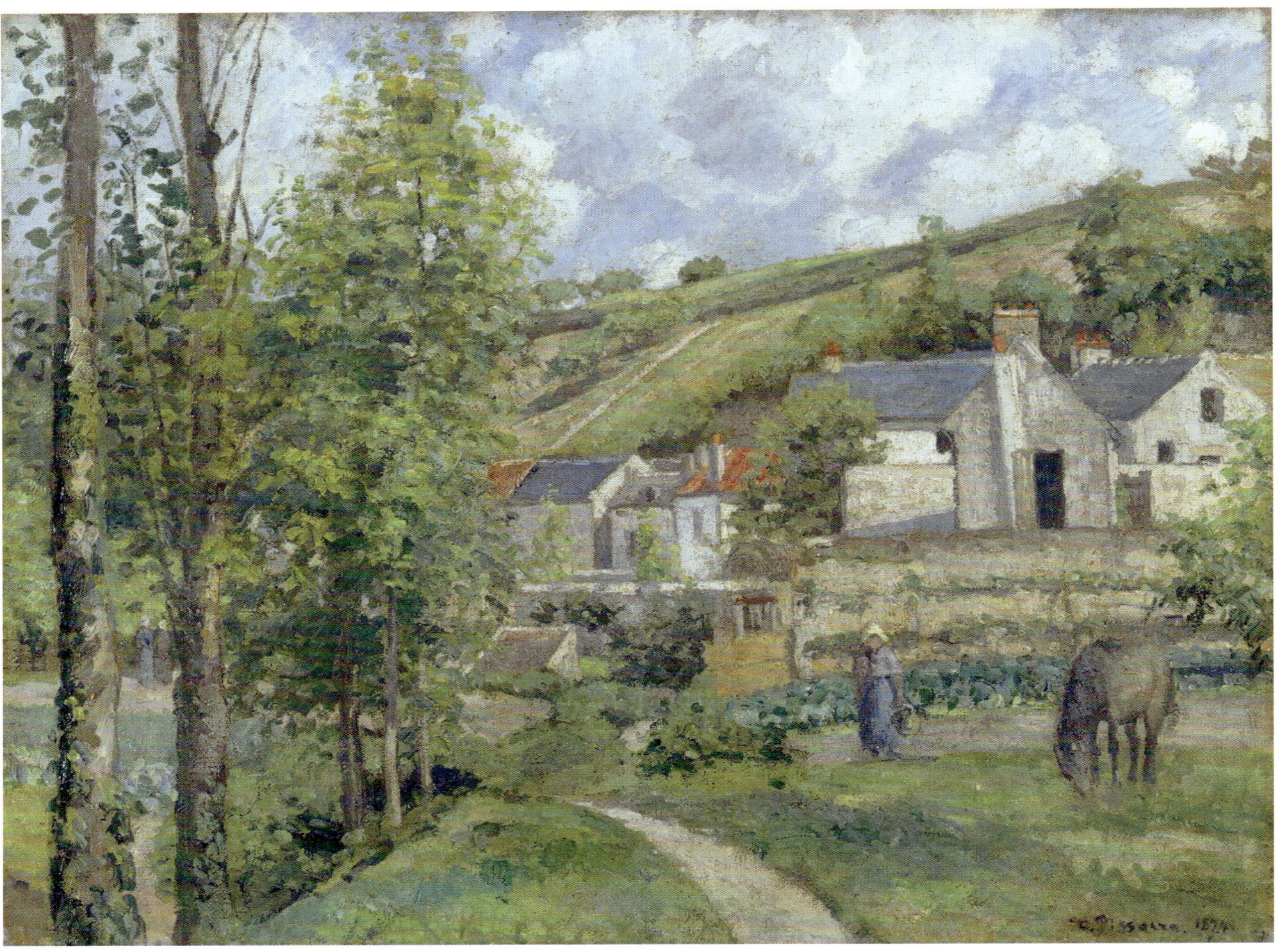

19. Camille Pissarro, *A View of L'Hermitage, Pontoise*, 1874, oil on canvas, 61 × 81 cm. The Swiss Confederation, Federal Office of Culture, Oskar Reinhart Collection 'Am Römerholz', Winterthur

the 'properly' Impressionist works, but also those by artists affiliated with the movement and who had made significant contributions to it. For instance, he became a champion of Camille Pissarro, whose work he deeply admired for its serene and lyrical beauty as well as for its unwavering commitment to capturing the effects of light and the atmosphere (fig. 19). He was also fascinated by the paintings of Alfred Sisley, whose landscapes captivated him with their delicate, ethereal beauty (cat. 15).

But the Impressionist artist he collected the most was Renoir. Over the years he acquired a number of works from the whole span of Renoir's career, encompassing his entire artistic development. Reinhart's collection ranges from *Lily and Greenhouse Plants* (cat. 17), an early work from 1864 that reveals the influence of Courbet and predates Renoir's Impressionist period, to *La Grenouillère* (fig. 20), all the way to the monumental nude *After the Bath* from 1913. It includes also two important bronzes, which Renoir created with

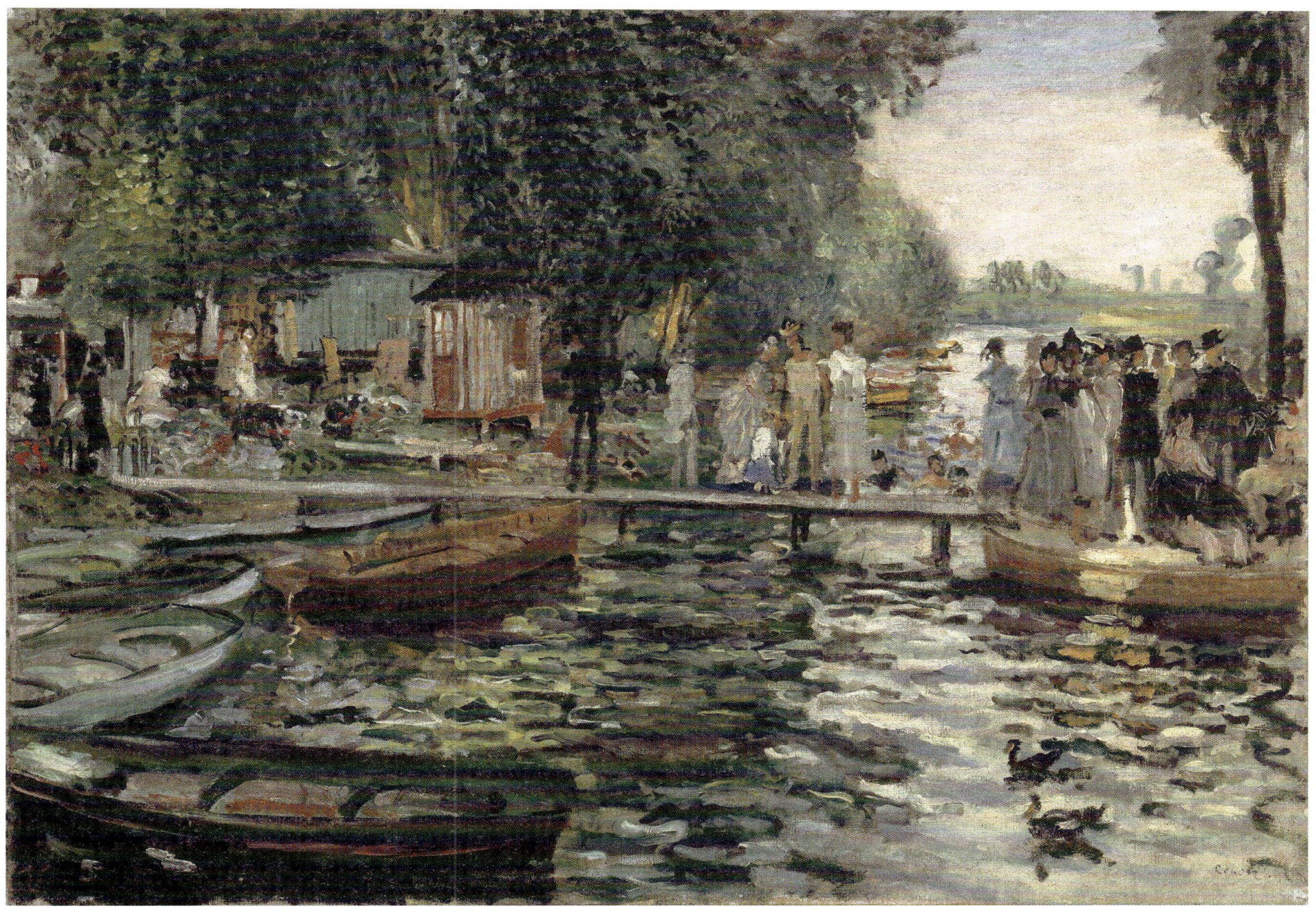

20. Pierre-Auguste Renoir, *La Grenouillère*, 1869, oil on canvas, 65 × 92 cm. The Swiss Confederation, Federal Office of Culture, Oskar Reinhart Collection 'Am Römerholz', Winterthur

Richard Guino during the First World War, the *Small Washerwoman* and *Large Kneeling Washerwoman*, from 1916 and 1917 respectively; the latter was the last work of the Renoir-Guino partnership.

In those very active years Reinhart also amassed a significant collection of prints and drawings, as well as sculptures, probably with the aim of reaching a more comprehensive understanding of the artists and their creative processes. Reinhart sought out works that would offer insights into the artists' working methods, their sources of inspiration and evolving styles.

In 1923, following a trip to Copenhagen, Reinhart was able to purchase twelve paintings from the Hansen collection, followed by seven more in the same year (see, for example, fig. 21); this coup would be the most significant triumph of his collecting career.[12] In the following year Reinhart left the family business and moved into his own house, villa 'Am Römerholz', nestled by a wood on the outskirts of northern Winterthur, where he could finally devote

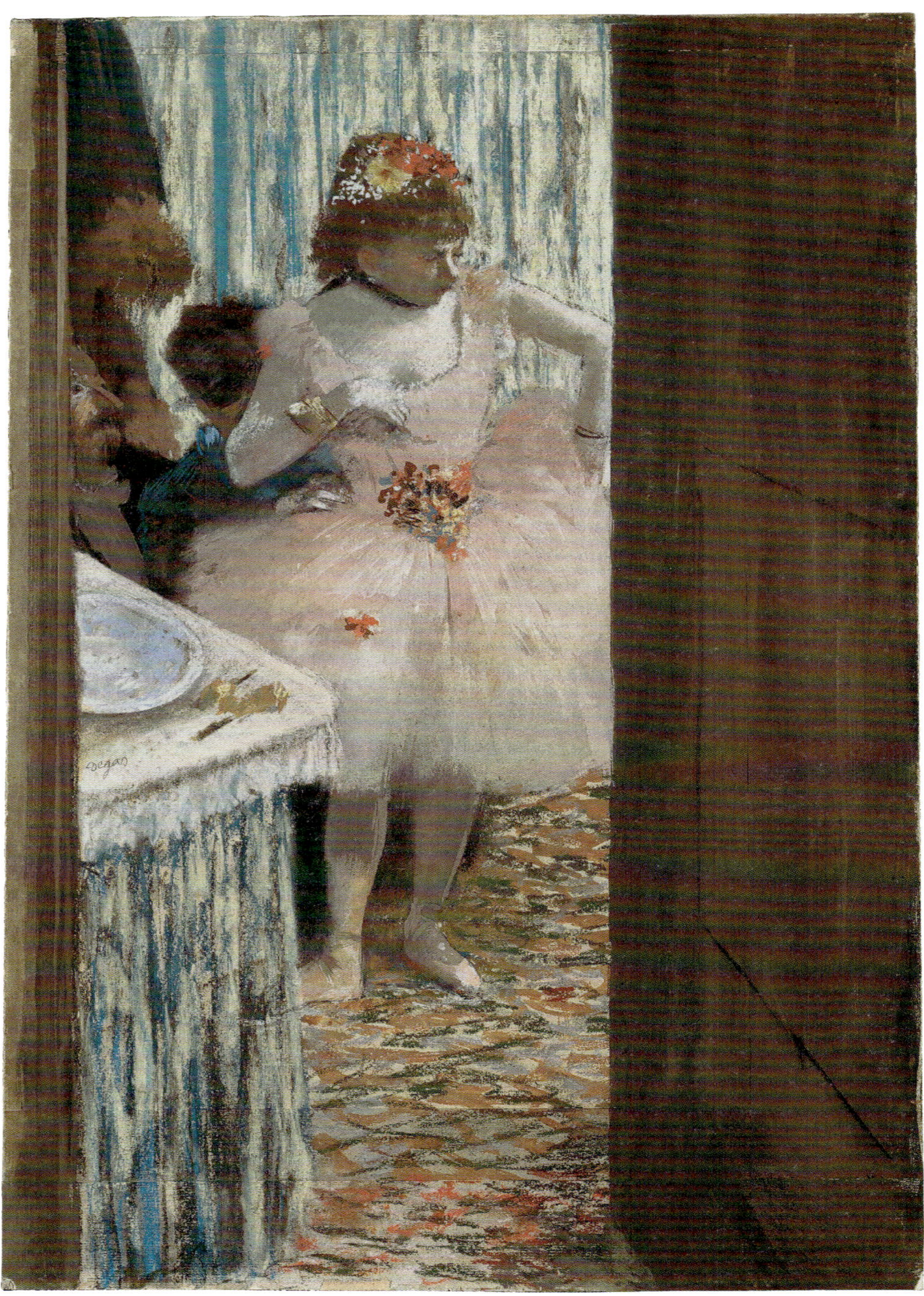

21. Edgar Degas, *Dancer in the Dressing Room*, c. 1878–79, pastel and bodycolour on paper, 60 × 40 cm. The Swiss Confederation, Federal Office of Culture, Oskar Reinhart Collection 'Am Römerholz', Winterthur (previously in the Hansen collection)

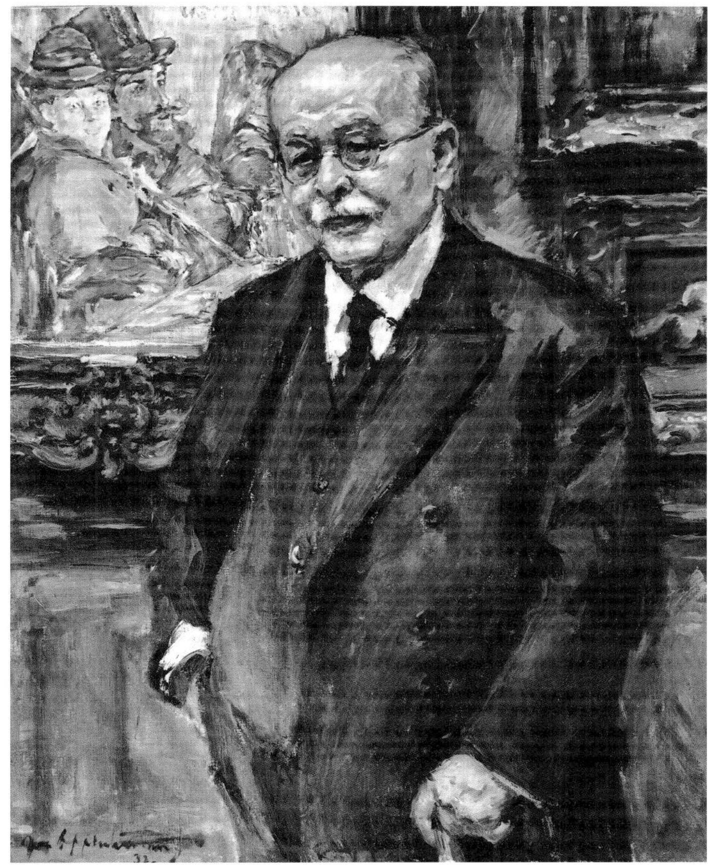

22. Oskar Reinhart's wishlist of artworks, written after his visit to Otto Gerstenberg's collection in 1923. Single sheet added to Notebook 10. The Swiss Confederation, Federal Office of Culture, Archive of the Oskar Reinhart Collection 'Am Römerholz', Winterthur

Édouard Manet's 'Au café' ('Cafeszene') appears at top-left of the sheet.

23. Photograph of the portrait painting by Max Oppenheimer (1885–1954) of the collector Otto Gerstenberg in front of *Au café* by Édouard Manet, undated. The Swiss Confederation, Federal Office of Culture, Archive of the Oskar Reinhart Collection 'Am Römerholz', Winterthur

himself fully to art. In the following years he further expanded his collection, acquiring works by both German and French artists, with particular attention for the precursors of Impressionism, such as Gustave Courbet and Jean-Baptiste-Camille Corot (see cat. nos. 3, 5–6). At the same time, he continued to pursue paintings by the artists he had included in his early wishlists (fig. 22), developing over the years remarkable stamina when it came to securing the most coveted pieces. When in 1923 he visited Otto Gerstenberg in Berlin (fig. 23), an art collector and head of a large insurance company, Reinhart stood in front of Édouard Manet's *Au café* (cat. 8) for the very first time; he instantly realised that he was looking at one of the most outstanding works of modern French art. The desire to one day own this work haunted him for a good thirty years, until he was finally able to acquire it after long endeavours for his 'Am Römerholz' collection in 1953.

A Tireless Traveller: Oskar Reinhart's Trips to London

Throughout his career as a collector Reinhart travelled incessantly. His travel diaries – he used separate diaries for his daily notes and his travel reports – are a wonderful testimony of his visits to galleries, museums and art collections all over Europe and the United States.[13] He visited London several times; an entry from March 1932 is especially noteworthy. On 6 March he notes: '10 days in London. I am starting to feel satisfied. If possible, I will travel home next Thursday. You can do everything in 12 days, especially if you minimise your social commitments.'[14] He continues the entry the following day:

> *Monday 7 March. Got up at 9am. Lefranc phones to say he's not coming. Hairdresser. Fitting at McDogall. Back at the hotel. 1pm lunch[15] at Samuel Courtauld's with Mrs Mayer and another woman. The most important paintings in the Courtauld collection are in the French exhibition.[16] In the flat I saw Cézanne's Man with Pipe (first-rate, one of the most beautiful Cézanne I have ever seen). Cézanne's Landscape. Still life. Still life with plaster putto. Manet Sketch for Dejeuner. Renoir Vollard (not special), also many Degas, Monet, Seurat, van Gogh Self-portrait with bandaged ear (important) Landscape etc. Beautiful Adam house, all very stylish. Butler + footmen. At 3.30pm farewell to Courtauld. Fritz Büsser, Swiss Federal Railways, 11b Regent Street, London. Spoken. Burlington Arcade. It starts to rain. Back to the hotel. Car accident in front of hotel entrance. A man from the hotel staff run over. Fortunately, injury not serious. Siesta on the terrace. Dinner alone at Café Royal. Very cosy place, French atmosphere. Food was good. Afterwards cinema Empire 'Arsène Lupin'. 11pm back to the hotel. Whisky.[17]*

Cast from a Similar Mould: Oskar Reinhart and Samuel Courtauld

The document quoted above is the only entry in Oskar Reinhart's diaries that reports a direct encounter with Samuel Courtauld (1876–1947). Reinhart's refined eye had immediately identified some of the stars of Courtauld's collection, among them Cezanne, especially *Man with a Pipe*, and Van Gogh's *Self-Portrait with Bandaged Ear* (fig. 43, p. 102) and *Peach Trees in Blossom;* interestingly, despite his interest for portraits and his fondness for Renoir, Reinhart was unimpressed with the painter's portrait of the Parisian art dealer Ambroise Vollard (1866–1939).[18]

Reinhart's library, now part of the museum's archives, includes the catalogue of Samuel Courtauld's collection that was published in 1954.[19] Later, pictures from Reinhart's collection were photographed for the Courtauld Institute's photo library (the Witt Library), as a short entry from 14 March 1958 in Oskar Reinhart's attests: 'Mrs Pariser from the Courtauld Institute photographs pictures for the Institute, especially Delacroix'.[20]

What Meier-Graefe (fig. 24) was to Reinhart, Roger Fry (1866–1934) was to Samuel Courtauld; Meier-Graefe's influential 1904 *History of the Development of Modern Art* had also struck a chord with Fry.[21] Roger Fry became a key proponent of modernism in Britain, and in 1910–11 he organized the landmark exhibition *Manet and the Post-Impressionists* at the Grafton Galleries in London. This groundbreaking show introduced British audiences to the work of avant-garde

Cat. 18 (detail)

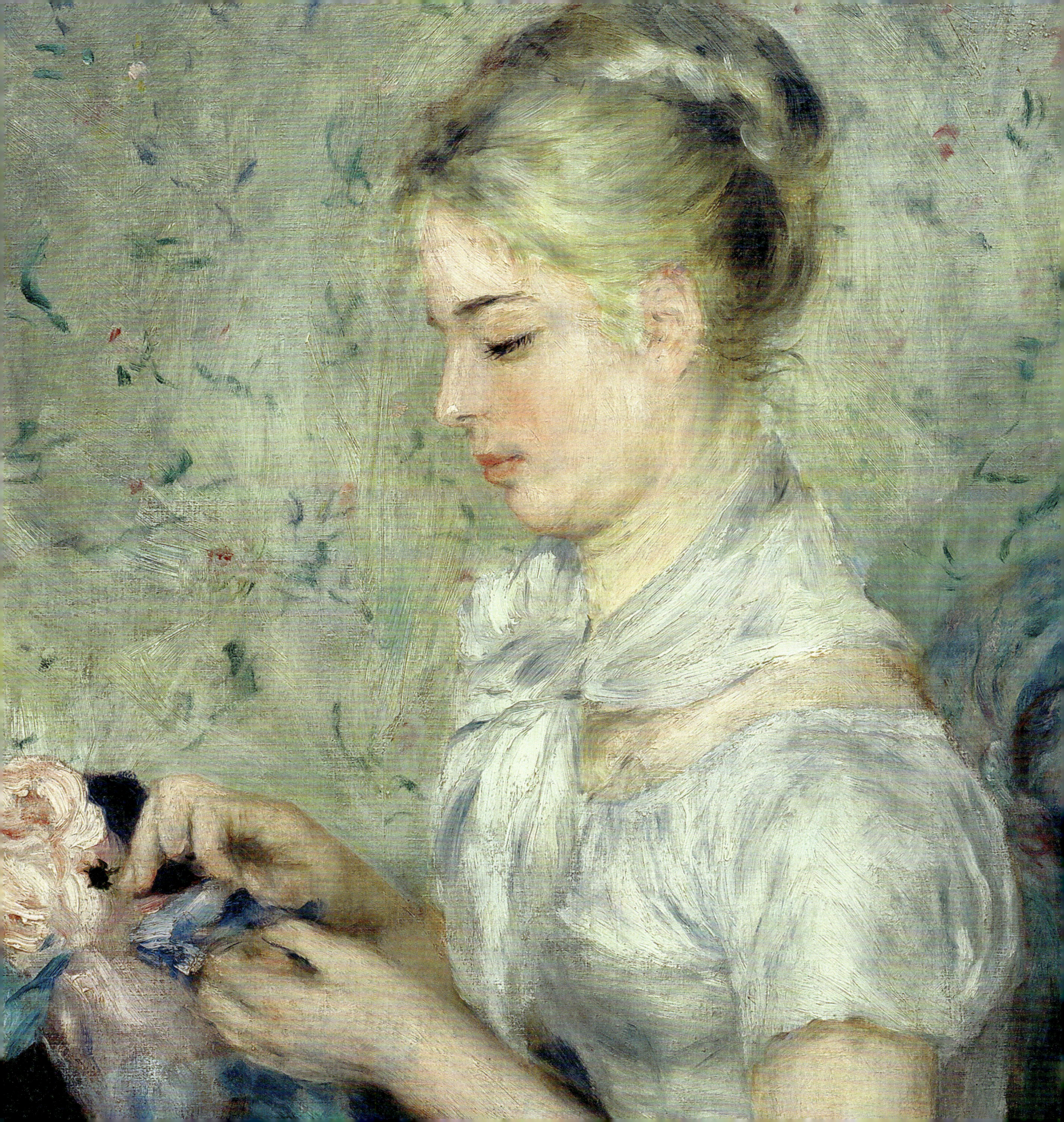

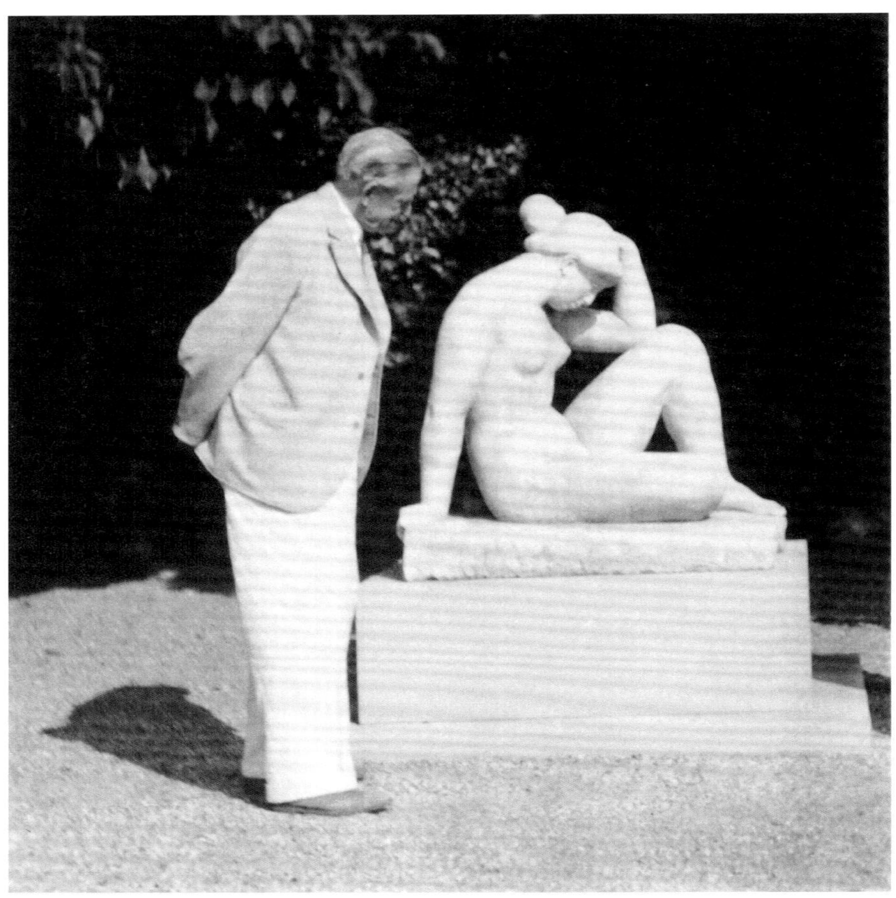

24. Julius Meier-Graefe looking at *La Méditerranée* by Aristide Maillol in the garden of the villa 'Am Römerholz', 1932. The Swiss Confederation, Federal Office of Culture, Archive of the Oskar Reinhart Collection 'Am Römerholz', Winterthur

artists such as Van Gogh, Cezanne, Gauguin and Matisse, significantly shifting perceptions about modern art. Fry's commitment to promoting modernism stemmed from his belief that art should not merely imitate nature but also convey emotional and intellectual responses. As an art critic, Fry's writings championed the importance of innovation in art. He argued for the necessity of viewing modern art in a broader historical context, linking it to earlier traditions and European artistic styles. His ardent advocacy allowed artists who were previously quite unheard of in Britain to gain recognition, and encouraged collectors – above all Samuel Courtauld – to appreciate and acquire their works. The collection assembled by Courtauld, and the artworks he secured for the National Gallery in London, also unmistakably reflected Fry's taste.[22]

No documents have yet come to light to prove that Reinhart saw Fry's pivotal exhibition at the Grafton Galleries – although one can assume that he did, or that he was aware of it, given that he stayed in London periodically between 1910 and 1911 and that he was so keenly attuned to the art scene. When acquiring individual works, Courtauld did not attempt to create a historically complete collection, but was guided above all by his own aesthetic

judgement. In this respect, Reinhart and Courtauld shared a similar vision
for their collections. Both had an eye for quality and wished to acquire the
finest works of art – Reinhart with a focus mainly on Pre-Impressionism
and Impressionism, Courtauld on Impressionism and Post-Impressionism.
Courbet and Corot played a major role in the Reinhart collection, while major
works by Seurat and Gauguin are today in the collection of The Courtauld.
Each collector contributed significantly to the appreciation and promotion
of the Impressionist movement as a whole, and aimed to enhance its public
understanding. Both Reinhart and Courtauld were motivated by their unique
taste, aesthetic sensibility and knowledge, but relied also on the opinions of
intellectually daring art historians of their time, such as Meier-Graefe and Fry.

Reinhart's Lasting Influence as a Collector

Reinhart's journey into Impressionism was not a sudden conversion; it was
a process of gradual discovery, a careful and insightful exploration of a new
artistic language. He began by acquiring works by the Impressionists, starting
with smaller pieces, especially works on paper, and carefully studying their
techniques and the nuances of their aesthetic. He spent time in galleries,
engaged in conversations with art historians and curators, seeking to deepen
his understanding of the movement. His early purchases reflected his evolving
taste, often focusing on works that showcased the Impressionists' mastery of
light and colour, or that illustrated an artist's distinct interpretation of a subject.

Reinhart's legacy extends far beyond building a collection for his own
appreciation. He believed that art should be accessible to everyone, not just
a privileged few, and donated the artworks he cherished so they could be
appreciated by the wider public. Reinhart built a collection that reflects the
breadth of his artistic knowledge and his appreciation for the beauty and
painterliness character of French Impressionist pictures. Today, the 'Am
Römerholz' collection of Impressionist paintings is regarded as one of the most
significant, once private and now public, collections of its kind in the world.
For the first time it is seen and appreciated at the Courtauld Gallery, in the very
place that is considered the home of the Impressionists in London.

Notes

1   See Reinhard-Felice 2005, p. 22.

2   Oskar Reinhart owned 212 prints by Muirhead Bone, which are today part of the Stiftung Oskar Reinhart at the Kunst Museum Winterthur.

3   The letter, addressed to his parents and dated 2 June 1908, is in the Archive of the Oskar Reinhart Collection 'Am Römerholz'; see Reinhard-Felice 2005, p. 26.

4   Ibid., p. 29.

5   Ibid., p. 31. In a letter dated 7 May 1912, Oskar Reinhart's brother Georg wrote: 'I saw your little Renoir at Durand-Ruel's; it's very pretty. But you know the truth will emerge! You've made a deep impression on all the Paris art dealers by reserving paintings for Papa. But this bluff won't work more than once, and if Papa doesn't take any of them you'll have to think up some other trick for next time.' Archive of the Oskar Reinhart Collection 'Am Römerholz'.

6   Notes 1.1, Archive of the Oskar Reinhart Collection 'Am Römerholz'.

7   Oskar Reinhart relied heavily on Julius Meier-Graefe's second revised edition of *History of the Development of Modern Art* (1914–15).

8   Notes 24, Archive of the Oskar Reinhart Collection 'Am Römerholz'. See also Reinhard-Felice 2005, p. 33.

9   This painting (Dauberville 1968, cat. 834), illustrating the surroundings of Vernon, is no longer in the Oskar Reinhart collection.

10 Hedy and Arthur Hahnloser's motto was 'To live our time'; they were keen on collecting works by artists of their own generation, such as Pierre Bonnard, Félix Vallotton, Edouard Vuillard and Aristide Maillol. They shared a close friendship with many of the artists whose works they collected; those artists visited them in Winterthur, and more than a few paintings were created at their residence Villa Flora, now part of the Kunst Museum Winterthur. However, the Hahnlosers were also able to acquire some key paintings by the artists of the previous generation, such as Van Gogh and Cezanne. See Hahnloser-Ingold 2011.

11 Displaying old masters side by side with nineteenth-century works is very much in line with Tschudi's thinking; see Reinhard-Felice 2005, p. 30; Krahmer 1996, pp. 374–75.

12 This major acquisition was made possible through the Hansens' misfortune. The collapse of the Danish Landmandsbanken in 1922 compelled the couple to sell approximately half of their precious French collection to pay off the debts. They offered the Danish nation the chance to buy the collection at a bargain price, but their offer was not met with interest. Reinhart took his chance and was successful.

13 The diaries are in the Archive of the Oskar Reinhart Collection 'Am Römerholz'.

14 The original document, in German, is in the Archive of the Oskar Reinhart Collection 'Am Römerholz', Reisetagebuch, Reise III, transcribed from the original handwritten text by Harry Joelson-Strohbach and translated by the author.

15 The word 'lunch' is in English in the original document.

16 This refers to the exhibition *French Art, 1200–1900*, which was held at the Royal Academy, London, in January–March 1932.

17 Reisetagebuch, Reise III, Archive of the Oskar Reinhart Collection 'Am Römerholz'; here transcribed by Harry Joelson-Strohbach from the original handwritten text in German and translated by the author.

18 For these paintings, see exh. cat. Paris 2019, cat. nos. 42, 71, 72, 26.

19 Cooper 1954.

20 Oskar Reinhart, Tagebücher, Tagebuch XXX, November 1957–December 1959, Archive of the Oskar Reinhart Collection 'Am Römerholz'; here transcribed by Harry Joelson-Strohbach from the original handwritten text in German and translated by the author.

21 See Barnaby Wright in exh. cat. Paris 2019, p. 61.

22 Ibid., pp. 60–66.

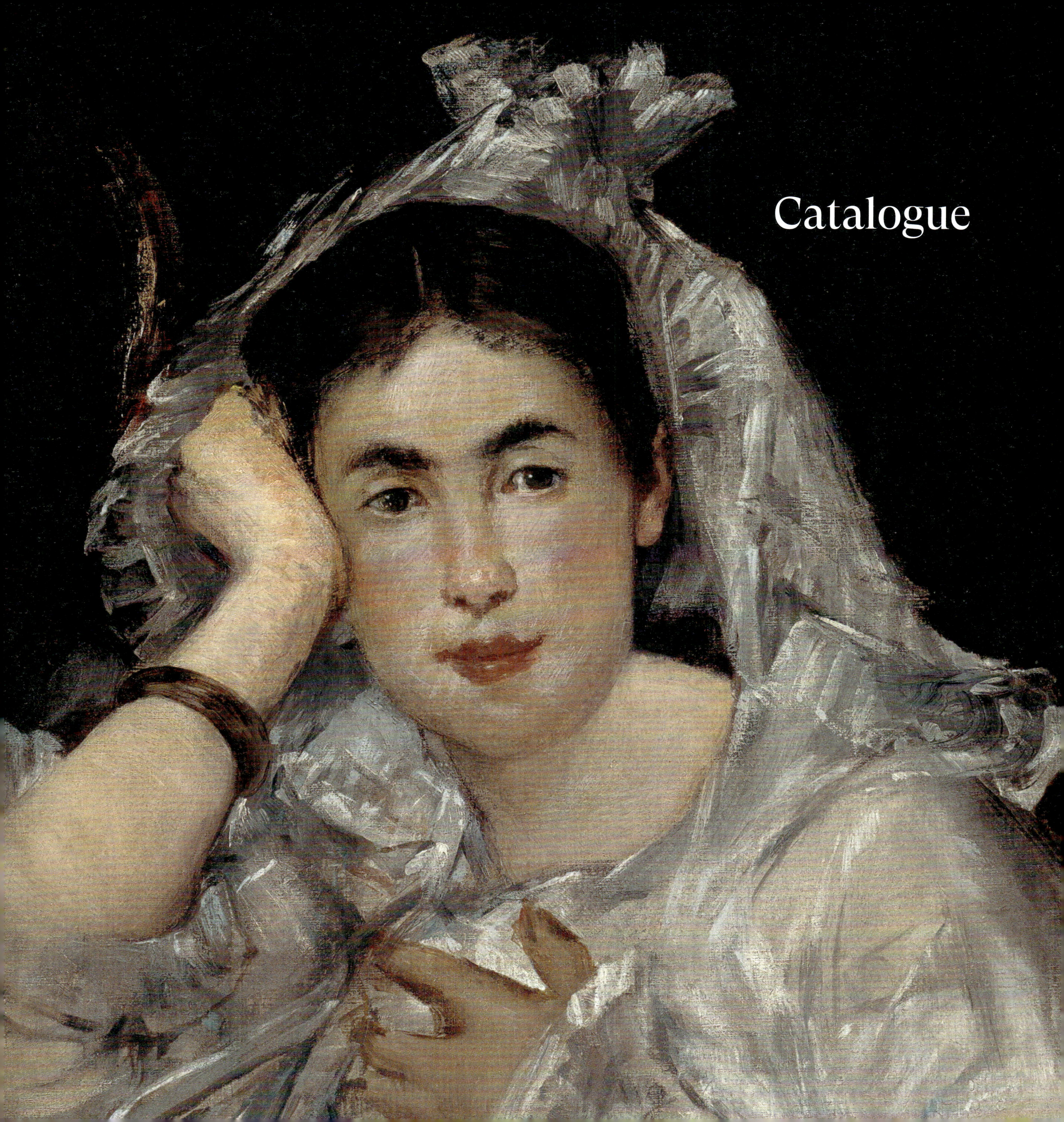
Catalogue

1

FRANCISCO DE GOYA
(1746–1828)
Still Life with Three Salmon Steaks,
1808–12

Oil on canvas, 45 × 62 cm
Inv. 1937.3
The Swiss Confederation, Federal Office of Culture,
Oskar Reinhart Collection 'Am Römerholz',
Winterthur

Provenance Acquired by Oskar Reinhart from the
Galerie Paul Rosenberg, Paris, 1937

In this painting, Goya has deliberately isolated three salmon steaks from any details that might visually compete with them. The artist has placed them against a dramatic dark background, lying on a bare surface made of stone or marble, on to which blood has dripped from their shimmering silvery skin. No other details are given, allowing the viewer to guess the setting: a kitchen counter or a fishmonger's shop?

Given the steaks' remarkable freshness, it seems implausible that Goya painted them in a single session, before they dried out and changed colour. While it is possible that he began the painting from life, it is more probable that he completed it from memory. The steaks' striking rawness is comparable to the artist's treatment of animal parts in his *Still Life with a Mutton's Head and Ribcage* (fig. 25). Both compositions are part of an extraordinary series of twelve still life pictures painted by Goya around the same period.[1] Another work from the series is also in the Oskar Reinhart Collection 'Am Römerholz', *Still Life with Bottles, Fruit and an Olive Jar* (fig. 26), and is the only one that does not depict animal parts. Goya painted these works towards the end of his life; prior to this, no comparable subjects are known to have featured in his oeuvre. While *Still Life with Bottles, Fruit and an Olive Jar* is more conventional and appears to evoke the Spanish Golden Age genre of *bodegones* (seventeenth-century kitchen still lifes), as well as the still lifes by Luis Meléndez (1716–1780), as scholars have suggested, the remainder of the series marks a departure from that tradition. The work's visceral quality is at odds with the sensibility and refinement evident in Meléndez's style, and foreshadows instead the dismembered bodies depicted by Théodore Géricault (1791–1824), marking a radical transformation of the still life genre. It also evinces similarities to the broadly painted still lifes of Paul Cezanne (1839–1906) and Édouard Manet (1832–1883).

Still lifes form a unique group within Goya's oeuvre, and thus present a conundrum for art historians, who have struggled to explain how the artist came to paint them. The Peninsular War (1807–14), which was fought in the Iberian Peninsula by Spain, Portugal and the United Kingdom against the French Empire, is often cited as a probable motivation for the production of these works. This is because addressing more obvious political subjects at such a heated time would have been risky. Furthermore, from 1809 onwards Goya's household in Madrid was compelled to accommodate a French officer as a guest.[2] In those unsettling circumstances, painting still lifes would have prevented unwanted scrutiny. During this period of upheaval, however, the artist was also engaged in the creation of the *Disasters of War* print series (c. 1810–15), which does not shy away from the disturbing depiction of mutilated human bodies to elicit a powerful emotional response.[3] This politically charged series was, out of necessity, made in private, and was only published in 1863, 35 years after the artist's death.

As documented in an inventory compiled in October 1812, following the death of the artist's wife, Josefa Bayeu (1747–1812), the twelve still lifes were legally designated as the property of Goya's son, Francisco Javier (1784–1854), but they remained in the artist's possession until his death in 1828.[4] The series hang in the dining room of Goya's residence in Calle Valverde, Madrid, until 1819, when the artist relocated to the Quinta del Sordo, on the outskirts of

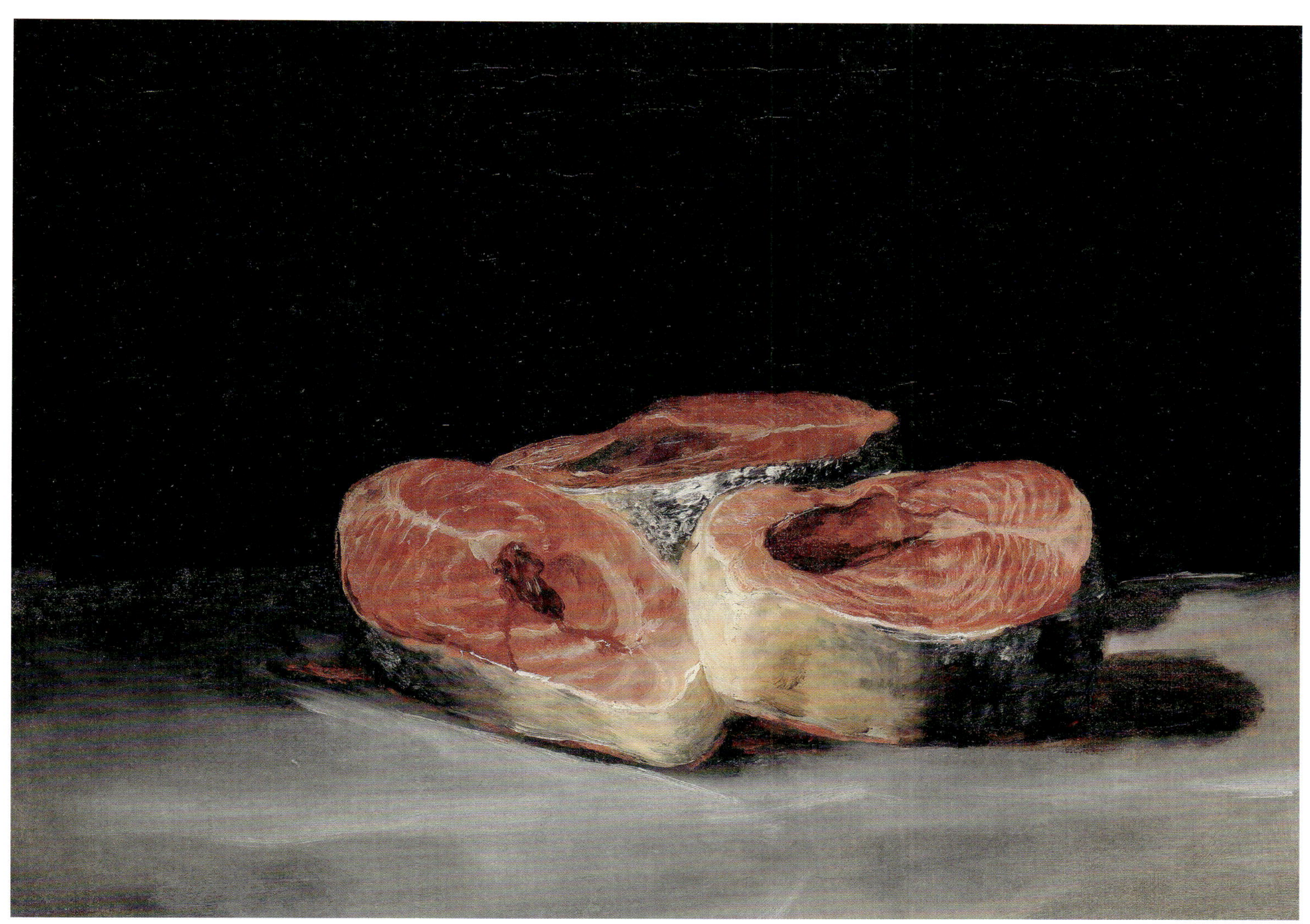

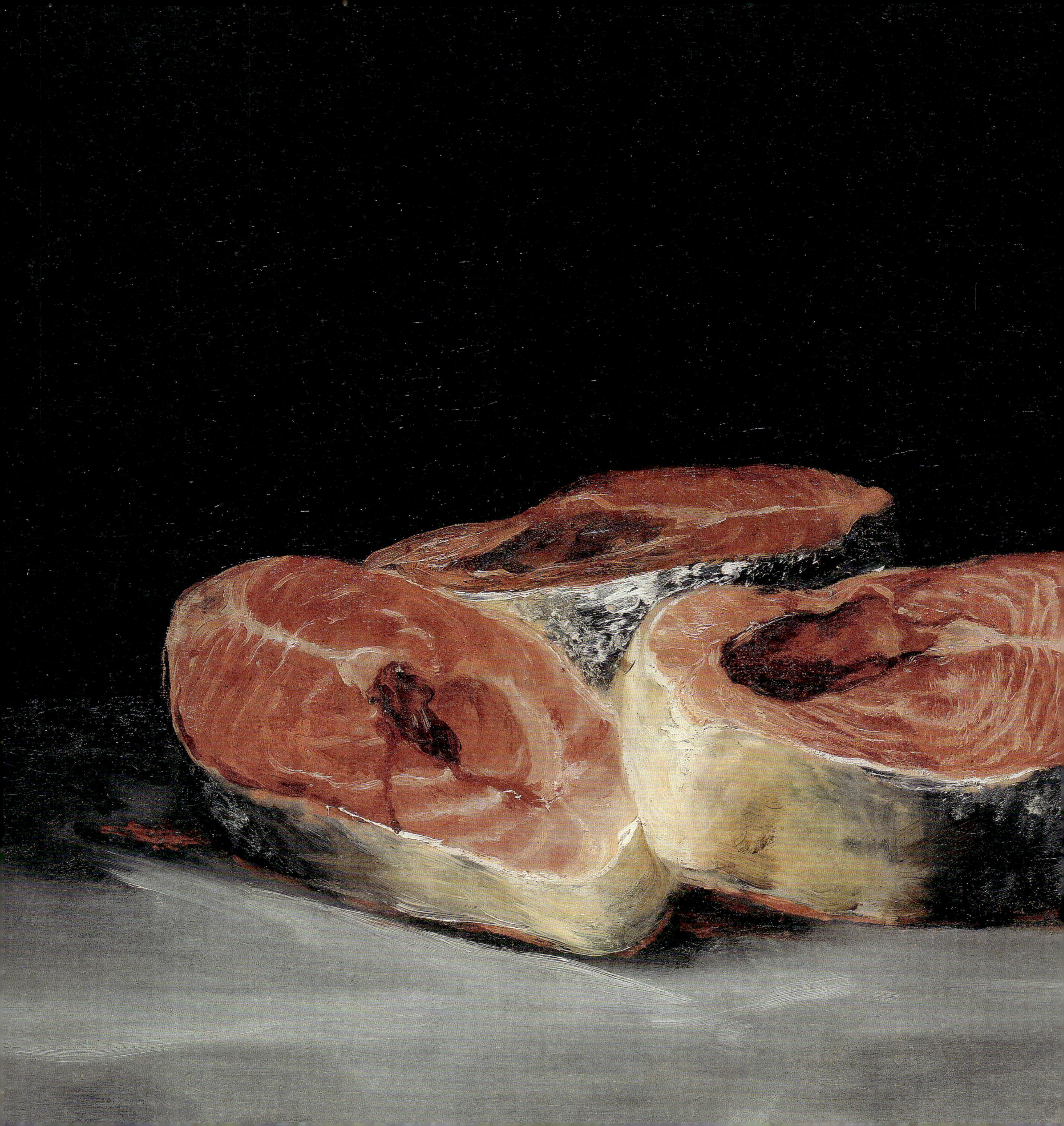

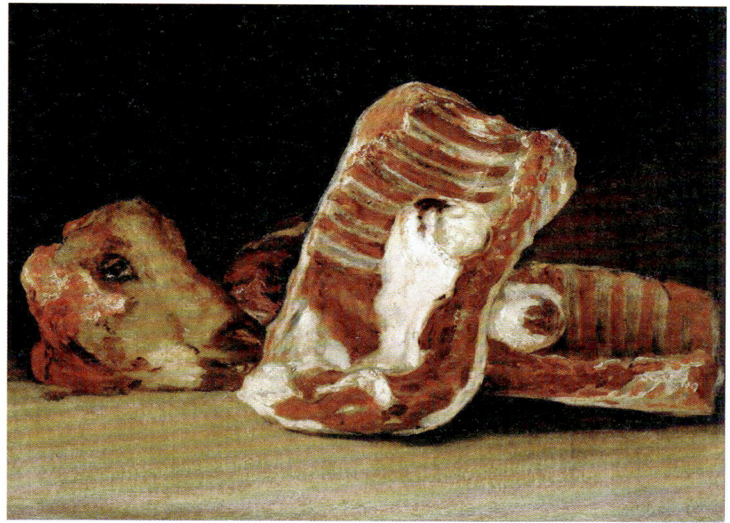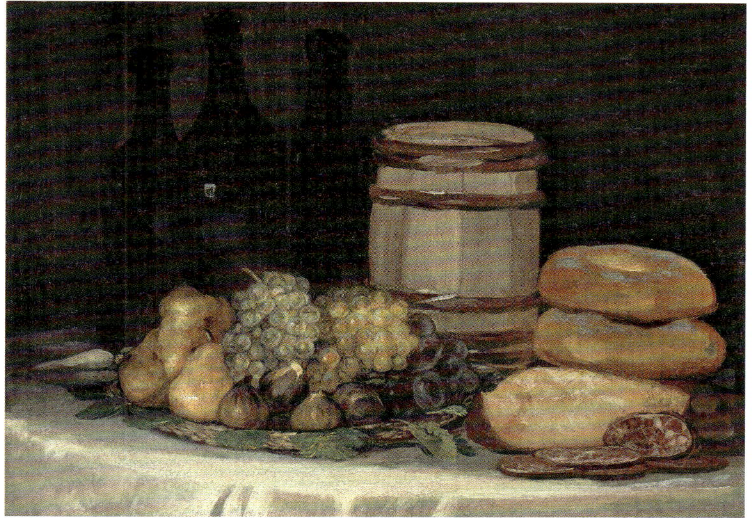

25. Francisco de Goya, *Still Life with a Mutton's Head and Ribcage*, 1808–12, oil on canvas, 45 × 62 cm. Musée du Louvre, Paris

26. Francisco de Goya, *Still Life with Bottles, Fruit and an Olive Jar*, 1808–12, oil on canvas, 45 × 63 cm. The Swiss Confederation, Federal Office of Culture, Oskar Reinhart Collection 'Am Römerholz', Winterthur

the city, and started work on a series of decorations for his new dining room, collectively known as the Black Paintings (*Pinturas Negras*). The still lifes remained in the possession of Goya's heirs until they were pledged in exchange for a monetary loan in 1851 and entered the collection of the first Count of Yumuri (1793–1865), after which they were dispersed. Today, only ten of the original twelve paintings have known whereabouts. The modernity of these pictures had not escaped the collector's sharp eye, and in 1937 Oskar Reinhart acquired *Still Life with Three Salmon Steaks* and *Still Life with Bottles, Fruit, and an Olive Jar* from the Galerie Paul Rosenberg in Paris.[5] **KG**

2

THÉODORE GÉRICAULT (1791–1824)
A Man Suffering from Delusions of Military Rank, c. 1819–22

Oil on canvas, 81 × 65 cm
Inv. 1924.7
The Swiss Confederation, Federal Office of Culture
Oskar Reinhart Collection 'Am Römerholz',
Winterthur

Provenance Acquired by Oskar Reinhart from an
unknown source between 1924 and 1926

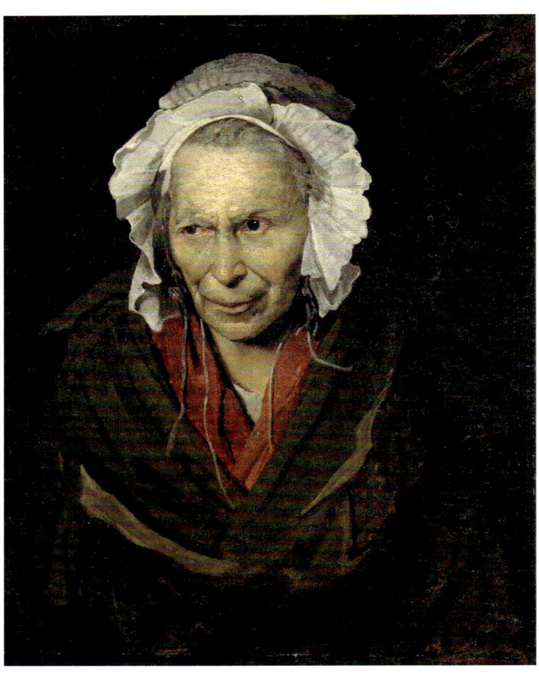

27. Théodore Géricault, *A Woman Suffering from
Obsessive Envy* (*The Hyena of the Salpêtrière*),
c. 1819–20, 72 × 58 cm. Musée des Beaux-Arts, Lyon

In the early nineteenth century the term 'monomania' was coined to describe a type of mental disorder in which a patient suffers from a form of partial insanity, conceived as a single delusional obsession. In this extraordinary painting Théodore Géricault seems to have depicted such a patient, a man suffering from delusions of military rank. This poignant work is one of a group of portraits in which the artist is thought to have depicted various fixations: *A Child Snatcher*, *A Kleptomaniac*, *A Woman Addicted to Gambling* and *A Woman Suffering from Obsessive Envy* (fig. 27).[6] These portraits are thought to have been painted around the same years, after the artist completed his most celebrated painting, *The Raft of the Medusa* (1818–19; Musée du Louvre, Paris). These works have since been interpreted in the context of the emergence of the new discipline of psychiatry. Although by the end of the nineteenth century the term monomania had lost its scientific rigour and was no longer used, the term 'monomaniac' remained attached to this group of paintings.

The art critic and dealer Louis Viardot discovered the pictures in Baden-Baden in 1863; the following year he published a letter in the *Gazette des Beaux-Arts*, arguing that the portraits represented 'alienated figures' suffering from mental disorders.[7] The series, which, according to Viardot, originally consisted of ten portraits (although he only saw five), was owned by Dr Adolphe Lachèze, who in turn bought them from Dr Étienne-Jean Georget (1795–1828). Georget, who had been a student of Dr Jean-Étienne-Dominique Esquirol (1772–1840), the father of psychiatry in France, was thought to have been the chief physician of the Salpêtrière asylum for women in Paris and an acquaintance of Géricault. Accounts of Géricault's personal difficulties in completing the dauntingly large and complex *Raft of the Medusa* (1818–19, Musée du Louvre Paris) and suggestions that some of his close family members may have suffered from mental illness, have for years cemented the belief that the artist had personal reasons for undertaking these works, which would have brought him close to Georget and his teacher Esquirol.[8] According to this interpretation, the series was painted as an illustration of mental illness; the portraits were a sign of gratitude for the medical help Géricault's family members had received. But scholars have since questioned the role previously attributed to Georget in commissioning and owning the series, or even whether he was the chief physician of the asylum.[9]

Despite the uncertainty surrounding their exact origin, commission or even the existence of the other five canvases, these portraits represent a unique body of work in early nineteenth-century painting and in Géricault's oeuvre. If they are true portraits of real people suffering from mental illness, Géricault is to be commended for the sensitivity and dignity with which he captured them. Set against dark backgrounds, the figures are bust-length, looking directly out of the picture, their hands not visible; all appear to be dressed in winter clothes. The present portrait, slightly taller than the others, is the only one to show specific accessories that would help to identify the nature of the sitter's delusional thoughts: a police cap with red piping and a tassel.[10] A tag with the number 121 hanging from a simple cord around his neck – probably a hospital ward badge – is worn proudly like a medal for military merit. The gaunt figure, emaciated cheeks and lost gaze conjure the powerful image of a person who has lost touch with reality. **KG**

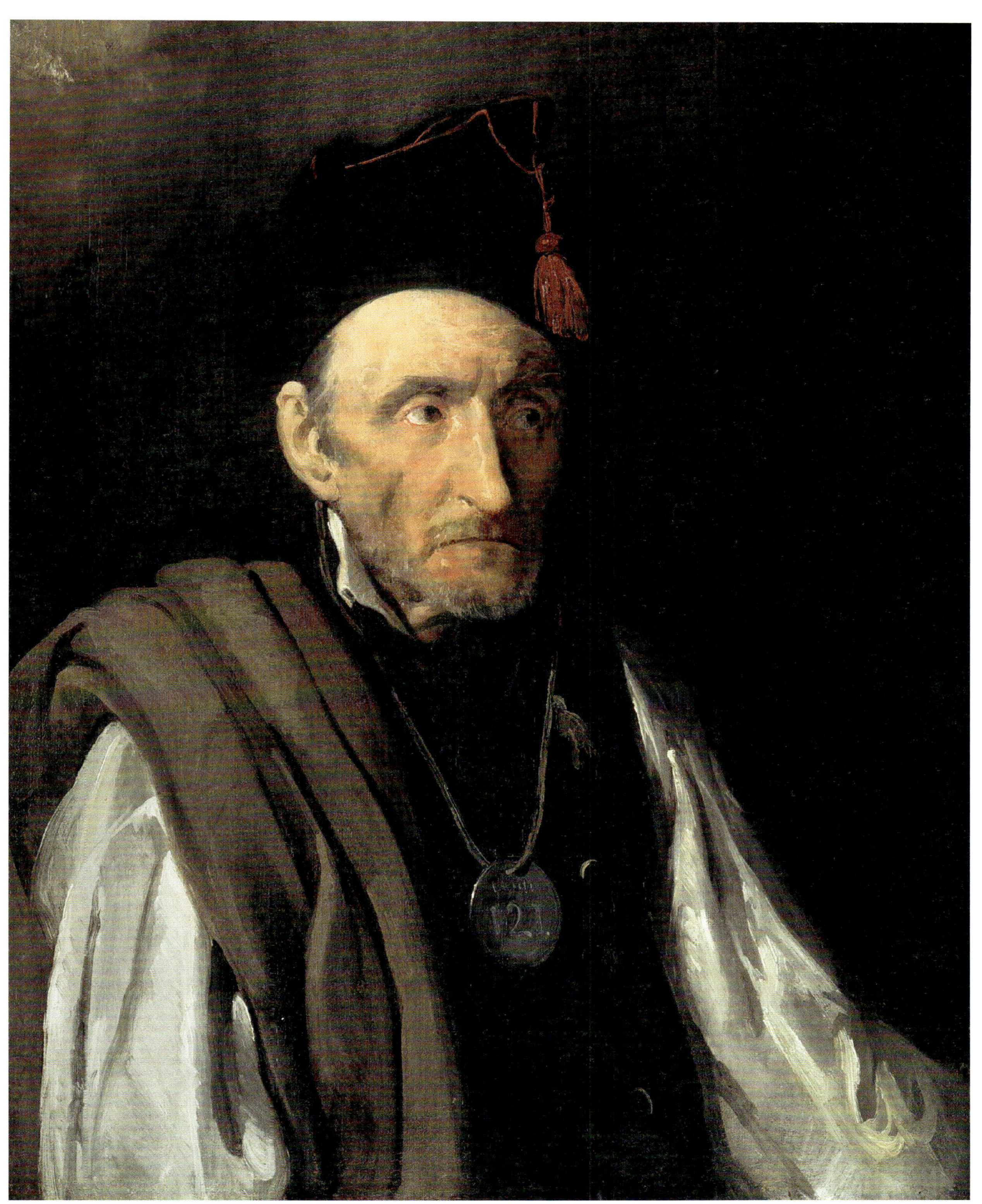

3

JEAN-BAPTISTE-CAMILLE COROT
(1796–1875)
Girl Reading, c. 1850–55

Oil on canvas, 46 × 38.5 cm
Inv. 1938.4
The Swiss Confederation, Federal Office of Culture
Oskar Reinhart Collection 'Am Römerholz',
Winterthur

Provenance Acquired by Oskar Reinhart from the
Galerie Paul Rosenberg, Paris, 1938

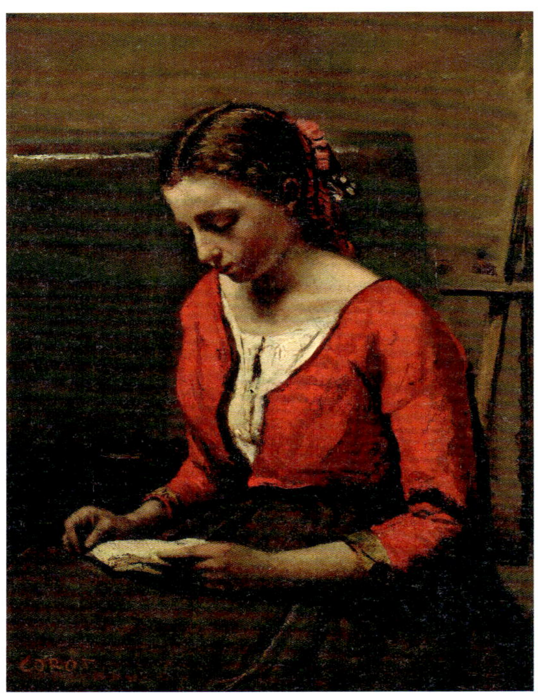

28. Jean-Baptiste-Camille Corot, *Girl Reading*,
c. 1845–50, oil on canvas, 42.5 × 32.5 cm. Emil Bührle
collection, on loan to the Kunsthaus Zurich

Although his reputation rests on his landscapes, Corot was always passionately interested in the human figure. His landscapes are frequently animated by finely rendered staffage: mythological or literary figures in historic landscapes and peasants and other rural labourers when he worked in a more realistic mode. The figure studies he made during his 1825–28 sojourn in Italy, however, presaged an important strand of his later oeuvre: highly finished paintings of single figures that fuse naturalism with the classicising influence of Raphael (1483–1520). These figures, often depicted reading or lost in thought, are not portraits in the traditional sense, and have more in common with the *tronies* pioneered by seventeenth-century Dutch artists like Rembrandt (1606–1669). By the early 1850s Corot had developed a new genre that fuses aspects of portraiture, genre painting and allegory; *Girl Reading* is both a typical example of these *figures de fantaisie* and one of Corot's finest such paintings.

Seated with her head bowed and eyes cast down over a book, the girl's costume – a striped apron or overskirt folded back over a crimson skirt, a white blouse and a black waistcoat – and the diminutive flock of sheep in the background at right suggest that she is a shepherdess.[11] Her pale face, framed by her loose hair, recalls that of an Italian Renaissance Madonna, yet Corot has rendered it in an unidealised manner that retains the model's individuality. Despite the suggestion of an outdoor setting, the even fall of the light and the flatness and summary handling of the background, reminiscent of a theatrical backdrop, point to the painting's execution in the studio. Corot depicted reading figures in both open air and studio settings, the latter of which he used in a somewhat earlier painting of the same subject (fig. 28). The present work seems to elide the distinction between the two. Rather than creating a realistic setting, Corot's focus is squarely on the model, who fills the canvas, and especially on capturing her contemplative pose and expression and the dreamlike atmosphere they evoke.

Reinhart's admiration for Corot is demonstrated by his acquisition of no less than ten canvases by the artist, spanning most of his long career. *Girl Reading* is one of three figure paintings by Corot in his collection and is arguably the most accomplished. **RS**

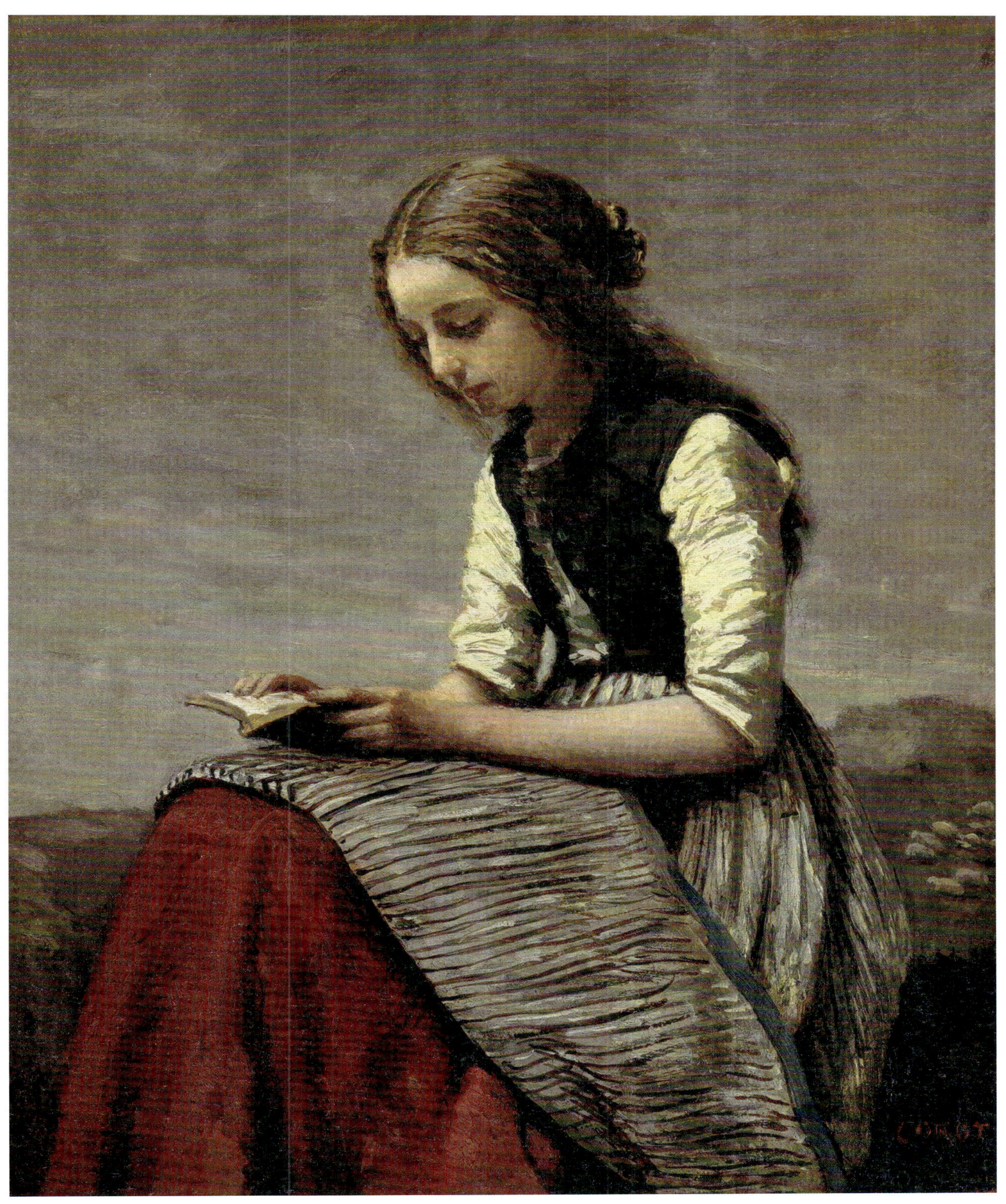

4

HONORÉ DAUMIER (1808–1879)
Don Quixote and Sancho Panza,
c. 1865–70

Oil on panel, 29.7 × 45 cm
Inv. 1923.14
The Swiss Confederation, Federal Office of Culture
Oskar Reinhart Collection 'Am Römerholz',
Winterthur

Provenance Acquired by Oskar Reinhart from
Wilhelm Hansen, Copenhagen, 1923

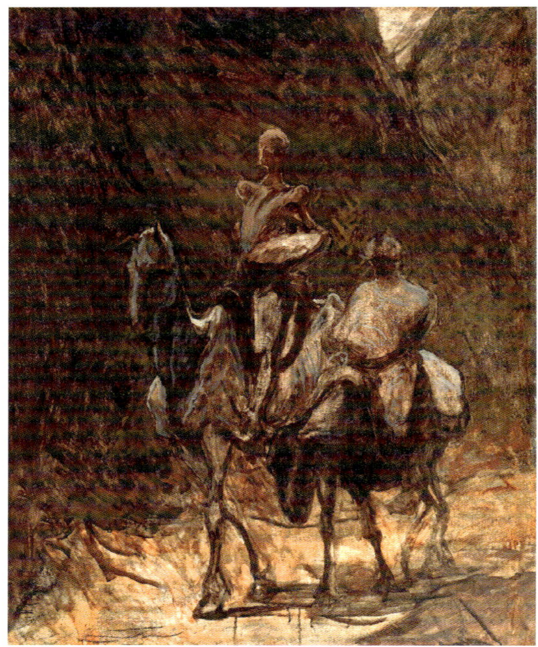

29. Honoré Daumier, *Don Quixote and Sancho
Panza*, 1868–72, oil on canvas, 100 × 81 cm. The
Courtauld, London (Samuel Courtauld Trust)

Daumier was already well-known as a caricaturist of French nineteenth-century society by the time his work was showcased at the Galerie Durand-Ruel in Paris in 1878, the year before his death. The exhibition revealed a depth of inquiry into painting and drawing that was received with astonishment by the press: one commentator declared in ecstatic tones that 'He has everything: breadth of touch, design, colour, thought. Some canvases seem to have been drawn by Michelangelo and painted by Delacroix!'[12] The display included six paintings and five drawings related to Miguel de Cervantes's novel *Don Quixote*, part of a cycle of 29 paintings and 41 drawings that Daumier produced over twenty years.[13] The first volume of *Don Quixote* was published in Spain in 1605, the second in 1615; the novel later became a popular subject amongst French illustrators and artists. The Paris edition of 1836–37 featured 768 woodcuts by Tony Johannot (1803–1852), and was followed in 1863 by an edition illustrated by Gustave Dóre (1832–1883). Jean-Honoré Fragonard (1732–1806) – an artist Daumier greatly admired – was said to have made over one hundred drawings based on *Don Quixote*,[14] three of which are held in the Oskar Reinhart Collection 'Am Römerholz'.[15]

The novel centres on the doomed pursuits of the knight errant Don Quixote and his squire Sancho Panza. Their antithetical physicalities – Don Quixote lean and lively, Sancho Panza corpulent and slouching (characteristics mirrored in their respective horse and donkey) – no doubt appealed to the mind and hand of the caricaturist, who 'exploited this contrast as the confrontation of opposing principals'.[16] Yet Daumier's depictions of *Don Quixote* venture far from caricature, or even illustration. Rather than concentrating solely upon the novel's more dramatic scenes, Daumier repeatedly chose to show the two men riding through the rugged, unpopulated Sierra Morena in moments of journeying between ill-fated adventures. The Winterthur picture, like that of The Courtauld (fig. 29), is one such work. In it, Don Quixote leads the two men through a craggy landscape towards the sunlit valley below. The broad, horizontal strokes of the sky, clouds and valley express the vastness of both the landscape and of their quest; the yellow downstrokes of the mountainside and the white, sinuous lines that describe the tense musculature of Don Quixote's workhorse Rocinante, and indicate the steep descent upon which they are embarking. Though Karl Eric Maison, author of the 1967 catalogue raisonné of Daumier's work, considered the painting unfinished, this is far from certain.[17] The modernity of Daumier's late paintings is revealed in his highly experimental use of loose, rapid brushwork, which suggests motion and feeling to extraordinary effect.

Daumier's interest in *Don Quixote* was 'seen from the outset as a psychological portrait of the artist himself'.[18] Indeed, a single print he made on the subject recasts Don Quixote as an artist, his lance replaced by a quill. The text accompanying its publication in 1867, written by Daumier's friend Alexandre Pothey (1820–1897), further emphasises the affinity between Don Quixote, the quintessential idealist, and Daumier: 'He has exchanged his lance for the modern weapon, the pen, in order to pierce the evils, the vanities and the platitudes that outrage his great spirit'.[19] **CN**

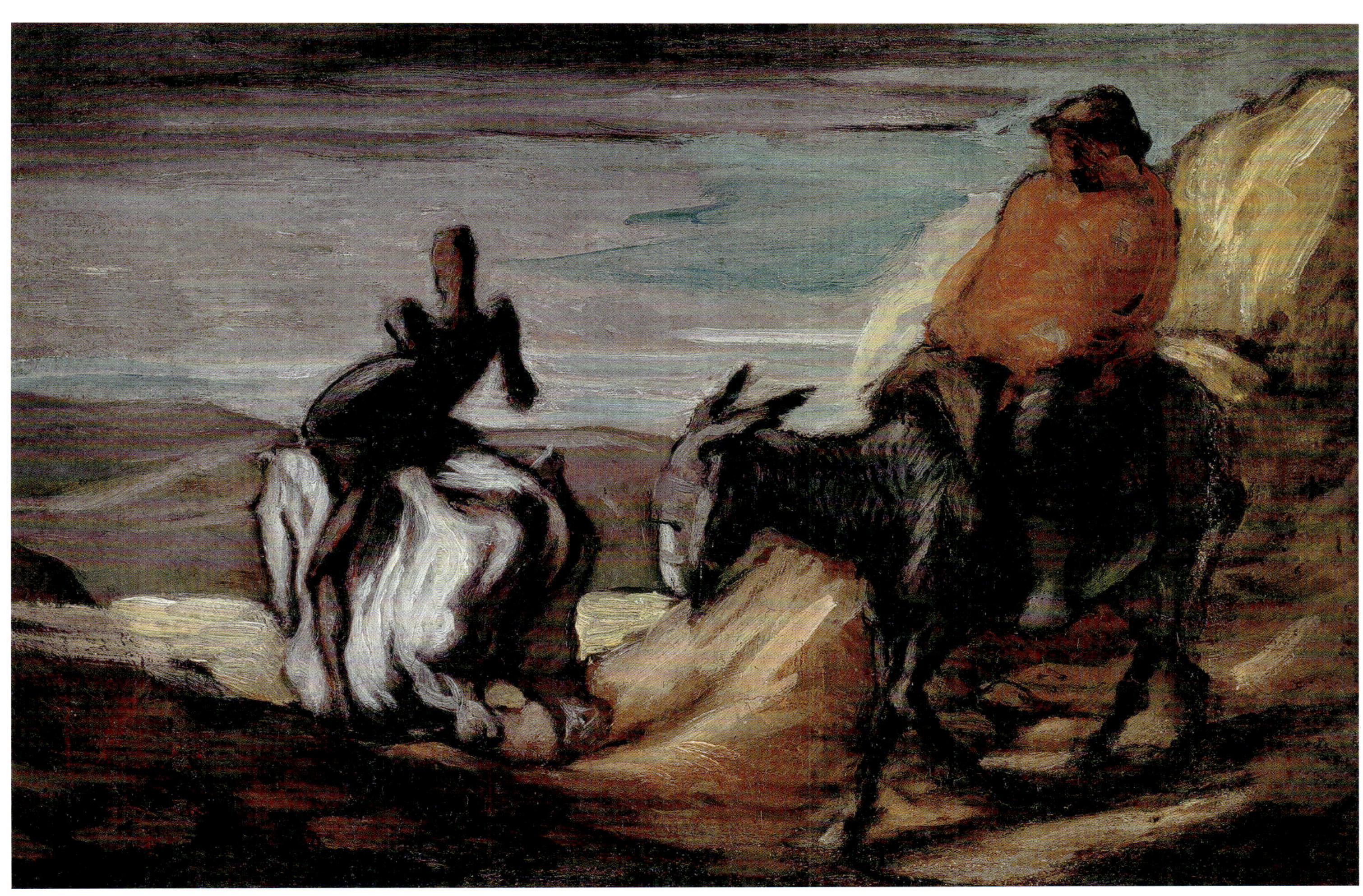

5

GUSTAVE COURBET (1819–1877)
The Hammock, 1844

Oil on canvas, 70.5 × 97 cm
Inv. 1924.11
The Swiss Confederation, Federal Office of Culture
Oskar Reinhart Collection 'Am Römerholz',
Winterthur

Provenance Acquired by Oskar Reinhart from the
Galerie Paul Rosenberg, Paris, 1924

The Hammock offers an early example of Courbet bringing together a female subject with ostensibly literary, allegorical or mythological connotations with modern dress – or lack thereof – to highly provocative effect.[20] The figure of the young woman asleep in a hammock strung over a stream in a forest glade, her long blonde hair wreathed with ivy like a Bacchante, would have called to mind for a contemporary viewer the poem 'Sara la baigneuse' by Victor Hugo (1802–1885), published in his collection *Les Orientales* (1829). In the poem, the beautiful Sara lounges in a hammock suspended over water, giving herself over to erotic reverie. 'Sara la baigneuse' served as a source of inspiration to numerous artists exhibiting at the Salon in the 1830s and 1840s.

When in 1845 Courbet submitted five paintings to the Paris Salon, *The Hammock* was one of the four that the jury rejected. Although reclining female figures in varying states of undress and degrees of coyness were a fixture at the Salon, it is not difficult to see why Courbet's overtly transgressive approach to the subject met with official refusal. Where Courbet erred – at least in the eyes of the jury – was in dressing his 'Sara' in modern clothing, her striped gown half-unbuttoned over a transparent chemise and her skirt hitched up to reveal her white stockings and yellow ankle boots, thus making it clear that this was no nymph or odalisque, but a contemporary woman. There is a hint of autoeroticism in the woman's unfastened bodice, in the position of her right hand and in the blush suffusing her cheeks; she seems to be revelling in her own semi-nudity, much as Sara does in the poem.

Courbet was a lifelong admirer of Hugo's poetry, and it is highly probable that 'Sara la baigneuse' served as the inspiration for *The Hammock*. Indeed, his friend and biographer, the critic Jules Castagnary (1830–1888), noted the connection between the two works, at the same time insisting that Courbet's painting depicts a contemporary woman with a painstaking attention to her costume that daringly courted accusations of vulgarity.[21] But Castagnary's assertion that *The Hammock* was a purely Realist work is complicated by the manner of its execution. The bright colours used in the woman's clothing, body and accessories, and the almost enamelled quality of the finely detailed brushwork are both characteristic of the *troubadour* style, a type of painting popular in France during the later Romantic period that usually focused on literary or historical subjects, and is at odds with the heavy impasto and darker palette Courbet adopted subsequently. It is also the first instance of another recurring theme in Courbet's later oeuvre, most famously epitomised by *Sleep* (1866, Petit Palais, Paris): pictures of sleeping women whose subjects appear to have been captured in the midst of erotic dreams. *The Hammock* and its sisters suggest that an interest in poetry and dreams were not as antithetical to Courbet's brand of Realism as was often claimed. **RS**

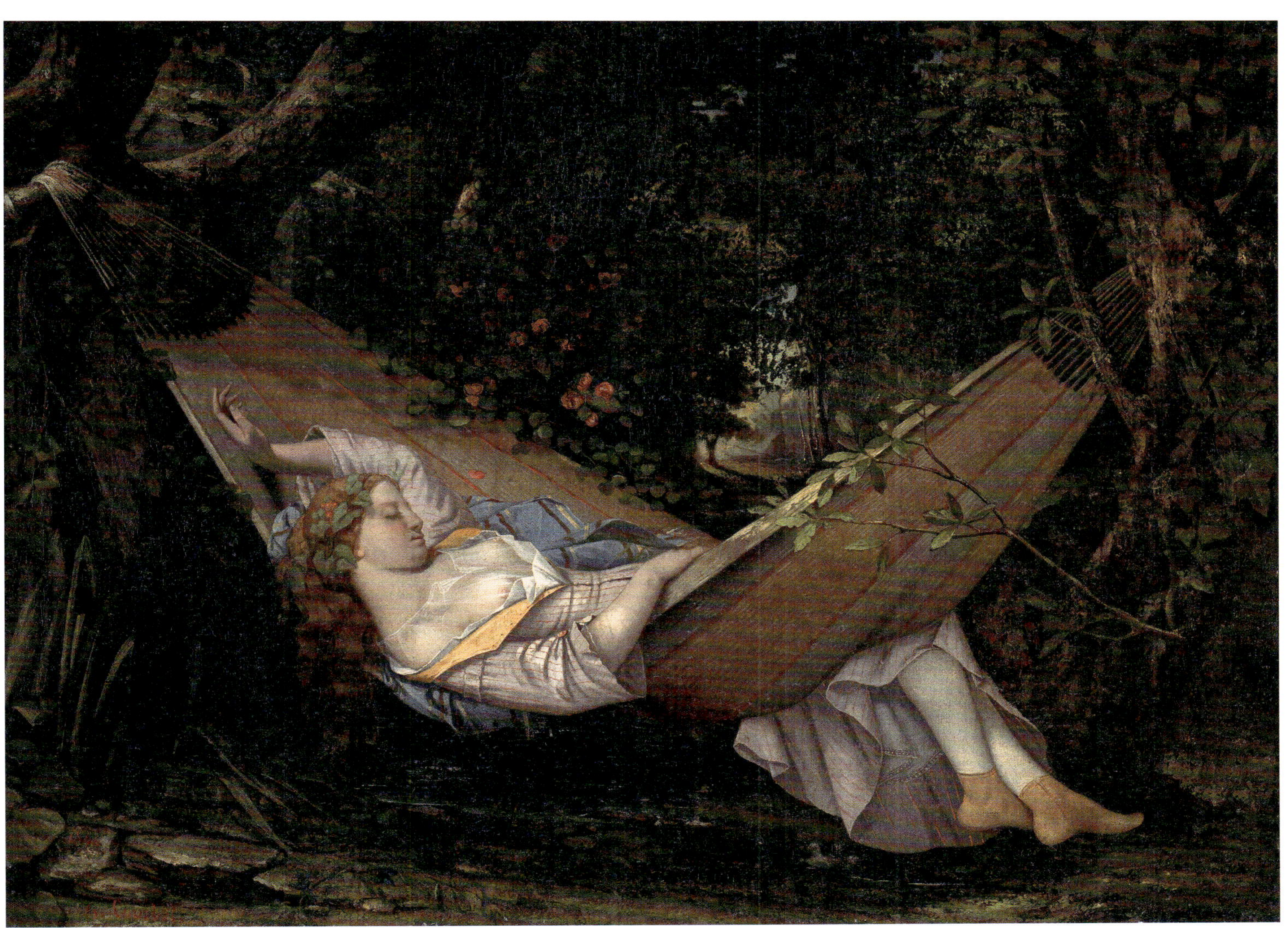

6

GUSTAVE COURBET (1819–1877)
The Wave, 1870

Oil on canvas, 80.5 × 99.5 cm
Inv. 1925.6
The Swiss Confederation, Federal Office of Culture
Oskar Reinhart Collection 'Am Römerholz',
Winterthur

Provenance Acquired by Oskar Reinhart from
the Galerie Paul Cassirer, Amsterdam, 1925

Although Courbet had begun painting seascapes during trips to the Normandy coast in 1865, when he spent three months in Trouville, the subject of the wave first appeared in his oeuvre in 1869. Between 1869 and 1870 he produced more than 60 variations on this theme, stripping the composition, in most cases, to its essentials: a thundering wave, often peaking in the centre; the rocks upon which it crashes; and a stormy sky filled with leaden clouds. He executed them primarily with a palette knife – or, in one case, according to the eyewitness account of the novelist Guy de Maupassant (1850–1893), with a kitchen knife.

Courbet's frequent repetition of the subject reflects both his enduring fascination with the elemental violence and destructive power of the sea and his keen commercial sense. He understood that these paintings sold readily and, given that such basic compositions were quick to execute, especially on a smaller scale, he could easily keep up with demand. His correspondence in the late 1860s details frequent sales of these pictures on the spot to collectors eager to take home a souvenir of their visit to Normandy.[22] He did, however, also produce seascapes on a larger scale, which were intended for exhibition at the Salon.

The *Wave* acquired by Reinhart is one of the larger versions of this composition; it exhibits similarities with the version now in the Brooklyn Museum, New York. The cresting wave in the foreground has a remarkable weight and solidity, a result of Courbet's use of the palette knife and something which became a common target of criticism during his lifetime. Such criticism notwithstanding, Courbet held a high place in Reinhart's esteem; over a period of more than 40 years he acquired no less than a dozen canvases by the artist, seeking to represent the full span of his career and subject matter.[23] He parted with one of them, *Choirboys* (now in a private collection) in order to acquire Corot's *Girl Reading* (see cat. 3); his diary and his correspondence with the dealer Paul Rosenberg indicate how reluctant he was to do so.[24] The presence of one of Courbet's *Wave* paintings in the collection has a particular resonance when we recall Paul Cezanne's admiration of both their subject matter and their facture. Cezanne emulated the older artist's use of the palette knife in his early work (see cat. 9) and, speaking of the *Waves*, declared that '[Courbet's] tide … appears to come from out the depth of the ages, it hits you right in the stomach. You have to step back. The entire room feels the spray.'[25] Given Courbet's foundational importance for the Impressionists and Cezanne, whom Reinhart regarded as the pinnacle of art, his prominence in the collection seems not only logical, but indisputable. **RS**

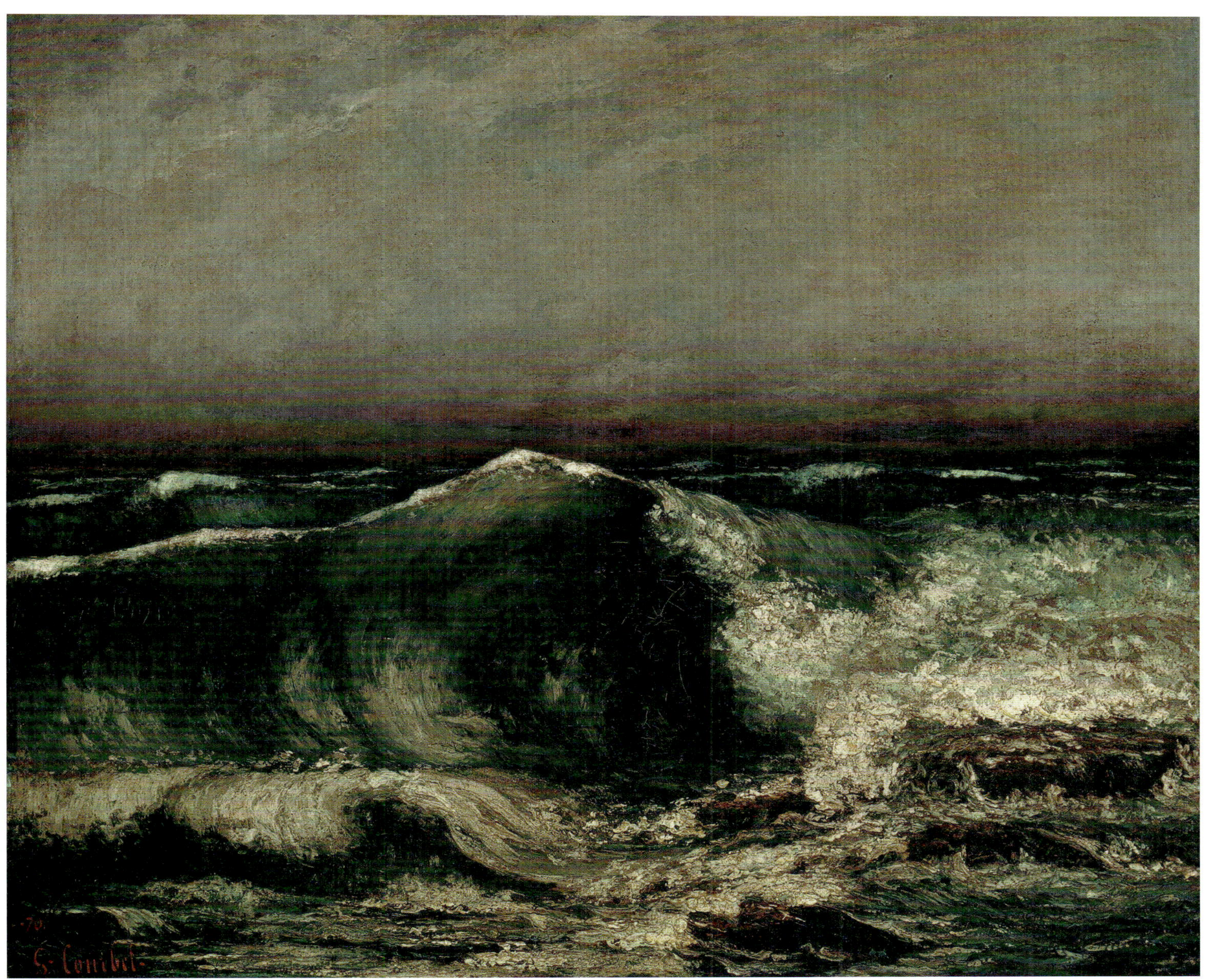

7

ÉDOUARD MANET (1832–1883)

Portrait of Marguerite de Conflans
Wearing a Mantilla, 1873

Oil on canvas, 55.5 × 46.5 cm
Inv. 1947.1
The Swiss Confederation, Federal Office of Culture,
Oskar Reinhart Collection 'Am Römerholz',
Winterthur

Provenance Acquired by Oskar Reinhart from
the dealer Alex R. Ball, New York, 1947

Marguerite de Conflans (b. 1856), the daughter of Manet's schoolfriend Foiet de Conflans, sat for Manet four times in 1873, when she was seventeen years old. Two of the resulting paintings were loose sketches, one of which can be tentatively identified as *At the Dance (Au bal)*, now in The Courtauld's collection; the remaining canvases are fully realised portraits.[26] The two finished portraits, evidently painted in quick succession, show Marguerite in the same informal pose, seated with her head resting on her hand. The earlier of the portraits (fig. 30) presents her as a modern young woman relaxing in a domestic setting, wearing a housedress and with her hair down. Although x-ray analysis revealed that Manet began the second portrait, ultimately acquired by Oskar Reinhart, in a very similar manner to the first, he soon altered it to create a dramatically different and overtly Spanish-inspired composition.

Restricting his palette largely to black and white, Manet made a work that is as much about the act of painting as it is about creating a likeness. A stark black background frames the translucent veil surrounding the sitter's pale face, which is similarly framed by her dark hair. The only touches of colour are the red of her cheeks and lips, the gold of her bracelet and the pale blue shadows in the folds of her white garment. The fine detail in Marguerite's face and right arm contrasts strongly with the free and vigorous brushwork Manet used to render her clothing. Inspired by James McNeill Whistler's (1834–1903) *Symphonies in White*,[27] Manet periodically painted his own portraits of women in white – notably those featuring his wife, Suzanne (1829–1906), his fellow artist and sister-in-law Berthe Morisot (1841–1895) and his student Eva Gonzalès (1849–1883) – in order to explore the possibilities of this challenging colour; both portraits of Marguerite de Conflans can be considered part of this strand of his oeuvre. However, her *mantilla* – albeit not a genuine Spanish shawl, but a part of her morning gown arranged around her head – as well as the dark background and striking chiaroscuro, place this portrait among the artist's homages to Spanish painting; there are especially notable parallels with his 1862 painting of the dancer Lola de Valence (Musée d'Orsay, Paris). Depicting Marguerite in Spanish costume may also subtly acknowledge Manet's friendship with her father, whose collection of Spanish prints and paintings offered him one of his first experiences of an art he would revere and emulate over the course of his career. **RS**

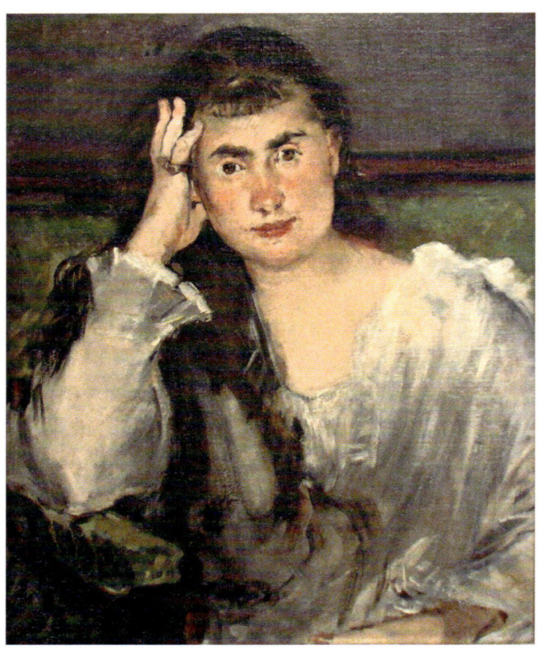

30. Édouard Manet, *Marguerite de Conflans*,
1873, oil on canvas, 53.4 × 44.5 cm. Smith College
Museum of Art, Northampton, Massachusetts

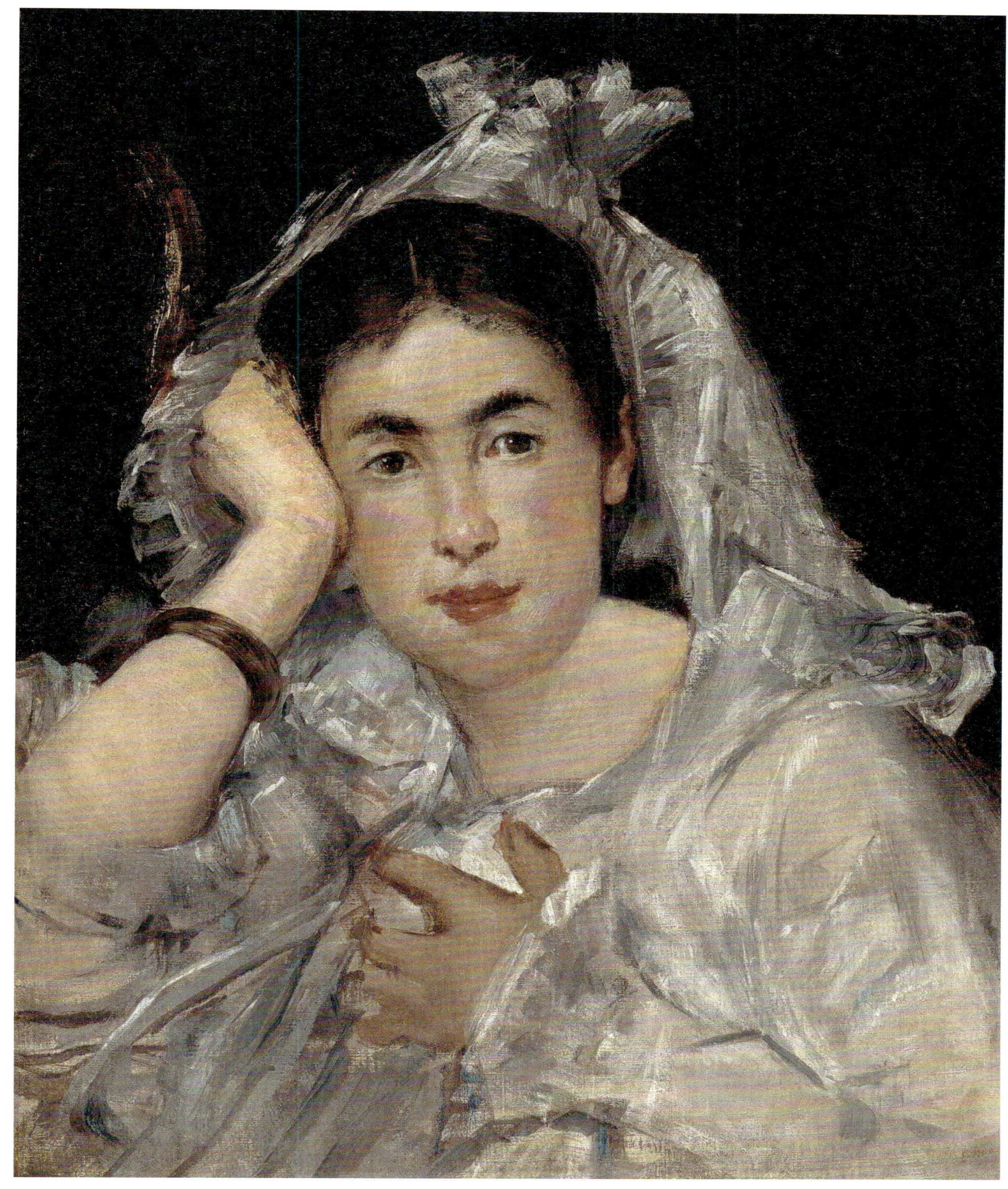

8

EDOUARD MANET (1832–1883)
Au café, 1878

Oil on canvas, 78 × 84 cm
Inv. 1953.3
The Swiss Confederation, Federal Office of Culture,
Oskar Reinhart Collection 'Am Römerholz',
Winterthur

Provenance Acquired by Oskar Reinhart from
Margarethe Scharf, Berlin/Oberstdorf, through Dr
Fritz Nathan, Zurich, 1953

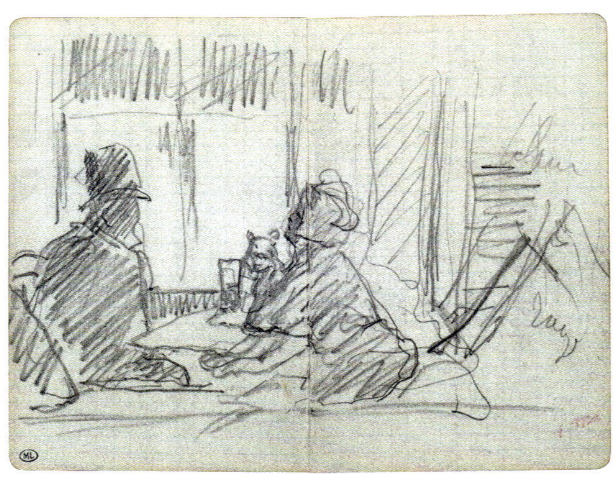

31. Édouard Manet, *Couple with a Dog on a Café
Terrace*, c. 1878, black chalk and graphite on
squared paper, 14.1 × 18.6 cm. Musée du Louvre,
Paris

In 1878 Manet began work on a large canvas that was originally titled *Reichshoffen*, the name of a Paris brasserie-cum-café-concert. He may have intended to show it at that year's Exposition Universelle, which was to open in July, either as part of the official fine art exhibition or in a one-man show, a second iteration of the one he had organised within the grounds of the previous Exposition in 1867. After struggling to resolve issues with the composition, Manet divided the canvas in two, to the dismay of at least one person who had seen the complete work: the artist Gaston La Touche (1854–1913), who later wrote that 'Like many other friends, I couldn't but regret this. … The composition had many great qualities and the painter's weak points were not in evidence.'[28] Manet then reworked both parts of the original composition, further cutting down and rearranging both sections of canvas. The right-hand portion of the canvas became *Corner of a Café-Concert*, now in the National Gallery, London (fig. 32); the left-hand portion became the present painting, *Au café*.[29]

The original composition appears to have begun as a small chalk and pencil drawing made across two pages of a pocket sketchbook of the type Manet often carried (fig. 31), depicting a top-hatted male café patron and a waitress on opposite sides of a table, observed in profile. By the time the artist began the painting, his initial conception had expanded to a large, multi-figure scene. The setting, the Café de Reichshoffen, was a brasserie located on the Boulevard de Rochechouart, on the southern border of Montmartre. Brasseries (literally, 'breweries') enjoyed great popularity in Paris in the second half of the nineteenth century; the term referred to an establishment that served Alsatian beer and that may have offered entertainment. In the wake of the Franco-Prussian War (1870–71), such places were charged with political significance, particularly as many of them were owned and staffed by Alsatians who had fled to Paris following Germany's annexation of Alsace and Lorraine, and the presence of a soldier – his scarlet kepi partially visible at left – undoubtedly alludes to the war and to France's growing appetite for *revanche*, or retaliation.

The two principal figures in *Au café* were modelled by the artist Henri Guérard (1846–1897), a painter and printmaker who was soon to marry Manet's student Eva Gonzalès (1849–1883), and by the actress Ellen Andrée (1856–1933), who had modelled the previous year for Manet's painting *Plum Brandy* (c. 1877, National Gallery of Art, Washington, D.C.).[30] The relationship between the two figures is unclear. It would have been uncommon for an unchaperoned woman to patronise a brasserie, and drinking alcohol in public may have raised questions about her morals, although beer was considered a less suspect drink than spirits.[31] The woman's modest dress and proximity to the man beside her might have invited the viewer to read them as a married or engaged couple, but Manet provides no other clues (for example, hands displaying rings) to substantiate this reading, and the figures' lack of engagement with each other makes it equally probable that they are two strangers who happen to be sharing the same space at a particular moment.

Manet rendered Andrée's face swiftly and economically; it is one of the only parts of the canvas that shows virtually no signs of reworking, and her blank expression and blurred features give the impression of a face

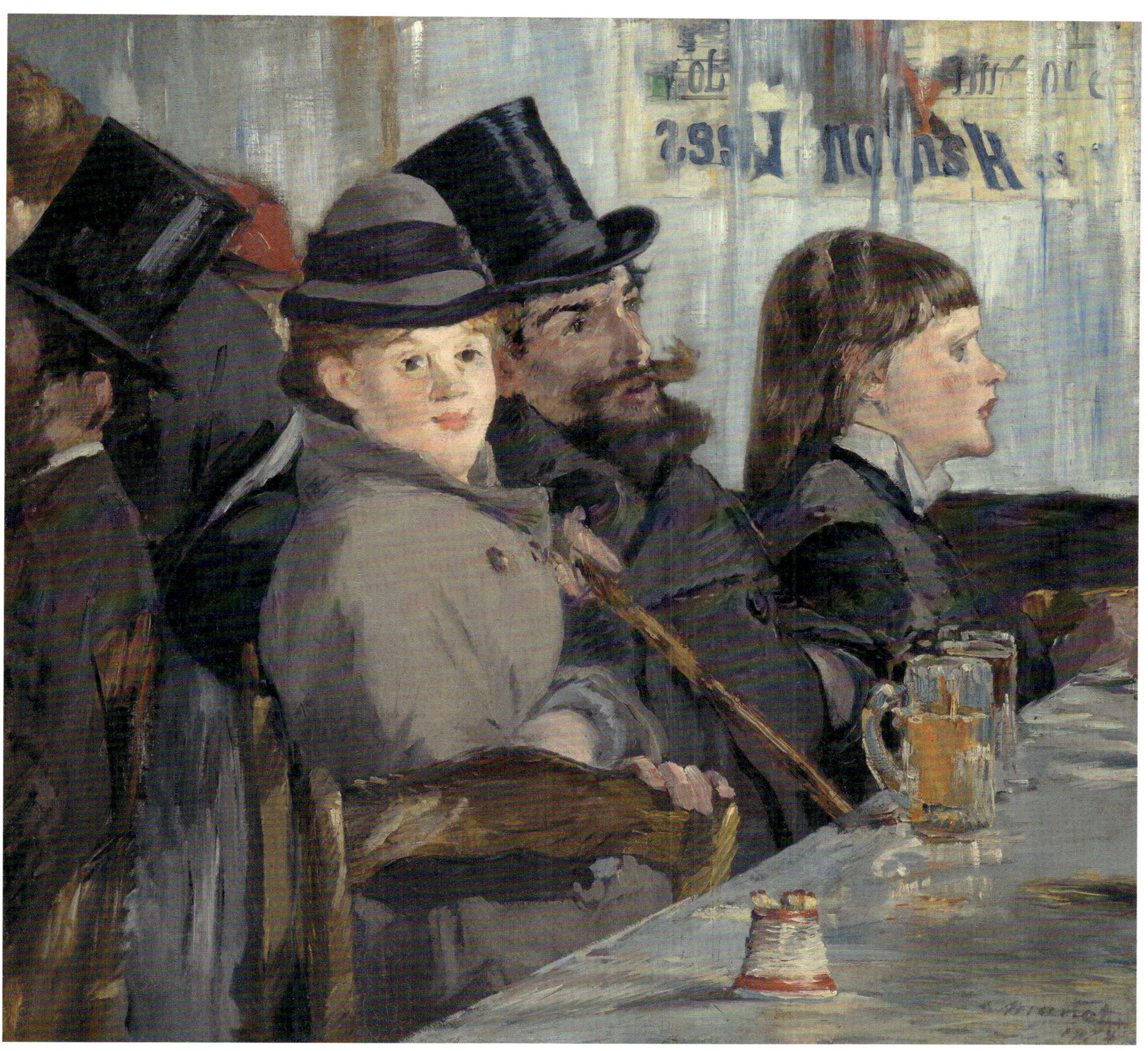

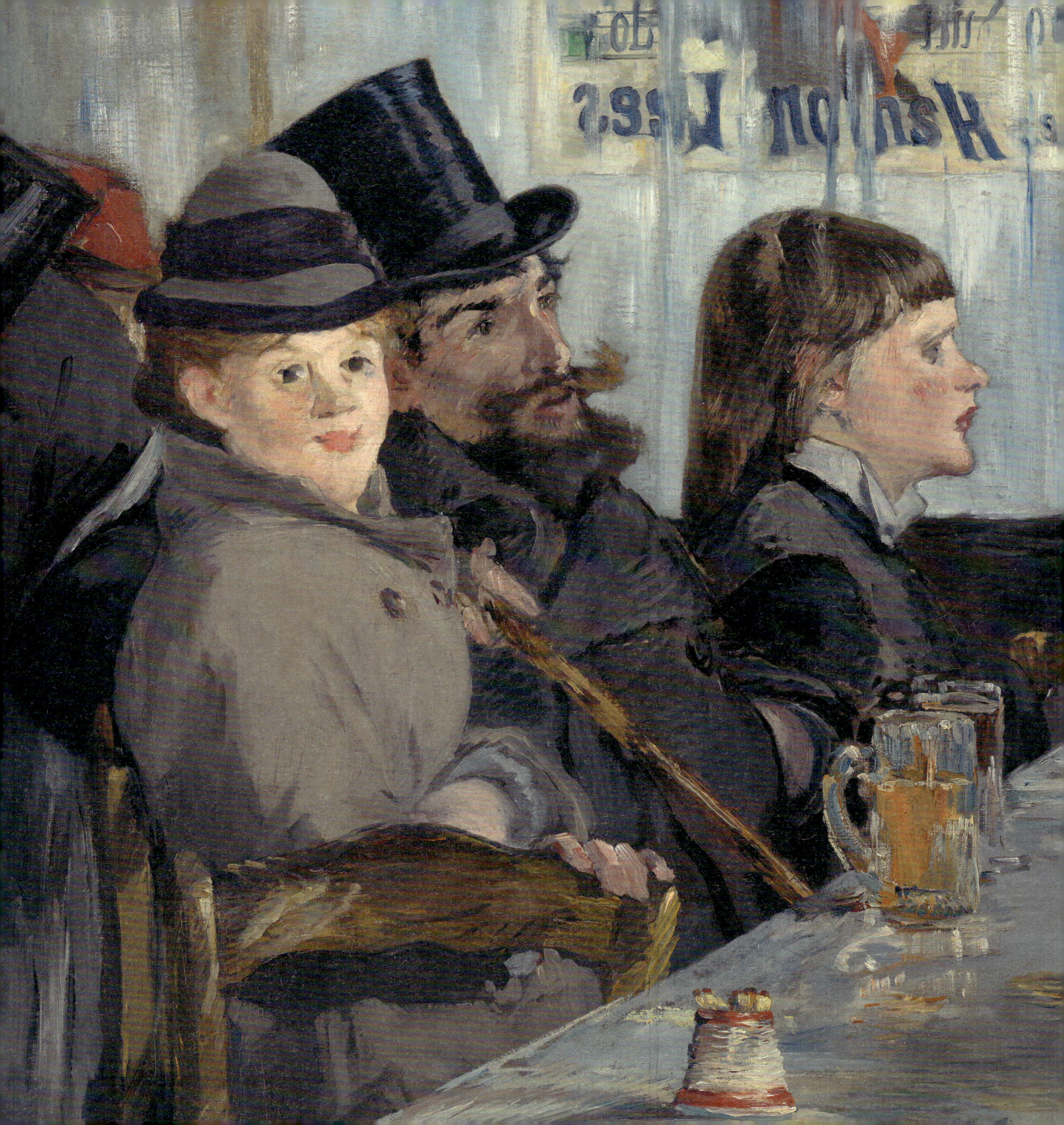
Hanlon Lees

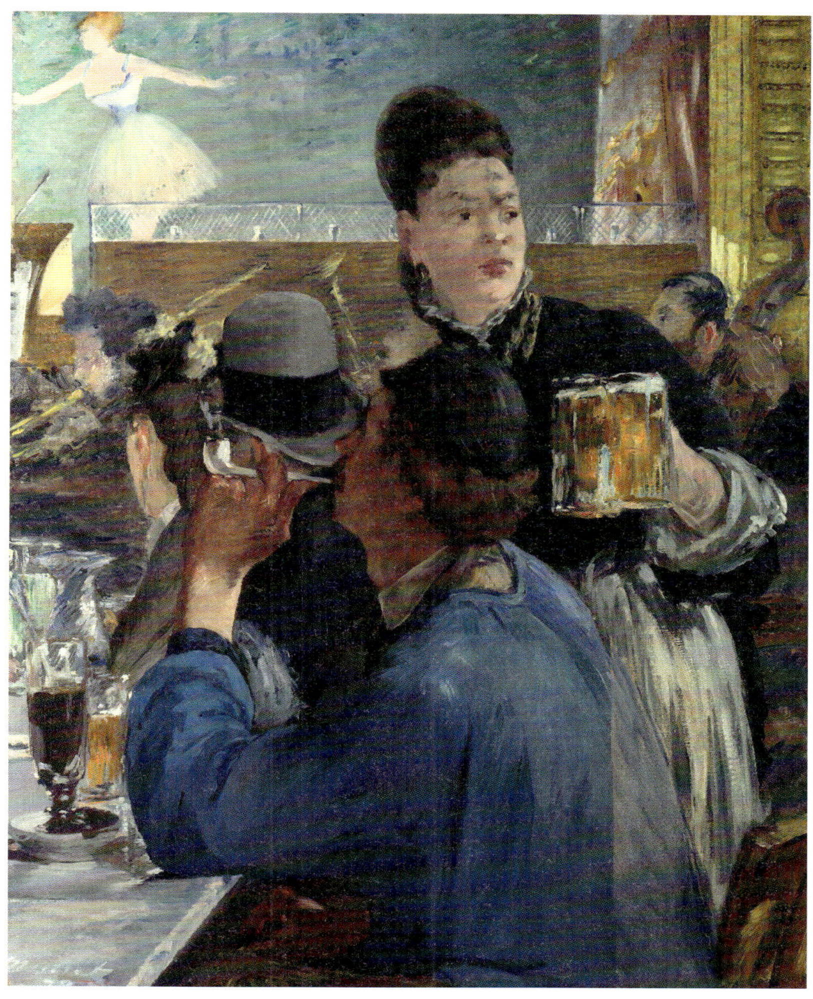

fleetingly glimpsed in a crowded room. The broad, fluid brushwork creates a disconcerting sense of unity and homogeneity among disparate elements, from the faces and clothing of the brasserie patrons to the sunlit surfaces of the table and beer glasses, to the semi-transparent curtain covering the window. In this way, Manet eloquently evokes rapid movement and, by extension, conveys the ephemeral and transitory nature of life in a modern city. The impression that we are observing a fleeting moment is reinforced by the fact that neither the man nor the woman have removed their overcoats; perhaps they have called into the brasserie for a quick drink en route to another destination, their chairs soon to be filled by another equally anonymous and equally hurried pair.

This sense of speed and verve belies the extent to which Manet reworked the rest of the composition. X-rays reveal that he made multiple changes to Guérard's body. His hands were originally placed in front of him, holding

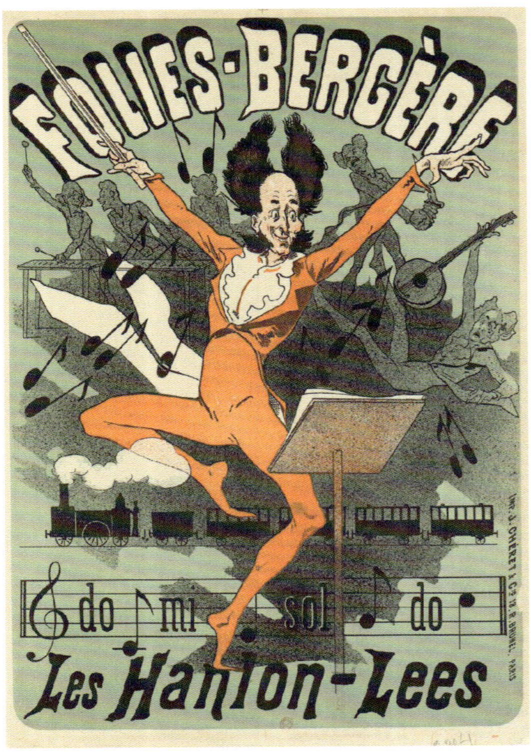

33. Jules Chéret, *Folies Bergère. Do-mi-sol-do. Les Hanlon-Lees* (poster), 1878, colour lithograph, 58 × 41 cm. Bibliothèque nationale de France, Paris

either a book or a glass of beer, but Manet later adjusted them so that one is thrust into his greatcoat and the other grasps a walking stick, a somewhat awkward pose that may have been dictated at least in part by practical concerns: the walking stick crosses and helps to mask a vertical join where the canvas was first cut. The third figure, to Guérard's left, proved the most difficult to resolve. Painted on a strip of canvas that was originally removed from the left-hand portion of the original composition and attached to *Corner of a Café-Concert* before being removed and reattached to the righthand edge of *Au café*, the figure initially had cropped hair, which, in combination with the stiff white collar, suggests that Manet intended to represent a young man. Later, however, he added a long fall of unbound hair, perhaps in an attempt to balance the figure's distinctive and outsize profile, with its pointed chin and long, upturned nose, but left the masculine attire untouched, thus leaving the figure's gender ambiguous. Elements of the table itself, which cannot be logically understood within the space of *Au café*, also point to the picture's origins as part of a larger composition and can aid our understanding of the join between the two paintings. For example, some of the apparently disembodied shadows in the Reinhart painting are cast by the glasses that appear in *Corner of a Café-Concert*.

The date at which Manet divided the canvas, or at the very least began to rework *Au café*, can be pinpointed quite precisely thanks to the poster stuck to the brasserie window, visible at upper right and cropped by the edge of the canvas. This has been identified as a poster by Jules Chéret (1836–1932) advertising the Hanlon-Lees, a renowned British troupe of acrobats who began a run at the nearby Folies-Bergère in late May 1878 (fig. 33), indicating that the painting must have been reworked after that month.[32] Despite the fact that both halves are signed and dated 1878, the reworking may have spilled into the following year. The 1879 Triennial Salon in Antwerp provides a useful cut-off date for Manet ceasing work; the artist wrote to his friend, the Belgian painter Alfred Verwée (1838–1895), on 10 July to inform him that he was 'sending two paintings to the exhibition in Antwerp – a *coin de café* and a *café concert*'.[33] As Manet had chosen not to submit any work to either the 1878 or 1879 Salons in Paris, the Antwerp exhibition (10 August–5 October) represents the public debut of both paintings; interestingly, they were displayed in separate rooms. Although a critic writing in the Paris magazine *L'Art* claimed that the paintings had 'created a scandal', their reception in the Belgian press was in fact largely favourable.[34] Following their return from Antwerp, the Marseille collector Étienne Barroil acquired both works. After his death in 1887, Barroil's son Fernand sold them to the Paris dealer Bernheim-Jeune, after which they took very different paths, with *Au café* passing through collections in Paris and Berlin before being acquired by Oskar Reinhart.

More than any other work in the collection, *Au café* exemplifies the common ground shared by Reinhart and Samuel Courtauld. Both collectors, in effect, purchased, or were involved in the acquisition of one of the two halves of the same painting. In 1923, *Corner of a Café-Concert* became the first (and ultimately, the most expensive) purchase made through the Courtauld

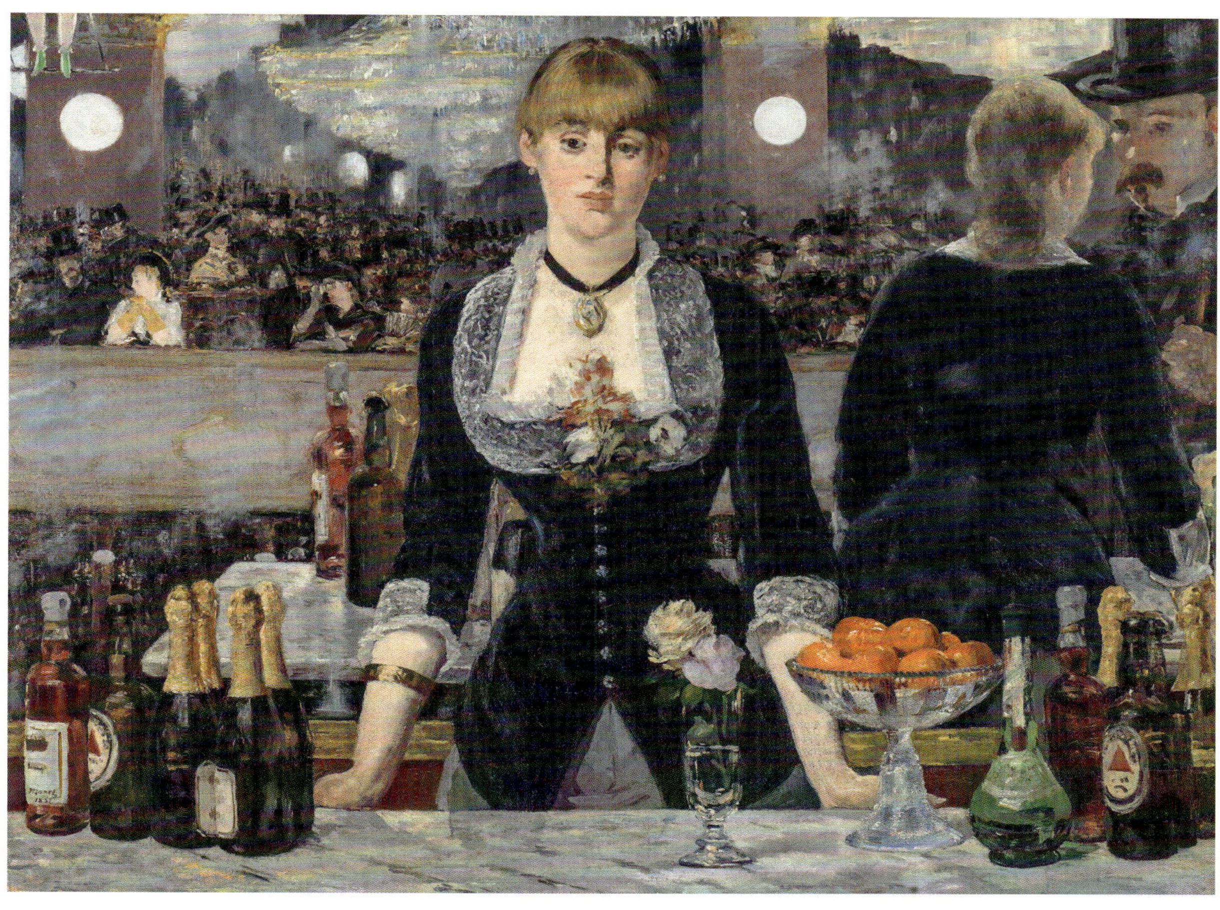

34. Édouard Manet, *A Bar at the Folies-Bergère*, 1882, oil on canvas, 96 × 130 cm. The Courtauld, London (Samuel Courtauld Trust)

Fund for the acquisition of Impressionist and Post-Impressionist paintings for the British national collection. Three years later, in 1926, Samuel Courtauld acquired Manet's last great depiction of Paris café life, *A Bar at the Folies-Bergère* (fig. 34) for his own collection. In 1953, with the acquisition of *Au café*, Oskar Reinhart added one of the most significant pictures to his collection of French modern art. He had coveted the painting for 30 years, since he first saw it in Berlin in 1923 in the collection of Otto Gerstenberg (1848–1935; see above, page 43). **RS**

9

PAUL CEZANNE (1839–1906)
Portrait of Dominique Aubert, c. 1866

Oil on canvas, 82 × 66 cm
Inv. 1938.8
The Swiss Confederation, Federal Office of Culture,
Oskar Reinhart Collection 'Am Römerholz',
Winterthur

Provenance Acquired by Oskar Reinhart from
Wildenstein & Cie., Paris/New York, 1938

Portraiture occupied an important place in Cezanne's career in the 1860s and served as a fertile ground for early experiments. None of these works, which offer invaluable insight into his early development as an artist, were the result of commissions; as he was seldom able to employ professional models, most of his sitters were family and friends, the latter of whom included Émile Zola (1840–1902). His maternal uncle, Dominique Aubert (b. 1817), a court usher, was an especially obliging model, sitting for him at least ten times in 1866. Although in a few instances Cezanne depicted him in a particular guise – as a monk or a lawyer, for example – in most cases, as here, Aubert posed in his own clothes. Seated with his elbow on his knee and his head propped on his clenched right fist, his body fills the canvas.

Aubert's massive physiognomy and confrontational pose are echoed and amplified by Cezanne's distinctive method: he applied the paint with a palette knife in slab-like strokes, building up a heavy impasto that stands proud of the canvas. His use of the palette knife, which carried iconoclastic connotations thanks to its association with the audacious Realism of Gustave Courbet (1819–1877), was inspired by his admiration for the older artist. But Cezanne takes Courbet's technique a step further, using it to construct a unified image that calls attention to the paint's materiality. The block-like paint application also heightens the intensity and the enigmatic quality of Aubert's expression, as does Cezanne's decision to make his face and hand the brightest points in an otherwise very dark composition. The cropping of the left arm and right knee is so abrupt that some scholars have speculated that the canvas was cut down at some point after the painting's completion. However, technical examination does not support this theory, suggesting that the unorthodox composition was intentional. The facture and the composition work together to create an image of immense power that transcends the conventions of portraiture, in which the task of capturing the sitter's physical likeness cedes place to conveying his personality.

Cezanne rarely, if ever, exhibited his early portraits, and one can only speculate on what their critical reception might have been had he shown them soon after completion. However, the present work found an early admirer and owner in Claude Monet (1840–1926), who purchased it in Paris probably in 1868. **RS**

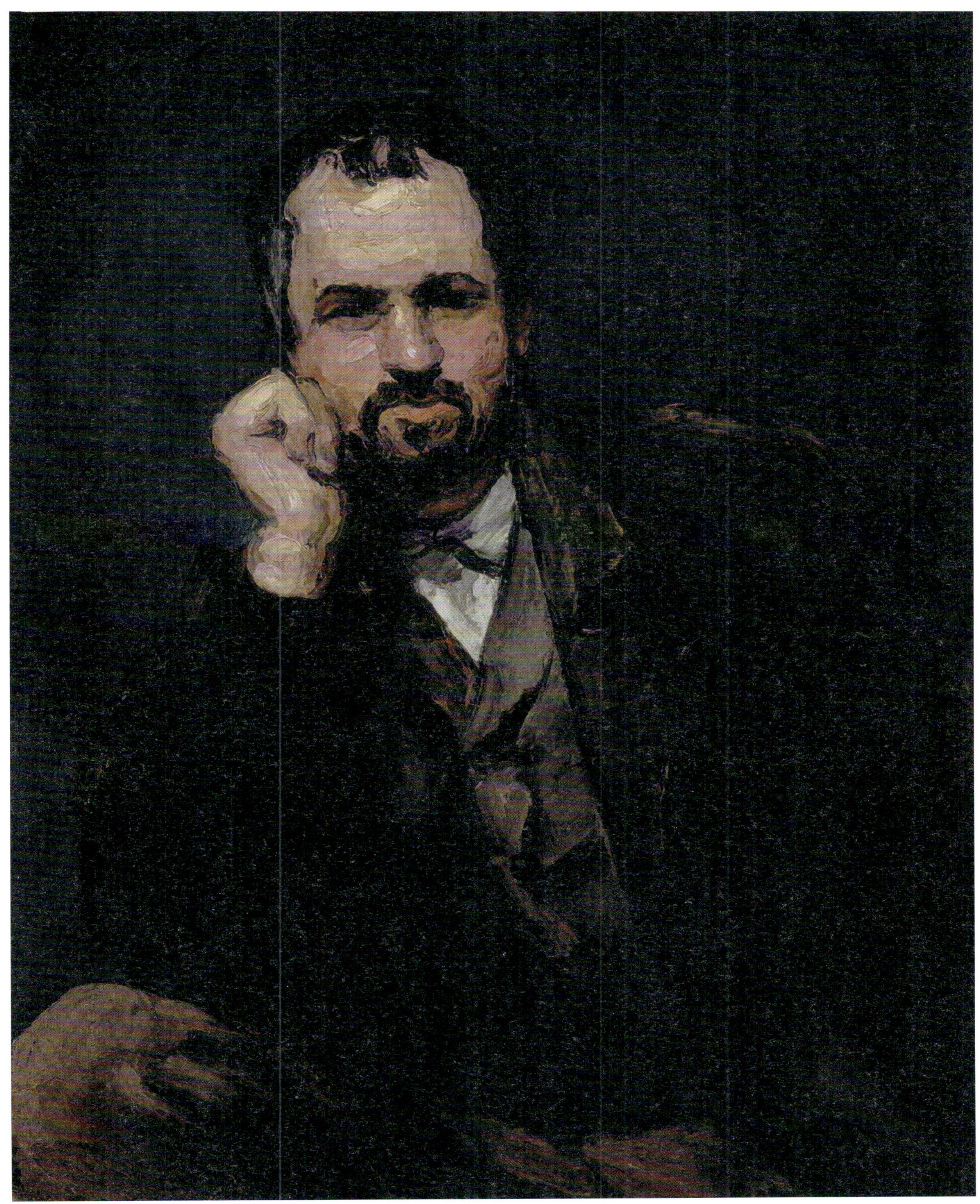

10

PAUL CEZANNE (1839–1906)
The Château Noir, c. 1885

Oil on canvas, 73.5 × 92.5 cm
Inv. 1926.5
The Swiss Confederation, Federal Office of Culture,
Oskar Reinhart Collection 'Am Römerholz',
Winterthur

Provenance Acquired by Oskar Reinhart from
the Galerie Paul Cassirer, Berlin/Amsterdam, 1926

One of Cezanne's favourite landscape subjects during the latter decades of his career was the Château Noir, an unfinished pseudo-Gothic folly begun by a local businessman in the second half of the nineteenth century that was situated in the countryside between Aix-en-Provence and the Montagne Sainte-Victoire on the road to Le Tholonet. He painted it so frequently that, from 1887, he rented a room in the Château to store his canvases and equipment; around 1899 he even considered acquiring the property. Although there is some dispute about its exact date, the picture purchased by Oskar Reinhart is thought by some scholars to be the first, or one of the first, in a series that extended to the last year of the artist's life.[35]

In contrast to later paintings of the Château Noir, which fully reveal the building and in which its status as ruined or unfinished is left tantalisingly unclear, here Cezanne has chosen to observe it from a viewpoint where it is largely obscured by trees. Only a small section of ochre wall, with a single lancet window and a vibrant red door, and what appear to be a group of unfinished columns beside it, can be glimpsed at the centre of the composition, and its identity and even its status as a single building are ambiguous.[36] Painted thinly on a grey canvas that lends a coolness to the palette, the composition is tightly structured, with the insistent verticals of the group of almost columnar trees at left and the diagonal branches of the lone tree at right alternately leading the viewer's eye towards the building and barring the way. Its power derives from two strong contrasts: on one hand, the polarity between blue and green and ochre and red; on the other, between the blocky vertical brushstrokes of the tree trunks and architecture and the flickering directional brushwork used in the foliage, undergrowth and sky, which gives the impression of leaves and branches rustling in the breeze. Although in other paintings of the Château Noir Cezanne observed the building from a vantage point that opened up on its wider surroundings, here his focus is very much on the dense web of undergrowth (*sous bois*), a favourite subject in his late landscapes. One of the most remarkable aspects of the Winterthur picture is the way Cezanne has created structure solely by means of colour. The overlapping planes of blue/green and ochre create a sense of depth and give a vivid impression of the forest's rich, almost impenetrable complexity, in which the natural and built environments blend into a harmonious whole. **RS**

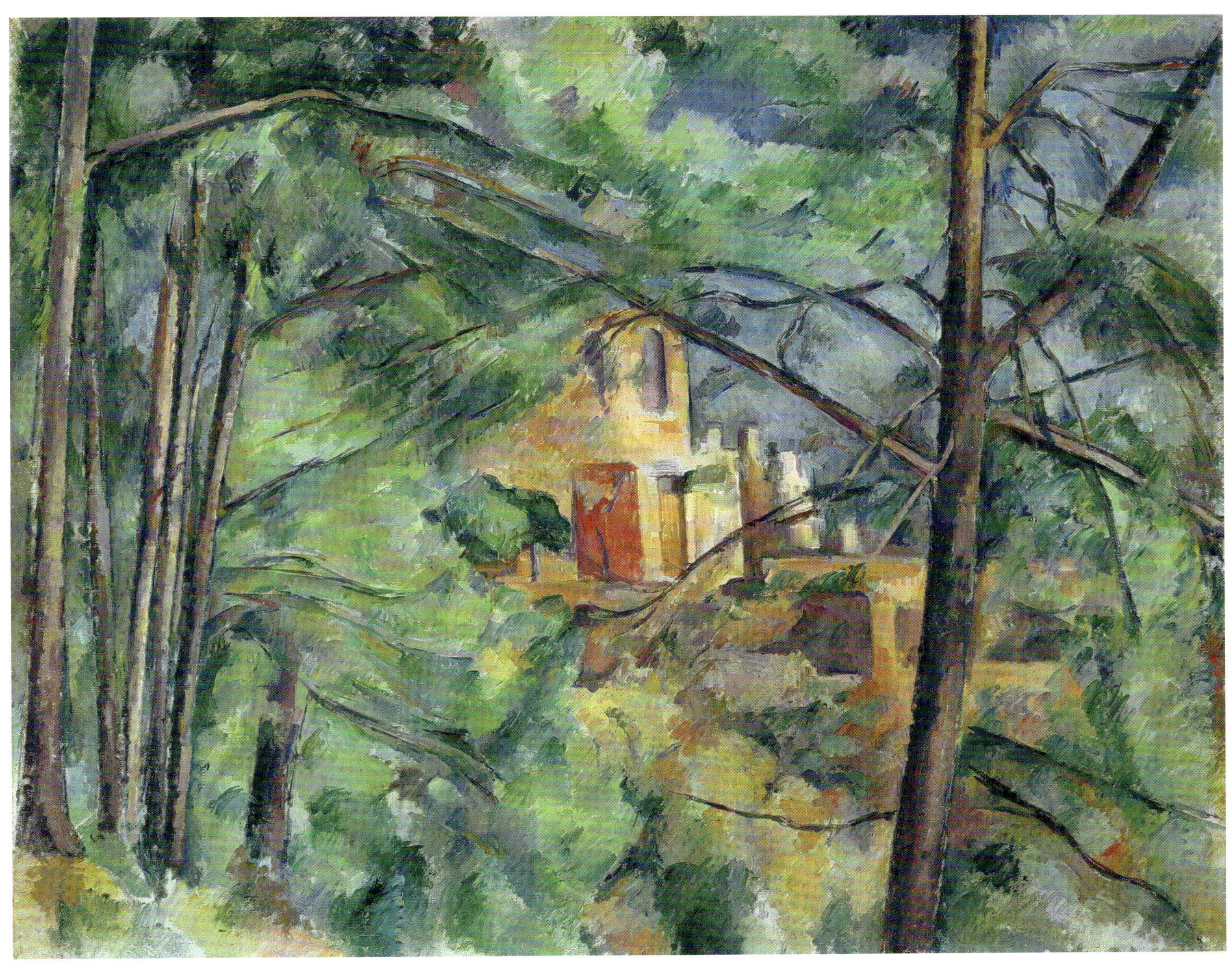

11

PAUL CEZANNE (1839–1906)
The Pilon du Roi, 1887–88

Oil on canvas, 82.3 × 101 cm
Inv. 1923.22
The Swiss Confederation, Federal Office of Culture,
Oskar Reinhart Collection 'Am Römerholz',
Winterthur

Provenance Acquired by Oskar Reinhart from
Wilhelm Hansen, Copenhagen, 1923

This landscape, which was first exhibited in the Salle Cezanne at the Paris Salon d'Automne in 1904, depicts the Pilon du Roi (King's Pestle). This rocky outcrop of the Étoile mountain range lies to the south of Aix-en-Provence, close to the estate of Cezanne's brother-in-law at Bellevue. In an earlier version (c. 1878–79, Kelvingrove Art Gallery and Museum, Glasgow), painted eight to ten years before the Winterthur picture, emphatic diagonals contribute to an impression of receding space. These are largely done away with in the present painting, in which Cezanne dispenses with typical rules of perspective to explore instead his personal apprehension of landscape and distance. In so doing, he constructs the receding fields and hills through striated bands of horizontal colour, deepening from light greens and yellows in the foreground to the dark blue outline of the hills on the horizon. As is characteristic of Cezanne's landscape paintings of this period, he intercepts a clear view with the introduction of a framing device: in this case, the overhanging tree that occupies the upper part of the canvas and the vertical patterning of deep-green maize crops that demarcate the foreground from the sweep of plain and hillside behind them. Yet fore-, mid- and background are all harmonised and brought into tonal dialogue through echoing patches of colour that recur outside of their immediate area of pertinence, such as the cool blue accents shadowing both the maize in the foreground and the field beyond.

Cezanne's bold mark, his 'constructive stroke',[37] unites almost the entire picture plane, and is differentiated only in the fluid deep-green ribbons of the maize plants. Though occasionally directed diagonally to describe foliage, as in the leaves and branches of the tree, the assertive brushstrokes with which Cezanne builds his picture largely run vertically, conveying a mirage-like impression of shimmering heat. Through this method of mark-making, Cezanne rejects illusionism: though he insisted upon the committed study of nature as vital to the artist, his project was not to produce beguiling verisimilitudes, but rather to aim at what he called a 'Harmony parallel to nature'.[38] As John House has argued, 'the parallel stroke was Cezanne's first mode of establishing that the work of art was categorically different from the experience of nature'.[39]

In 1921 Oskar Reinhart stated his ambition to acquire 'an outstanding landscape' by Cezanne.[40] His chance came two years later: *The Pilon du Roi* was one of nineteen paintings, along with further landscapes by Camille Corot (1796–1875) and Camille Pissarro (1830–1903), that he acquired from the Danish collector Wilhelm Hansen (1868–1936) after the dissolution of his collection was precipitated by the 1922 crash of Denmark's largest private bank, Landsmansbanken. Reinhart believed that he had acquired the 'jewels' of that collection, and expressed his delight at bolstering his own with 'very significant items and some works of everlasting value'.[41] **CN**

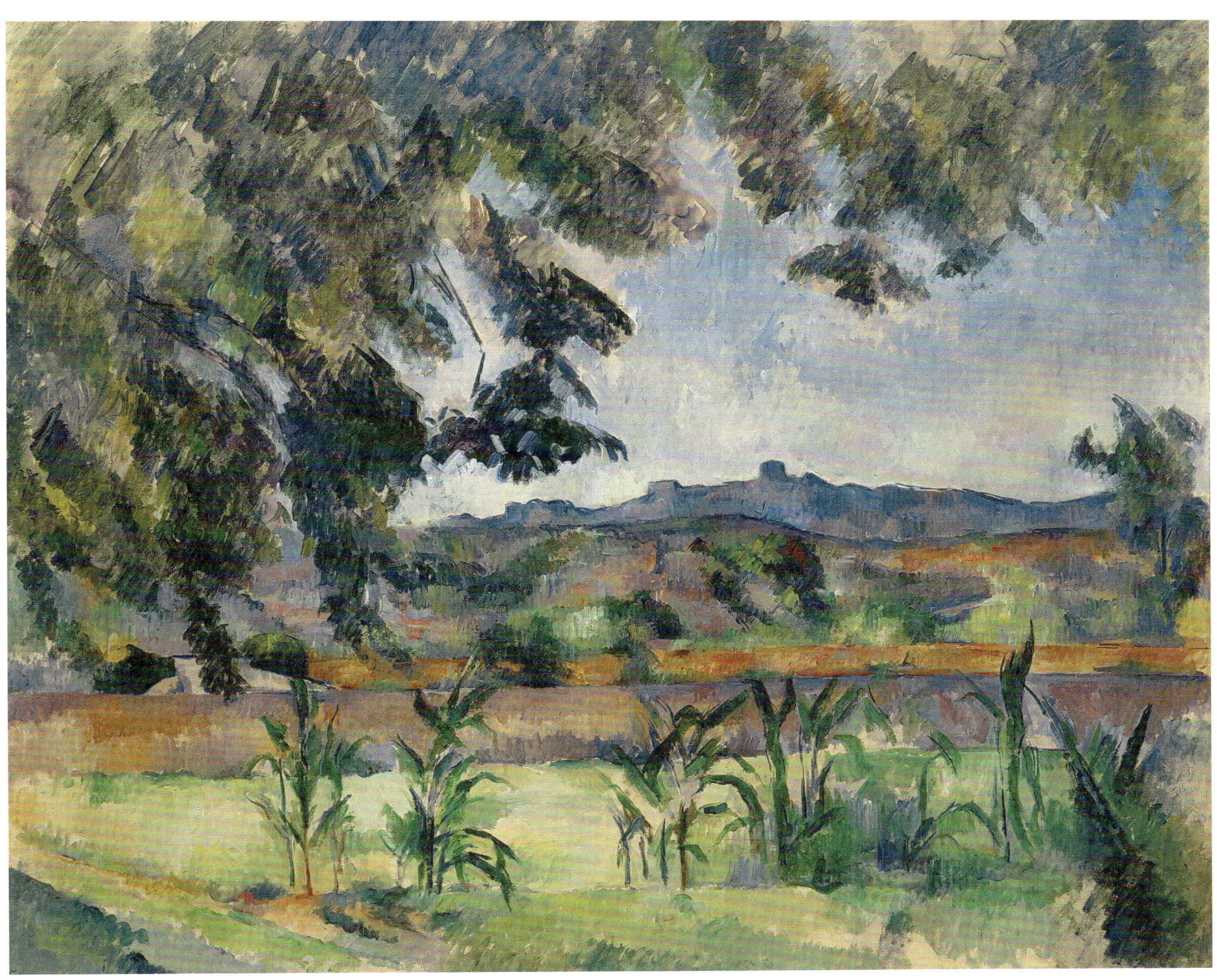

12

PAUL CEZANNE (1839–1906)
Still Life with Faience Jug and Fruit,
c. 1900

Oil on canvas, 73.7 × 101 cm
Inv. 1925.8
The Swiss Confederation, Federal Office of Culture,
Oskar Reinhart Collection 'Am Römerholz',
Winterthur

Provenance Acquired by Oskar Reinhart from
the Galerie Paul Rosenberg, Paris, 1925

Still Life with Faience Jug and Fruit was completed in the final decade of Cezanne's life, probably in Aix-en-Provence, and is one of a few paintings from the 1890s onwards that illustrate the same tin-glazed earthenware jug and patterned curtain fabric. Cezanne's exploration of still life spanned his entire career: numbering over two hundred, these works range from loose, reduced watercolours that invite the support to act as a vital component of the finished picture, to large-scale oil paintings such as this one, which are fully worked across the entire canvas. This, one of the largest still life paintings of his late years, is a critical example of his attainment of a monumental form that upturned notions of the genre's traditionally lowly status. Indeed, in 1906 the art critic Théodore Duret (1838–1927) observed the genre-defying power of Cezanne's still lifes, writing that by a 'force independent of the subject ... a few apples and a cloth on a table ... assume a presence equal to that of a human head or a landscape by the sea'.[42]

Painting arrangements of objects such as this allowed Cezanne to work slowly, remaining with his subject for extended periods of time and experiencing changing optical sensations that he sought to convey truthfully with his brush. Short, inquisitive brushstrokes – particularly notable in the heaped white cloth – testify to this continuous observation and responsive modification, and impart an impression of vibrating, ever-shifting visual phenomena. In the present painting, the table tilts towards the lower left corner, an eccentricity borne of the intention to capture sensory experience and overall harmony on the canvas above the illusion of visual accuracy.

Yet in spite of this sense of animation, the painting possesses a composed equilibrium much in the tradition of seventeenth-century Dutch still life. The table is equally weighted between two groups of fruit on its left and right sides, and punctuated at its centre by the faience jug that marks the highest point of the objects standing on the table. Bowl, jug and cloth form a white, cross-like structure that holds the composition evenly in place. The downward pull of the fruit, which threatens to roll from the sharply tilted bowl, is counterbalanced in the five verticals that run along the back wall, providing a structuring framework of uprights that operate in concert with the seeming upward growth of the curtain's leaf pattern.

An account of the manner in which Cezanne set up his still lifes, recorded by the painter Louis Le Bail (1866–1942), conveys the deep significance of colour to this overall search for balance: 'Cezanne positioned the peaches by opposing the tones next to one another, making the complementaries vibrate, the green with the reds, the yellows with the blues, tilting, inclining, balancing the fruits.'[43] In the present picture, the rich, burnished palette typical of Cezanne's late still lifes is contrasted with the arresting use of blue that is woven throughout the painting, particularly in its juxtaposition against the orange and yellow fruits, seemingly a combination of apples and peaches. Blue is perhaps most exquisitely employed in the glass, which is near-camouflaged against the wall's bruised palette of green, pink and lilac. Through the transparency of the glass, Cezanne plays upon an opposition between volumetric space and the picture plane – a concern that similarly animates the dialogue between the vegetal patterns of the fabric and jug, and the real fruits resting beside them.

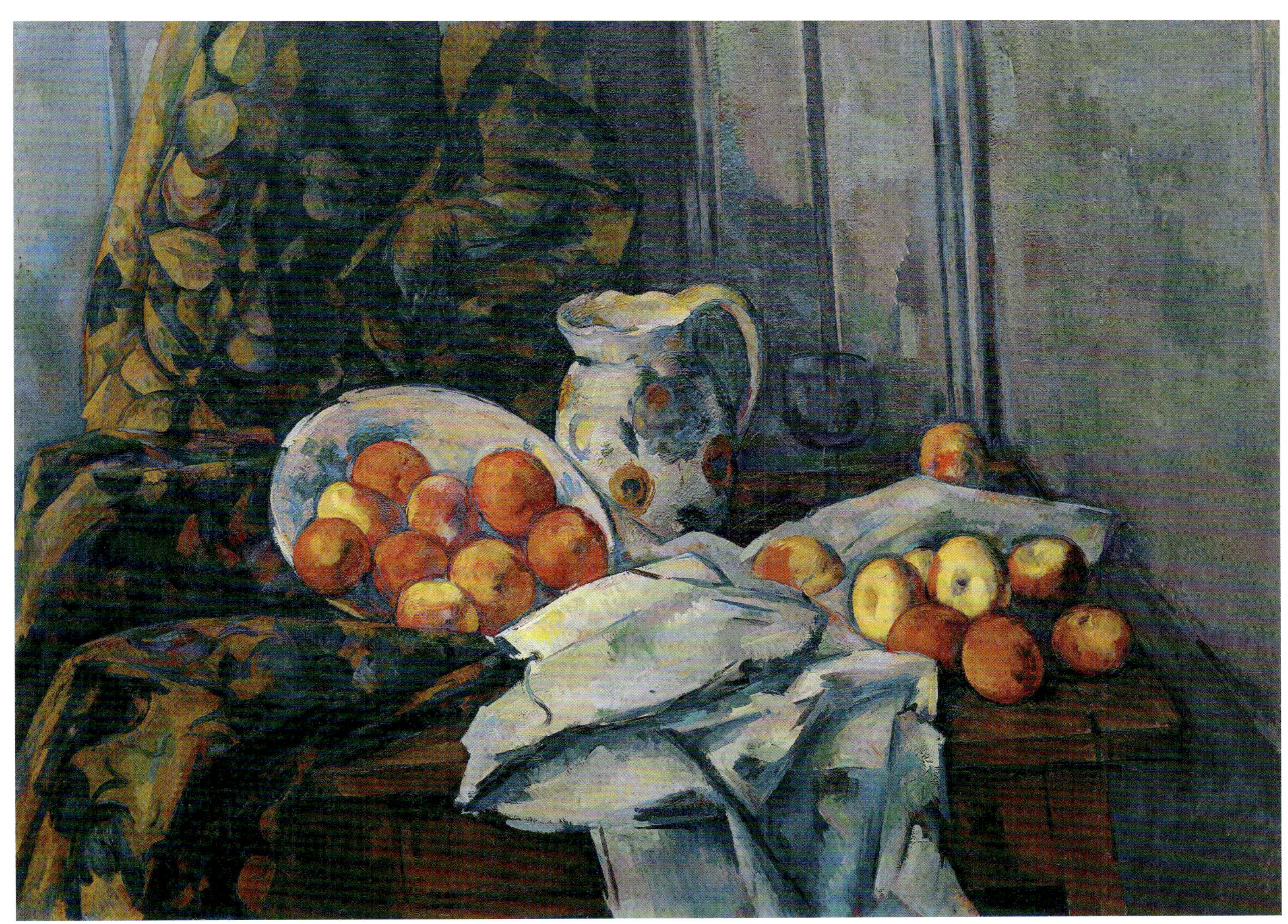

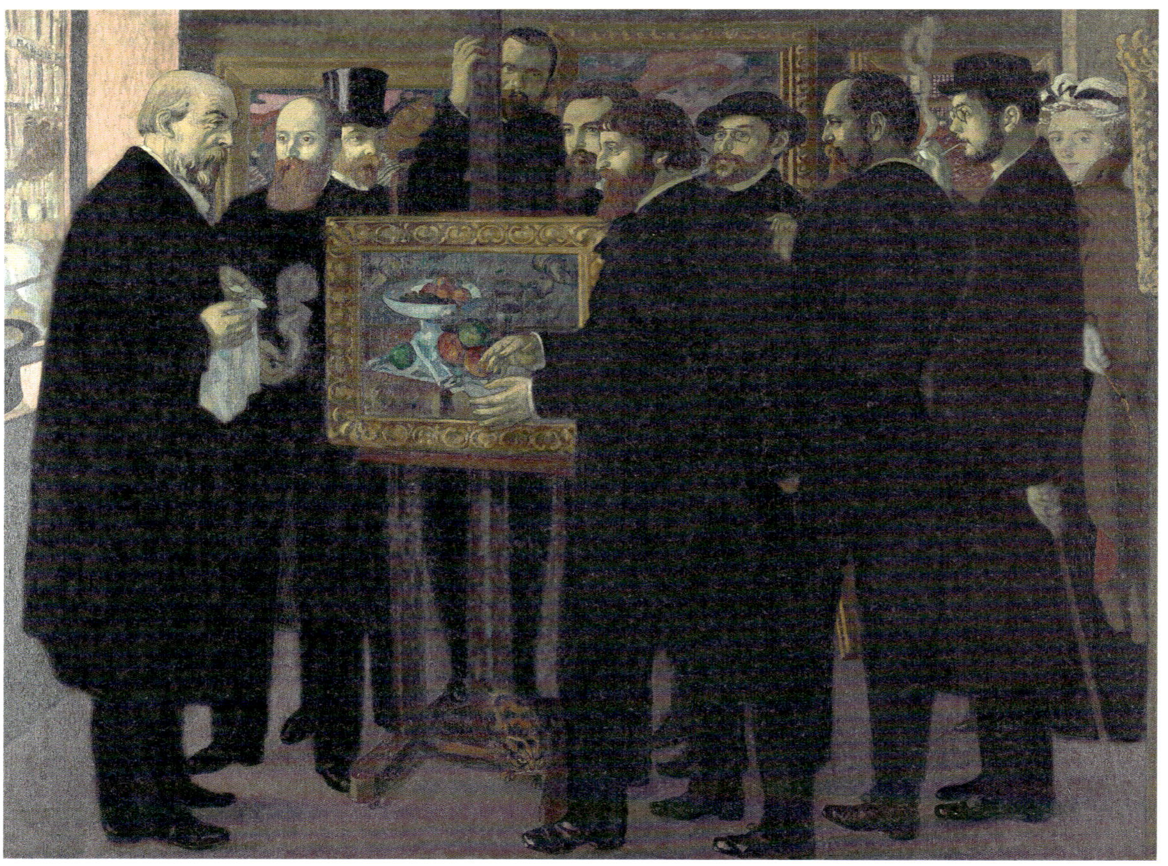

35. Maurice Denis, *Homage to Cezanne*, 1900, oil
on canvas, 182 × 243.5 cm. Musée d'Orsay, Paris

By the time Cezanne painted this work he had achieved a discreet success, especially among collectors and younger artists, and still life subjects had come to hold a special significance and centrality to his oeuvre.[44] Indeed, in the same year that *Still Life with Faience Jug and Fruit* is thought to have been painted, Maurice Denis (1870–1943) completed his *Homage to Cezanne* (fig. 35), an eloquent expression of Cezanne's immense influence on the genre. Denis's painting depicts Cezanne's *Still Life with Fruit Dish* (1879–80, Museum of Modern Art, New York) displayed on an easel in the Paris gallery of the art dealer Ambroise Vollard, while a group of fellow artists including Denis, Pierre Bonnard, Odilon Redon, Paul Sérusier and Édouard Vuillard gather to discuss it. For those artists, like so many others, Cezanne's innovations in the representation of perception itself and what he termed *sensation* – or sensory experience – offered a radical new path of artistic discovery.

Still Life with Faience Jug and Fruit was first exhibited in 1904 at Cezanne's inaugural solo exhibition in Germany, held at the Berlin gallery of the influential art dealer Paul Cassirer (1871–1926). There, it was shown alongside six further still lifes, including one of his earliest studies in the genre, *Still Life*

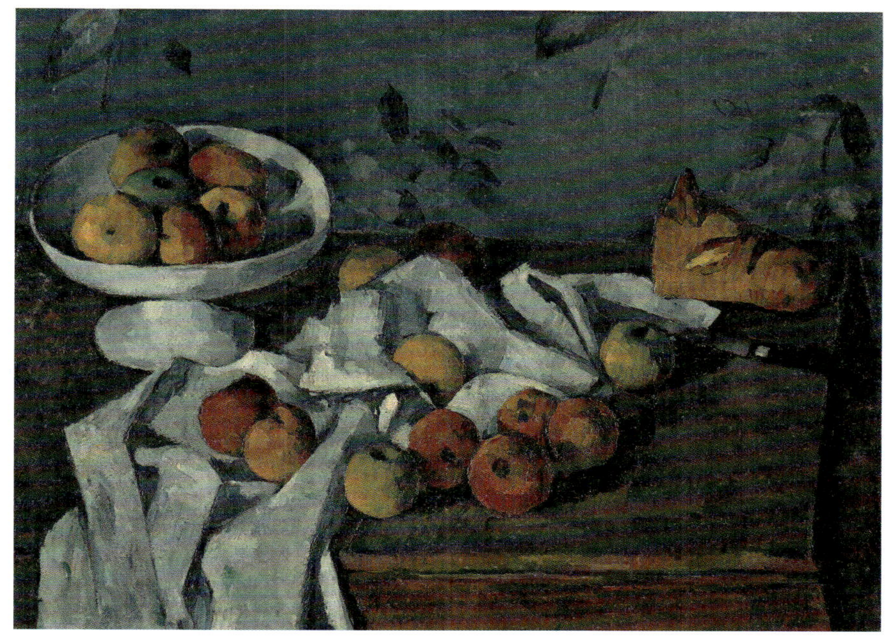

36. Paul Cezanne, *Still Life with Fruit Dish, Apples and Bread*, 1879–80, oil on canvas, 55.1 × 74.4 cm. The Swiss Confederation, Federal Office of Culture, Oskar Reinhart Collection 'Am Römerholz', Winterthur

with Bread and Eggs (1865, Cincinnati Art Museum). It was next shown at the same venue in 1912. On both occasions Cezanne was hailed as a mythic figure in the development of modern art by members of the German press. 'He reveals and transfigures nature to us', wrote one critic, 'just as clairvoyant people with sensitive organs have experienced unheard of and wonderful things and made them known to the general public'.[45] Later that year, responding to a different work, another critic commented that 'Cezanne painted apples in which the cosmos seems unleashed'.[46]

Oskar Reinhart had expressed the desire to acquire a still life by Cezanne as early as 1918. He succeeded in 1921 when he purchased an earlier work in the genre, *Still Life with Fruit Dish, Apples and Bread* (fig. 36), followed by *Still Life with a Plate of Peaches* (c. 1892) in 1923, before finally acquiring the present painting in 1925.[47] It stands as an exception to Reinhart's disinclination towards collecting large paintings that would disrupt the domestic character of his collection, and as such is a testament to his admiration for this imposing work.[48] CN

13

PAUL CEZANNE (1839–1906)
Bathers, c. 1900–06

Watercolour and opaque watercolour over graphite
on paper, 25.7 × 41.9 cm
Inv. 1925.7
The Swiss Confederation, Federal Office of Culture,
Oskar Reinhart Collection 'Am Römerholz',
Winterthur

Provenance Acquired by Oskar Reinhart from the
Galerie Ambroise Vollard, Paris, 1925

The subject of the bathers had occupied Cezanne since the mid-1870s, but they assumed a much greater presence in his oeuvre in his later years. His research culminated in the three *Large Bathers* (*Grandes Baigneuses*) paintings, of which the Philadelphia Museum of Art's 1906 canvas is considered one of the crowning achievements of Cezanne's career.[49] This group of paintings and watercolours, in which the artist ceaselessly revised poses and number of figures, was mentioned in the 1914 biography of Cezanne written by his dealer Ambroise Vollard (1866–1939), from whom Reinhart acquired this watercolour. With regard to the Philadelphia painting, Vollard wrote that the artist would have wished for nude models to pose for him in nature, but as this was not permitted, he resorted to sketches he had previously drawn while at the Académie Suisse in Paris in the early 1860s, and to paintings by other artists he had seen in museums. It was with the *Large Bathers* that the younger artist Émile Bernard (1868–1941) immortalised Cezanne in an iconic black-and-white photograph that depicts the elderly painter in his studio near Aix-en-Provence, the bathers behind him.

Oskar Reinhart's female *Bathers* is one of ten watercolours in which the artist studied female bathers as a group, revisiting poses he used in other drawings and paintings. Its composition is closely related to the painted female bathers of a slightly earlier date (fig. 37). The present watercolour differs, however, for its unusual *horror vacui* (fear of empty space) treatment of the background, which is almost entirely covered in shades of blue and green, an approach commonly found in Cezanne's late, highly finished watercolours. These multifigure compositions represent a departure from Cezanne's usual subject matter of landscape, still life and single figure studies. While at first his bathers were predominantly male, in his later works he focused instead on female bathers, as in the present work.

The top, right and lower edges present evidence that the sheet was initially larger and has been trimmed.[50] Characteristic of Cezanne's late watercolours, this work epitomises his formidable technique, a harmonious interplay of

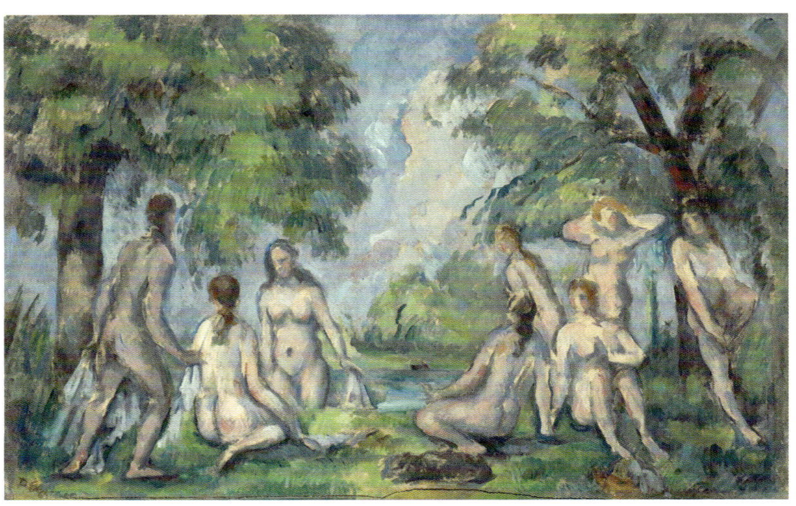

37. Paul Cezanne, *Baigneuses*, c. 1890,
oil on canvas, 29 × 45 cm. Musée d'Orsay, Paris,
on loan to Musée Granet, Aix-en-Provence

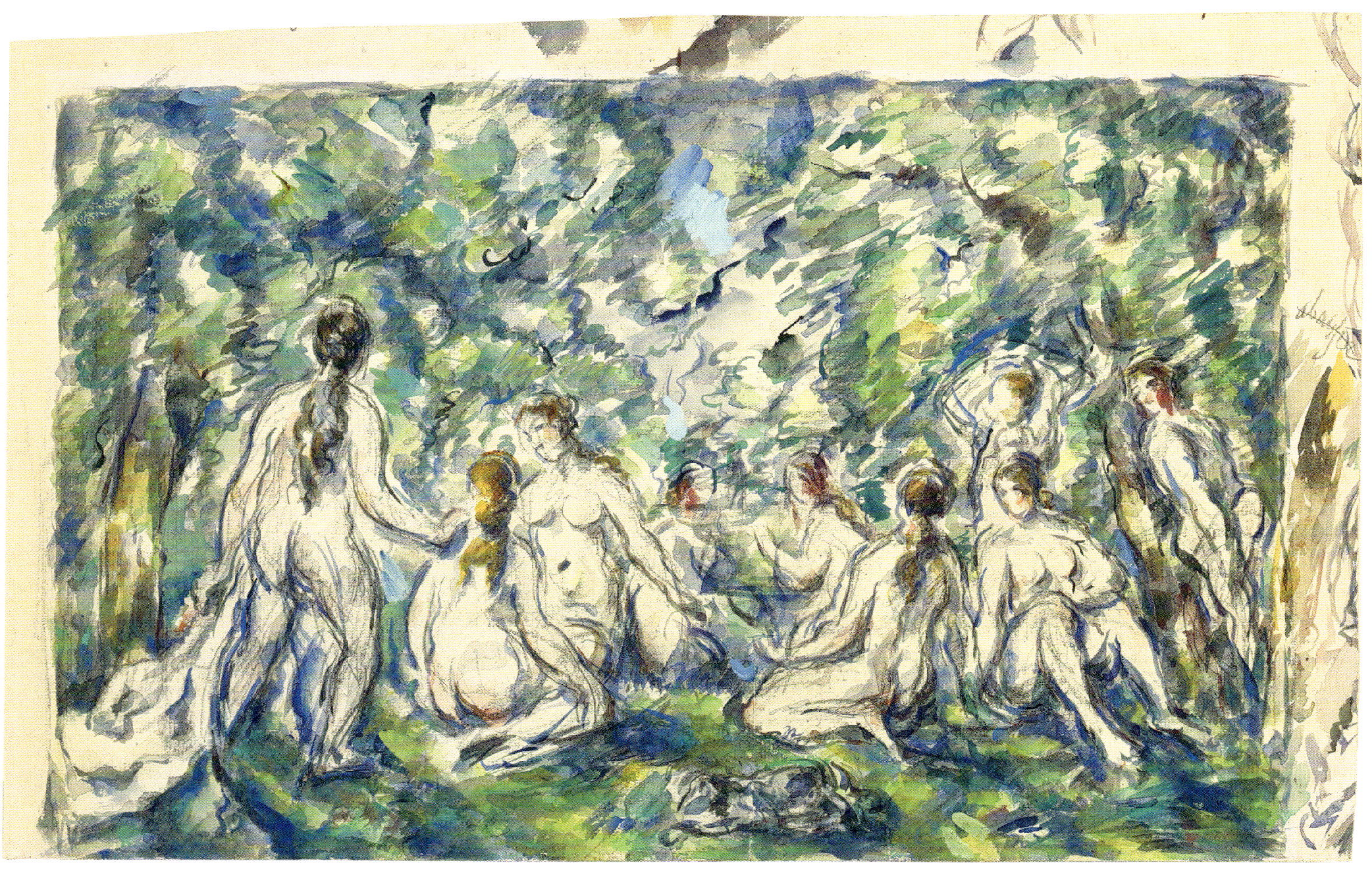

graphite and dashes of watercolour. Far from using watercolour to cover the underdrawing, the artist sometimes used graphite to correct a line he had already drawn in colour. Loose, expressive brushstrokes suggest the forms rather than defining them precisely. There is a sense of movement and fluidity, as if the figures are part of the landscape itself. In contrast to his late paintings of bathers, the distant mountains in this watercolour are barely visible, and are instead masked by the energetic strokes that define the tree branches and foliage. Viridian and cobalt blue dominate the sheet. Whilst the bodies are skilfully left in reserve, their outlines are delineated in blue, a reminder of what the artist told Émile Bernard in a letter from 1904 (which belonged to Samuel Courtauld and is today in The Courtauld collection) about the need to introduce 'into our vibrations of light, represented by the reds and yellows, a sufficient quantity of blue tones to give a sense of atmosphere'.[51.] **KG**

14

PAUL CEZANNE (1839–1906)
Mont Sainte Victoire, 1902–06

Watercolour and opaque watercolour over graphite on
paper, 48 × 63.2 cm
Inv. 1923.24
The Swiss Confederation, Federal Office of Culture,
Oskar Reinhart Collection 'Am Römerholz',
Winterthur

Provenance Acquired by Oskar Reinhart from the
Galerie Ambroise Vollard, Paris, 1923

This powerful, large and dynamic watercolour was acquired by Oskar Reinhart in 1923 from Cezanne's dealer, Ambroise Vollard (1866–1939). When it was still in his possession, Vollard used the artwork to illustrate the last pages of his biography of Cezanne, which he published in 1914.[52] Describing the last two days of the artist's life, the author recounts how, surprised by a thunderstorm while working 'on the motif', after being exposed to incessant rain for over two hours, Cezanne fainted; carried home by a passer-by, he would die just a few days later, aged 67.

That 'motif', Mont Sainte-Victoire, towers over the area around Cezanne's hometown of Aix-en-Provence. The artist drew and painted it numerous times throughout his career, from different viewpoints. Its profile, with its characteristic, and unmistakeable, jagged top, embodies the landscape of his native region, and Cezanne returned to it repeatedly in almost a hundred paintings, drawings and watercolours (two of which are at The Courtauld). He used colour to suggest the expansive distance in front of him. In the foreground and middle ground, greens, blues, warm yellows and a few dashes of light red depict the vegetation and the few buildings dotted around the landscape, while light blue is used to identify the imposing mountainous profile of the Sainte Victoire, which is otherwise largely left blank. Seen from Les Lauves, on the northern edge of Aix-en-Provence, where Cezanne had built a new studio in 1902 and where he worked until his death, the profile of the mountain appears as seen here, with its characteristic broken top, the Arc River valley occupying the middle ground.

Following his father's death in 1886 Cezanne spent most of his time in Aix, occasionally travelling to Paris until 1899, when he settled permanently in the south, thus making the landscape around his studio one of his main artistic interests. In fact, half of the almost one hundred representations of the Sainte-Victoire were executed in the last six years of his life, when his approach to nature and landscape became a personal investigation into the perception of the visible, focusing on this landmark that held great symbolic meaning for him.

In his late watercolours he used the underlying graphite to sketch a few, lightly drawn outlines, whereas patches of colour convey the elusive shapes of objects, or, in this case, the elements of nature. Generally executed on larger sheets of a full French *Raisin* sized paper (typically 63 × 48 cm), these watercolours push the boundaries of the medium, skilfully creating a dialogue between the pencil marks and the transparent brushstrokes, expertly exploiting the luminosity of the paper reserve. The use of translucent washes means there was also little margin for revision. In these late drawings Cezanne used colours composed essentially of pure pigments, as is evidenced by the ridges formed in areas where the wash is more densely applied. The emerald green, composed of copper and arsenic, seems particularly well preserved; the lovely blue is probably the result of the use of cobalt blue with some indigo. To his admirer and fellow painter Émile Bernard (1868–1941), Cezanne said that 'to read nature is to see through the veil of interpretation in terms of coloured touches that follow each other according to the law of harmony'.[53] **KG**

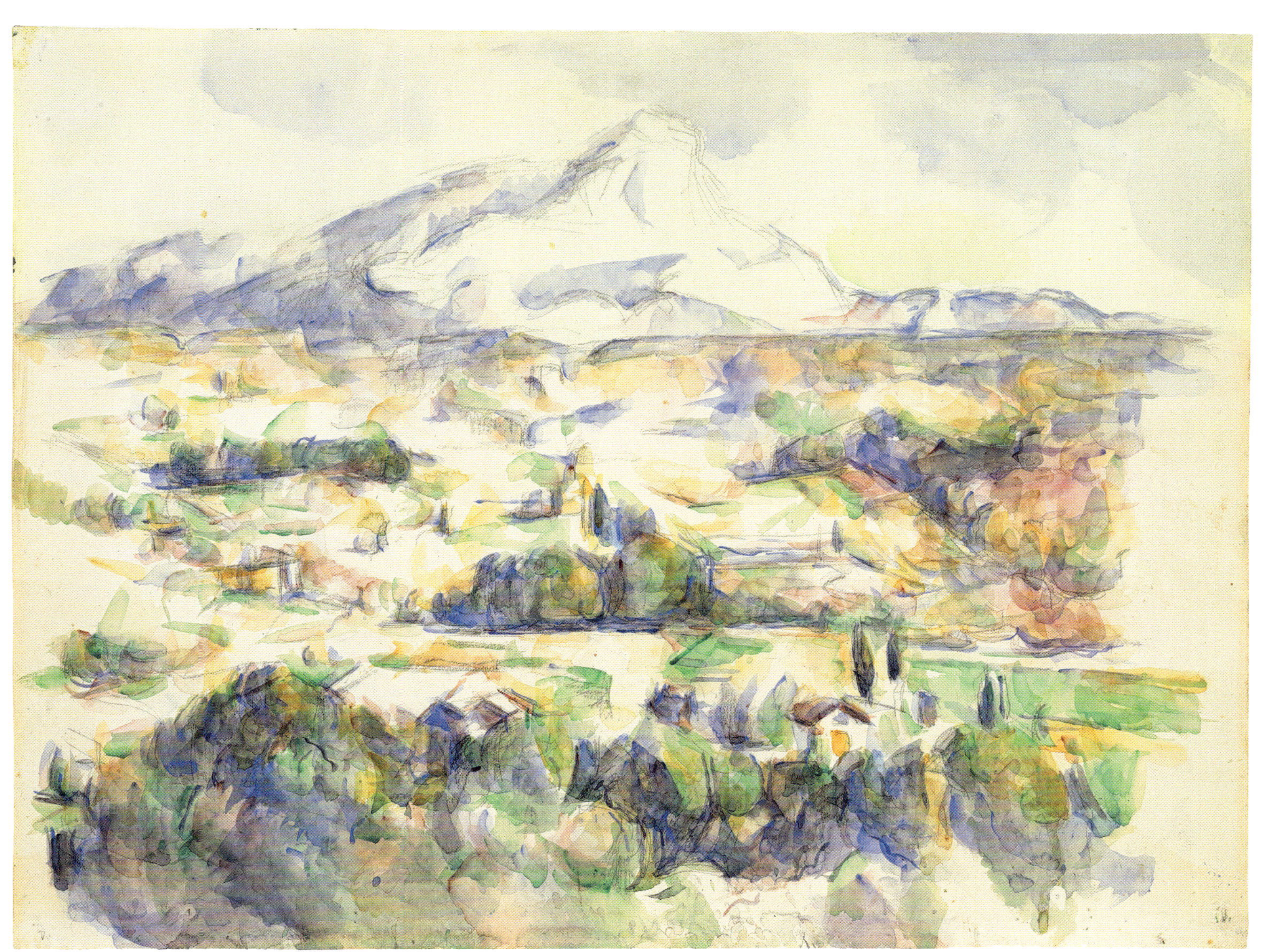

15

ALFRED SISLEY (1839–1899)
Barges on the Saint-Martin Canal, 1870

Oil on canvas, 54.5 × 73 cm
Inv. 1923.20
The Swiss Confederation, Federal Office of Culture,
Oskar Reinhart Collection 'Am Römerholz',
Winterthur

Provenance Acquired by Oskar Reinhart from
Wilhelm Hansen, Copenhagen, 1923

Though modern-day Paris was a favoured subject among artists in Alfred Sisley's circle such as Claude Monet, Pierre-Auguste Renoir and Édouard Manet, who first owned this painting, *Barges on the Saint-Martin Canal* is notable for its focus on a particularly workaday aspect of the metropolis. The canal, which stretches for almost 5 kilometres, was then a key route for the transportation of goods into the city. The subject was unusual for Sisley: aside from a small number of paintings of Paris, which includes a companion painting of the canal made in the same year, the artist soon became more interested in depicting the small towns and countryside to the city's southeast, where he lived from 1880, including at Veneux-Nadon and Moret-sur-Loing.

Both views of the canal were successfully submitted to the Salon of 1870. Perhaps due in part to their relatively small size and their novel employment of the visible, fragmented brushstrokes favoured by the Impressionists (a name the group would not adopt until 1874), the paintings remained overlooked by critics.[54] The other work (fig. 38), takes its viewpoint from the middle of a bridge, resulting in a composition dominated by the reflecting interplay of sky and water that opens into a limpid expanse of blue and white. Sisley seems to have aimed at a different mood in the Winterthur picture. Descending to the *quai*, here our view of the water is abridged by the banks, sloping wall at left and shed at right, and the two barges solidly moored side by side, while the dark band of apartment building roofs forms a hard edge cutting across the sky. This tightly enclosed structure combines with the darkening clouds and groups of briskly rendered figures to give a sense of the industry and activity of the canal that is missing in the serene view of the Musée d'Orsay picture. The present work exemplifies well Sisley's belief in the need for 'a variation of surface within the same picture' so as to render the material effects of light:[55] his application ranges from the staccato, choppy marks that imply the movement of water and rough-textured walls, to the

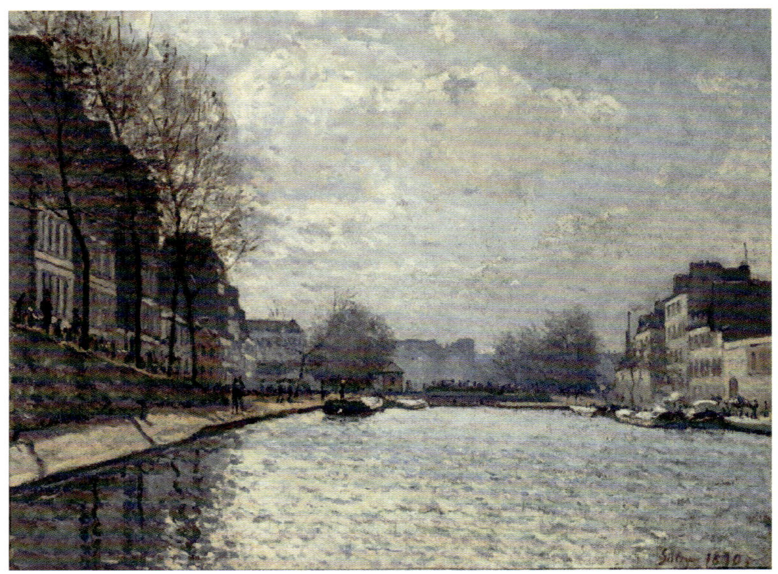

38. Alfred Sisley, *Vue du canal Saint-Martin*, 1870
oil on canvas, 50 × 65 cm. Musée d'Orsay, Paris

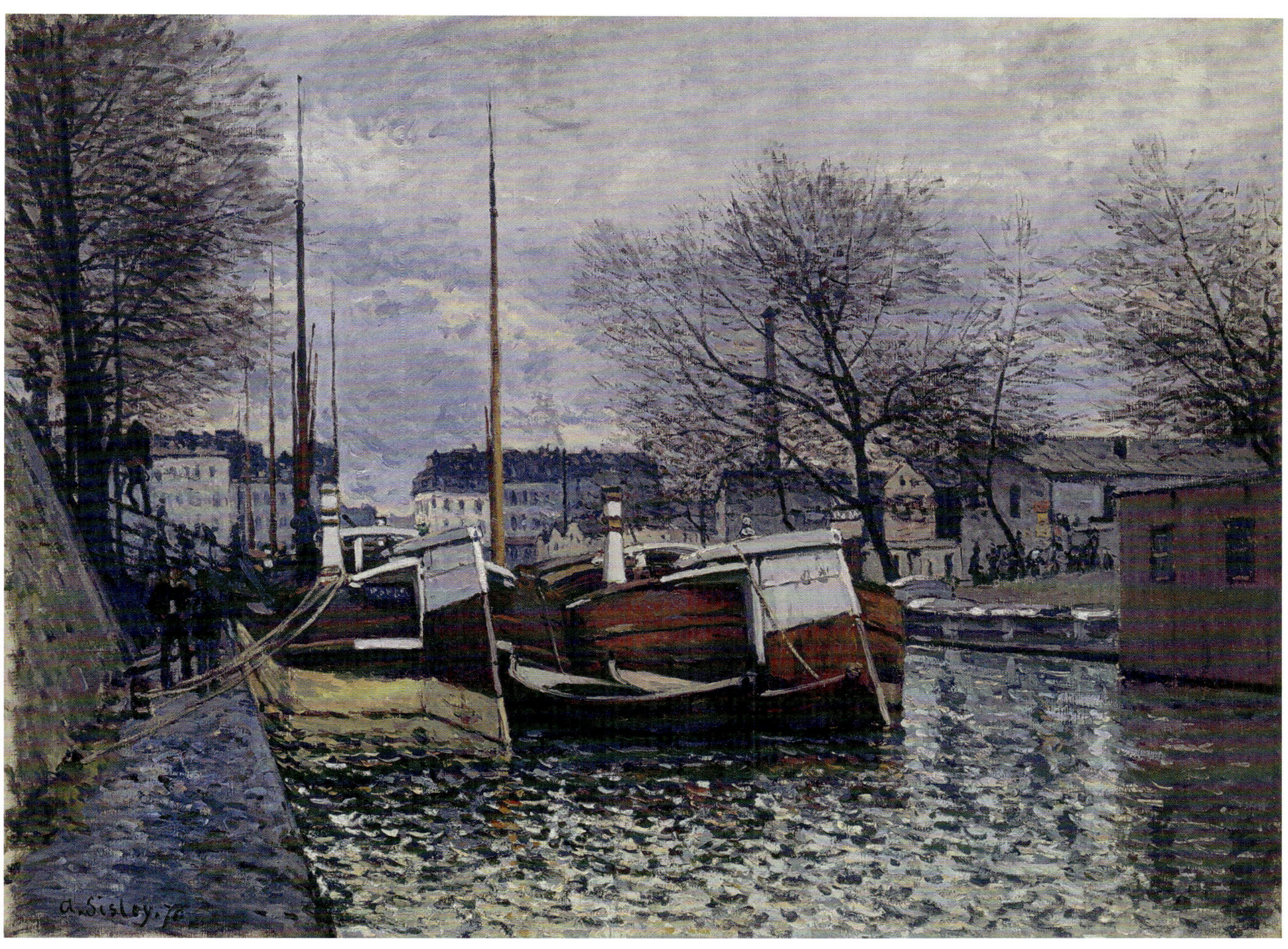

fine-veined tree branches made with a seemingly near-dry brush, to the broad, smooth strokes that construct the varnished wood of the barges.[56]

Though Sisley has often been regarded as holding a secondary status amongst the Impressionists, his unwavering dedication to the *en plein air* depiction of landscape, particularly its changing light and character, situates him as one of the group's most archetypal practitioners. Indeed, when Camille Pissarro was asked by Henri Matisse whom he would claim as 'a typical Impressionist', it was Sisley he chose to name.[57] **CN**

16

CLAUDE MONET (1840–1926)
The Break-up of Ice on the Seine, 1880–81

Oil on canvas, 60 × 99 cm
Inv. 1924.12
The Swiss Confederation, Federal Office of Culture,
Oskar Reinhart Collection 'Am Römerholz',
Winterthur

Provenance Acquired by Oskar Reinhart from the
Galerie Paul Rosenberg, Paris, 1924

During Monet's 1878–81 sojourn in Vétheuil, northwest of Paris, France experienced one of the coldest winters of the nineteenth century. The Seine froze over at the end of 1879, followed by a sudden rise of temperature at the end of the year that led to the explosive breakup of the 50 cm thick layer of ice, causing severe flooding. Monet recorded this dramatic event in some two dozen paintings made over the course of 1880–81. The present work is among his most experimental versions of the subject.

When he lived in Argenteuil in the 1870s Monet had painted numerous views of the Seine and its side channels from his studio boat. *La Débâcle*, or *The Break-up of Ice on the Seine* similarly places the viewer in mid-river among the ice floes. The view – looking upstream from Vétheuil towards an island in the middle of the river – is almost identical to that used in the more highly finished *Thaw at Vétheuil* (1880, Museo Thyssen-Bornemisza, Madrid). This clearly fictive vantage point, as well as the present painting's apparent completion in 1881,[58] reveal both the length of the working process – much of which must have taken place in the studio rather than *en plen air* – and the role played by the artist's imagination in realising the composition. While several of his earlier views of the frozen Seine included figures or other signs of human presence, here the scene consists wholly of a vast field of snow and ice mirroring the overcast sky and the bands of poplars and bushes lining the riverbanks. Monet rendered both the poplars and the ice floes in similar long, thin, smeary brushstrokes, intersecting at right angles as the reflections of the trees cross the floes on the surface of the river. The palette is restricted primarily to greys, whites and blue, with sparse touches of red in the trees, a very faint blush of pink in the clouds and areas of brown ground showing through the paint layer barely raising the chromatic temperature.

The Break-up of Ice on the Seine was the only painting by Monet that Reinhart ever acquired. A work by the artist had been on his wish list since 1914, and he was able to realise this goal when he acquired this canvas from Paul Rosenberg in 1924. However, both his correspondence and his private notebooks reveal a certain lack of enthusiasm for the painting. In 1930 he declared to the Galerie Paul Cassirer his wish to 'replace [my] late Monet with an early one'; following a visit to the Monet exhibition at the Zurich Kunsthaus in 1952, Reinhart reiterated his desire to 'sell *La Débâcle*' in order to acquire one of two works by Monet made in the first half of the 1870s.[59] Given Reinhart's preference for bold, well-structured compositions with clearly rendered forms, regardless of period or style, his lukewarm feelings about a painting defined by its sketchy handling and radical economy of execution are not entirely surprising. **RS**

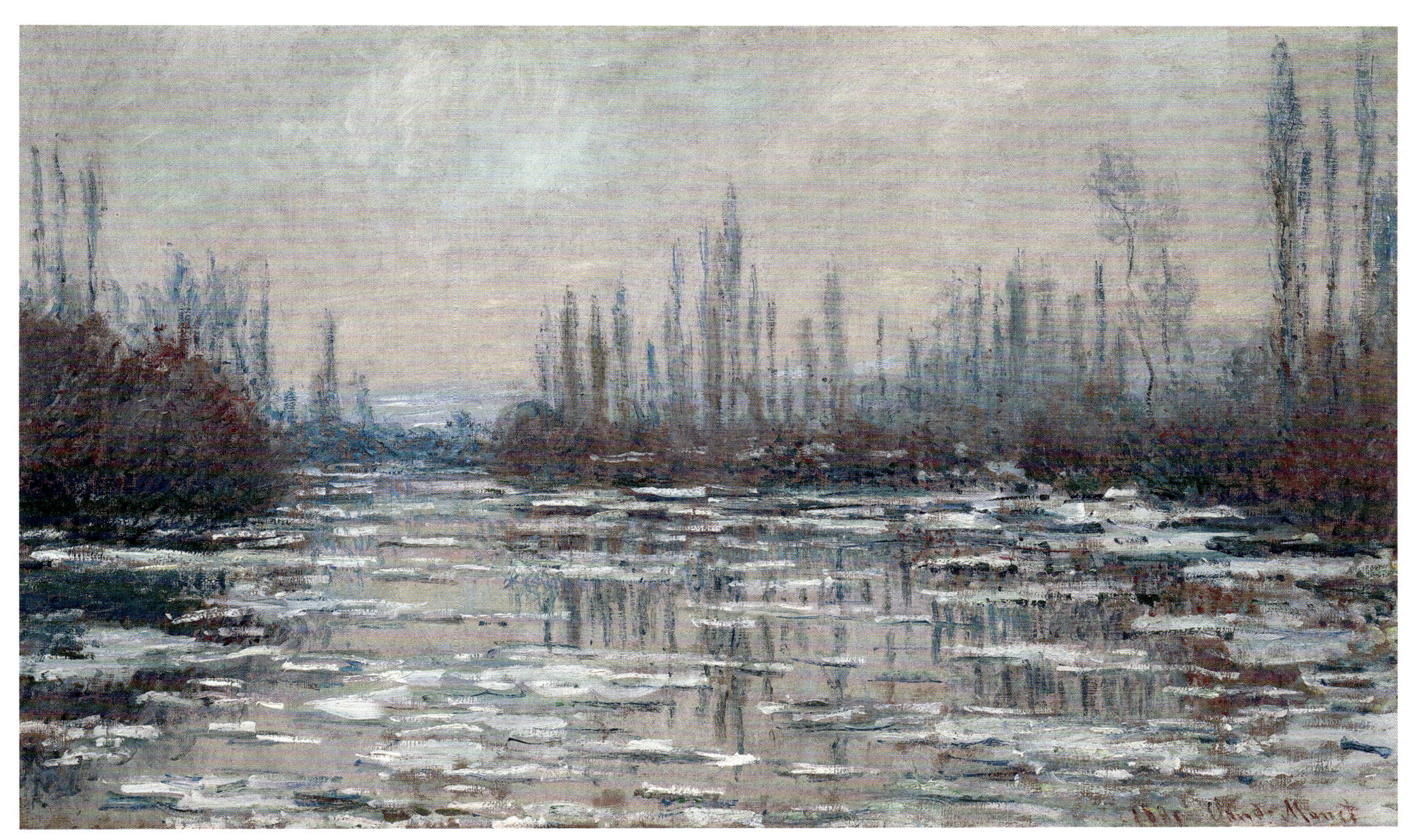

17

PIERRE-AUGUSTE RENOIR
(1841–1919)
Lily and Greenhouse Plants, 1864

Oil on canvas, 130 × 96 cm
Inv. 1927.4
The Swiss Confederation, Federal Office of Culture,
Oskar Reinhart Collection 'Am Römerholz',
Winterthur

Provenance Acquired by Oskar Reinhart from
the Galerie Fritz Gurlitt, Berlin, 1927

The 1860s witnessed a resurgence of interest in flower painting in France, sparked at least in part by an exhibition of seventeenth- and eighteenth-century Dutch and Flemish floral still lifes staged by the dealer Louis Martinet in his gallery on the Boulevard des Italiens in 1862.[60] In spite – or perhaps because – of the historically low regard in which still life was held within academic hierarchies, artists associated with the nascent avant-garde seized on flower painting with particular enthusiasm, so this type of subject features prominently in the work of Gustave Courbet, Henri Fantin-Latour and the young artists who would unite under the banner of Impressionism in the 1870s. For Monet, Renoir and Frédéric Bazille in particular, painting flowers offered a tantalising opportunity to experiment boldly with colour and form while producing pictures with commercial appeal. Renoir's remarkable *Lily and Greenhouse Plants* stands out from its peers, however, in its ambitious scale and composition, its unorthodox approach to a genre usually bound by narrow conventions, and in the insights it offers into social, botanical as well as art history.

Judging from the flowers included in the composition, Renoir must have begun *Lily and Greenhouse Plants* in the spring of 1864, shortly after his teacher Charles Gleyre (1806–1874) closed the atelier where he, Monet and Bazille had been training. The fact that he completed another version (now in the Hamburger Kunsthalle) that is only slightly smaller and less finished points to the breadth of his ambition.[61] Monet also chose to tackle a large-scale flower painting (fig. 39) around the same time; viewing both paintings side by side is instructive. Although Monet eschewed opulent receptacles for his flowers – some are piled in a willow basket, whilst the rest tumble and cascade across a neutral background – it is still an image of luxury, excess and romance, with peonies and tulips to the fore and old-fashioned flowers such as lilacs and wallflowers filling most of the remainder of the canvas, heaped informally as if they had just been gathered from a garden. It is a painting clearly made with exhibition and a potential sale in mind.[62]

Lily and Greenhouse Plants, although painted on the same large-scale format more commonly associated with grand-manner portraiture, presents an altogether more extraordinary tableau. A profusion of potted plants are clustered artlessly – some cropped by the edges of the canvas – in the shadowy interior of a greenhouse (a setting somewhat more clearly delineated in the version in Hamburg): a calla lily, daisies, a Keizerskroon tulip, a hyacinth, hydrangea macrophylla, lilac, pelargoniums, crocuses and primula obconica.[63] They are rendered without finicky detail but with enough sensitivity that their identities are mostly readily apparent. In place of the rich, harmonious and subtly modulated colour of Monet's flower painting, Renoir's palette is one of jarring contrasts, the clash of bright, mostly primary colours – the brilliant blue of the hydrangea, the flaming reds and yellows of the tulip, the cerise of the pelargonium, the stark white of the primula and hyacinth – thrown into sharp relief by the dark background and scarcely tempered by the pastel tones of the daisies and lilacs. No attempt has been made to disguise their status as the raw materials of the gardener's trade; they are presented in wooden boxes and clay pots, some displaying smears of earth, and the sinuous elegance of the calla is undercut by the visible piece of twine binding its stem to a stake. One of the

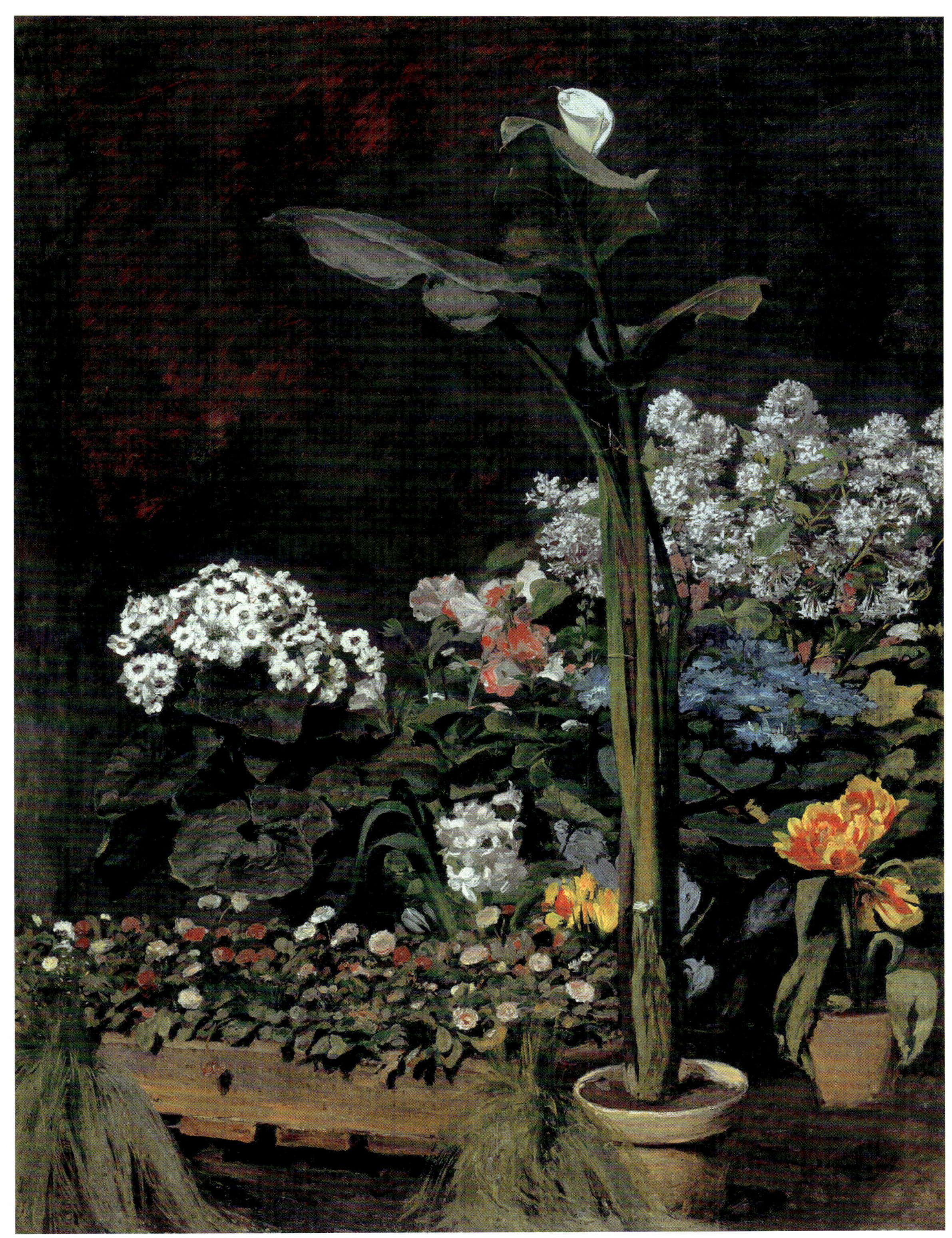

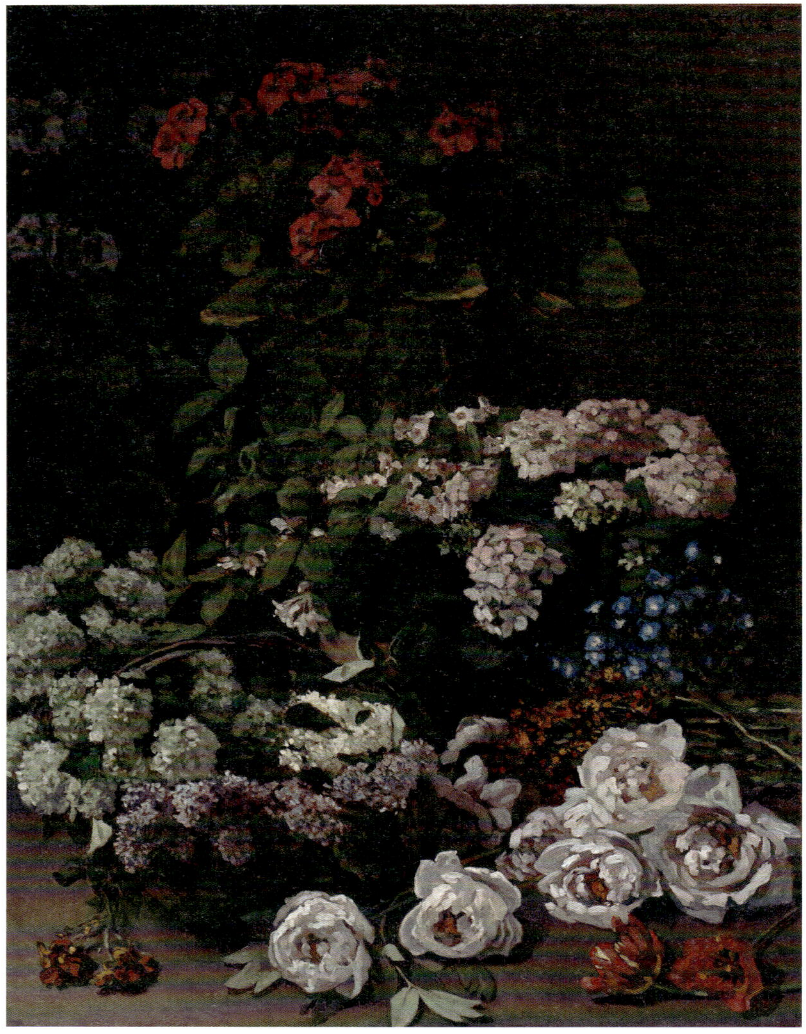

painting's few clear precedents is the flower pieces Courbet began painting in
the early 1860s, at least one of which (fig. 40), also owned by Oskar Reinhart,
depicts flowers growing in simple terracotta pots; two years later Bazille would
take up the challenge of making his own floral still life (1866, private collection)
in response to those of Courbet, Renoir and Monet, but his orderly rows of
pots seem timid in comparison. A less obvious ancestor is the work of the Lyon
painter and designer Jean-François Bony (1754–1825), who pioneered a floral
motif known as 'preparations for a celebration', in which extravagant masses
of flowers are gathered in an outdoor setting, awaiting further arrangement.[64]
Yet Bony's compositions invariably depict a classically influenced garden, the
flowers grouped on the edge of a fountain or around a plinth, cleansed of any
hint of behind-the-scenes dirt or labour.

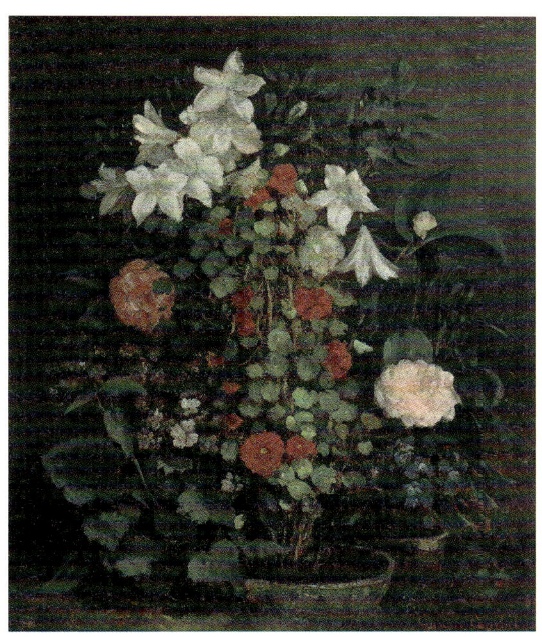

40. Gustave Courbet, *Still Life with Flowers*, 1863, oil on canvas, 65 × 54.5 cm. The Swiss Confederation, Federal Office of Culture, Oskar Reinhart Collection 'Am Römerholz', Winterthur

One other precedent is worth dwelling on. The lavish, symbolically and morally freighted bouquets of the Dutch Golden Age were botanical impossibilities, gathering together flowers that bloom at different times of year. Here, Renoir offers a very modern twist on this idea. Pelargoniums and calla lilies, for example, do not naturally bloom at the same time as spring bulbs – but they will do so if they are forced in a greenhouse. Furthermore, this combination of plants would never occur together in the wild – primula obconica and hydrangea are native to east Asia, callas and pelargoniums to southern Africa, the bulbs to west Asia and the Mediterranean (albeit widespread in Europe by this point). That Renoir was able to paint this florilegium at all is the result of the technological advances of the time and of Europe's ever-increasing colonial ambitions. The modern greenhouse was developed by Joseph Paxton at Chatsworth in 1840, the year before Renoir's birth; fifteen years later, as part of the wholesale remaking of the fabric of Paris, Baron Haussmann (1809–1891) and his chief gardener, Jean-Pierre Barillet-Deschamps (1824–1873), established a vast complex of greenhouses, the Fleuriste de la Muette, for the propagation of millions of plants for bedding out in the city's parks. Flowers – at least, some varieties – were no longer symbols of luxury, but objects of mass production. Many of the plants Renoir depicted here were, and still are, staples of municipal planting schemes, and the way they are presented, apparently ready for planting out, suggests that we may be looking at a corner of an official city greenhouse. Later in life, Renoir expressed a deep dislike of Haussmann's transformation of Paris, in particular the dull uniformity of its gardens and parks. Here, however, he appears emboldened by the possibilities offered by recent revolutions in horticulture to create a painting that both nods to and subverts the traditions of a genre not normally noted for audacity.

Renoir began his working life as a painter of porcelain before moving to paper and canvas, a background that undoubtedly informed the central place of flowers in his oeuvre. He famously confided to his biographer Georges Rivière (1855–1943) that 'I just let my brain rest when I paint flowers', a remark that is frequently taken out of context to erroneously suggest that he considered flower painting a mindless pursuit, to be indulged in between bouts of more ambitious work. In fact, as he further explained, 'When I am painting flowers, I establish the tones, I study the values carefully, without worrying about losing the picture. I don't dare do this with a figure piece for fear of ruining it. The experience which I gain in these works, I eventually apply to my [other] pictures.'[65] Painting flowers, in other words, offered Renoir fertile ground for experimentation, formal and otherwise. It is therefore fitting that *Lily and Greenhouse Plants* was one of the most radical paintings he ever produced. **RS**

18

PIERRE-AUGUSTE RENOIR
(1841–1919)
The Milliner, c. 1875

Oil on canvas, 59 × 49 cm
Inv. 1949.7
The Swiss Confederation, Federal Office of Culture,
Oskar Reinhart Collection 'Am Römerholz',
Winterthur

Provenance Purchased by Oskar Reinhart from the
Galerie Paul Rosenberg, New York, 1949

The model for this charming genre scene was probably Nini Lopez, with whom Renoir worked frequently during the latter half of the 1870s. She sat for numerous half-length studies, some of them very similar to this composition, as well as some of his most ambitious works such as *La Loge* (fig. 41) and *The Dance at the Moulin de la Galette* (1876, Musée d'Orsay, Paris). Depicted in the act of sewing an artificial flower on to a hat, Lopez poses in profile before a wall covered with pale green floral wallpaper, a background that locates the painting in Renoir's studio in Rue Cortot in Montmartre, where he moved in 1875. The same background appears in the portrait of his patron Victor Chocquet, probably painted the following year (cat. 19).

Despite the painting's relatively small size and simple composition, Renoir's skill and astute handling of colour are evident. The background is broadly brushed, leaving small areas of canvas visible, contrasting with the fine strokes used to render the individual strands of the girl's hair – particularly the wisps at the nape of her neck – as well as her delicate features and long, curving eyelashes. The position of her hands is particularly finely observed. The shadows on her white blouse and scarf and the highlights on her blonde hair are rendered in subtly modulated blues.

In late-nineteenth-century Paris millinery grew into a significant and modern industry that employed thousands of women, producing hats for men and women. The son of a tailor and a dressmaker, Renoir owned many hats, which his models would wear. Although milliners and other women employed in the fashion industry are a subject more often associated with Edgar Degas (1834–1917), who used it repeatedly in his paintings and pastels from the 1880s, Renoir had gravitated towards such imagery earlier.[66] The present work is one of several depicting milliners he made in the 1870s, including *At the Milliner's* (1878, Harvard Art Museums) and *The Milliner* (1877, The Metropolitan Museum of Art, New York). In contrast to his other portrayals of milliners and their assistants, which are explicitly set in a shop or in the street directly outside a shop, in this painting Renoir makes no attempt to disguise the studio setting in which his model is posed. His chief concern here seems to be with the figure and with colour, rather than with incidental detail and implied narrative. **RS**

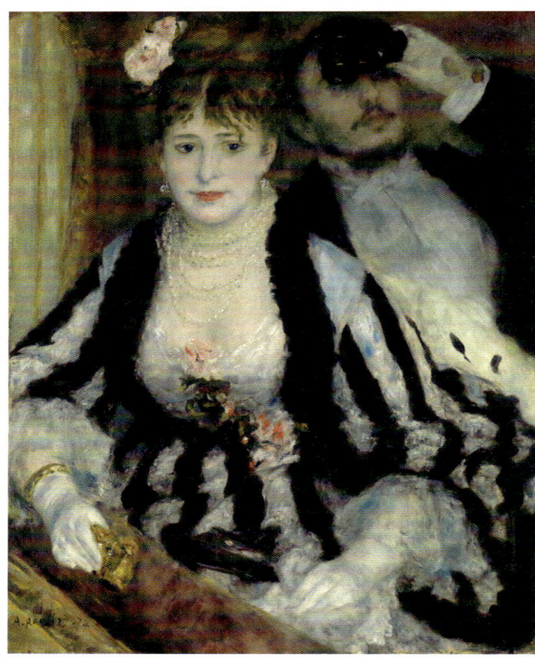

41. Pierre-Auguste Renoir, *La Loge*, 1874,
oil on canvas, 80 × 63.5 cm. The Courtauld,
London (Samuel Courtauld Trust)

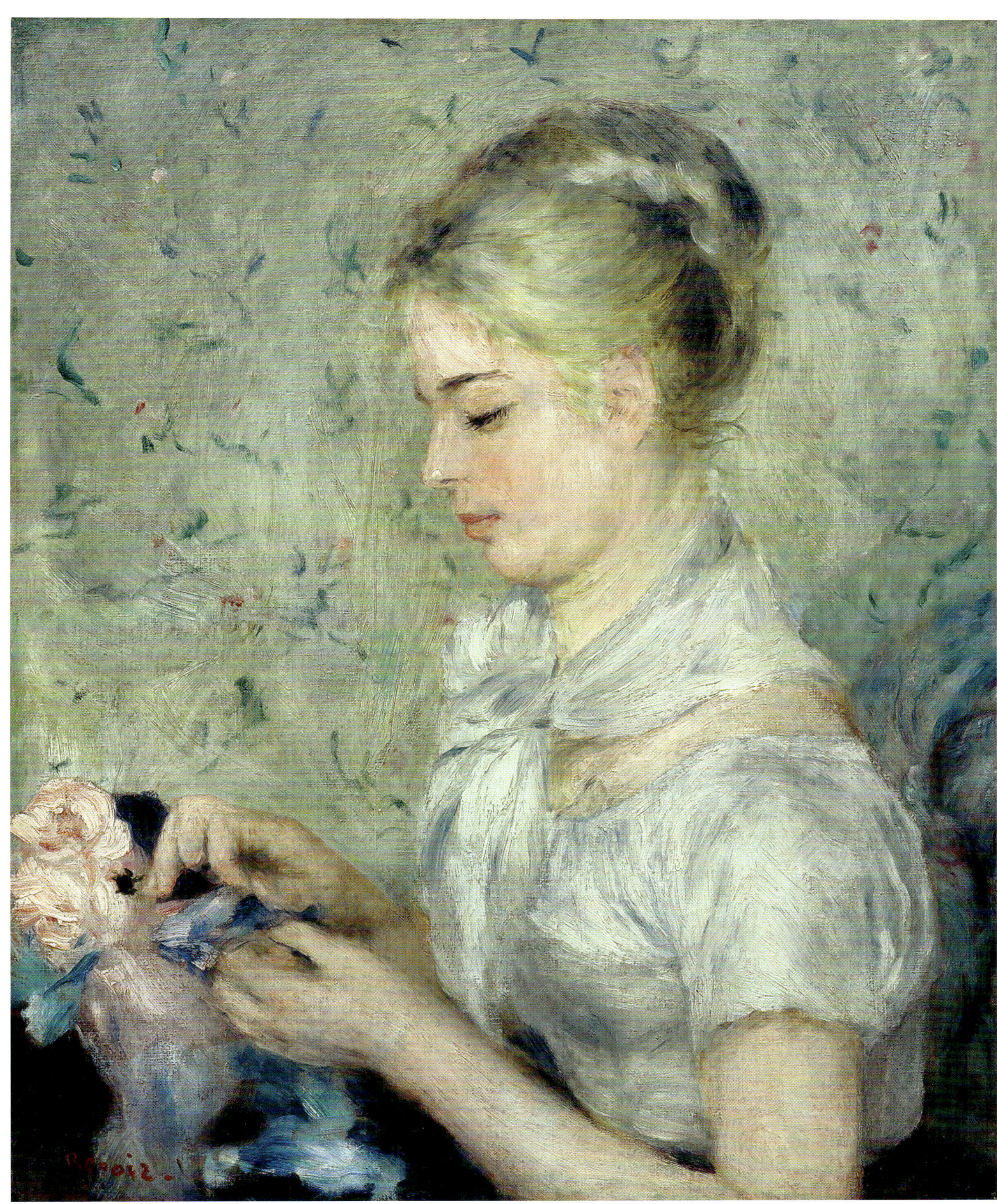

19

PIERRE-AUGUSTE RENOIR
(1841–1919)
Portrait of Victor Chocquet, c. 1876

Oil on canvas, 46 × 36 cm
Inv. 1925.9
The Swiss Confederation, Federal Office of Culture,
Oskar Reinhart Collection 'Am Römerholz',
Winterthur

Provenance Purchased by Oskar Reinhart from the
Galerie Durand-Ruel, Paris/New York, 1925

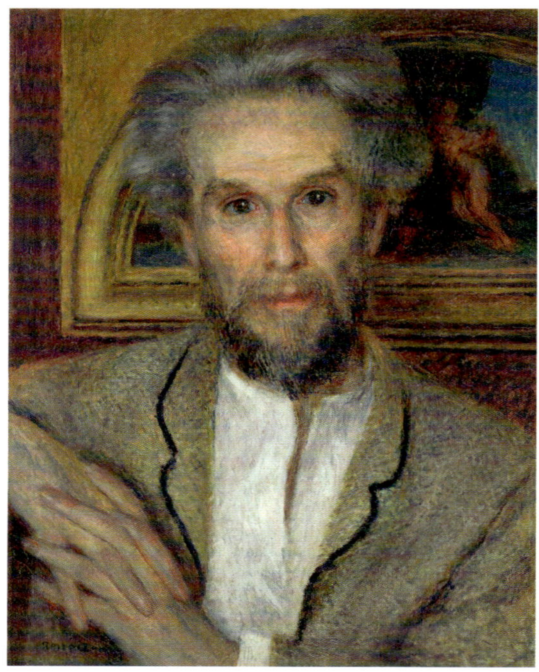

42. Pierre-Auguste Renoir, *Victor Chocquet*, c. 1875,
oil on canvas, 53 × 43.5 cm, Harvard Art Museums,
Cambridge, Massachusetts

Victor Chocquet (1821–1891) was one of Renoir's earliest and most dedicated patrons and an ardent supporter of Impressionism. Despite his modest income as a customs employee – later supplemented, from 1882, by his wife's inheritance – he managed to assemble an art collection of great quality, in which works by Renoir, Monet and Cezanne took pride of place. Having first become acquainted with Renoir at an unsuccessful sale the artist organised at the Hôtel Drouot on 24 March 1875, Chocquet soon commissioned the artist to paint portraits of him and his wife (the latter now in the Staatsgalerie Stuttgart). Renoir painted two of Chocquet: one in which he sits with clasped hands in front of a sketch by Delacroix in his own collection (Harvard University Art Museums; fig. 42), and the present work.[67] Although the order in which the portraits were executed is not clear, it seems plausible that the more formal portrait was painted first. The present work, which is striking in its informality and suggests a degree of familiarity between artist and sitter, probably followed later.

Chocquet poses in a Louis XV armchair in Renoir's studio in the Rue Cortot, Paris, which the artist had moved into in 1875, identifiable by the pale green wallpaper patterned with pink and red flowers; the same setting features in *The Milliner* (cat. 18), a slightly larger painting. The composition is very tightly cropped, with Chocquet's unruly shock of grey hair almost grazing the upper edge of the canvas. Renoir depicts his distinctive features – hollow cheeks, high forehead, long nose and piercing dark eyes – in extreme closeup. The gesture of his hand touching his beard and his informal attire lend him the air of a philosopher. His relaxed pose and the hint of a wry smile playing about his lips suggest a sense of ease, even complicity, between artist and sitter; indeed, Renoir later described it as a 'portrait of a madman, by a madman'.[68]

That Chocquet was pleased with his portrait is suggested by the fact that he lent it, along with four other paintings by Renoir, to the second Impressionist exhibition in April 1876. Critics greeted it with a combination of derision and incomprehension, complaining that the sitter's hair was 'green and sky blue' and his beard was 'pink', revealing the same misunderstanding of the Impressionists' approach to colour that characterised the early response to their landscapes.[69] Notwithstanding this critique, the portrait remained in Chocquet's collection until his death. Paul Durand-Ruel acquired it from his sale (following the death of his widow) in 1899 and kept it for 25 years, until Oskar Reinhart acquired it from his gallery in 1925. **RS**

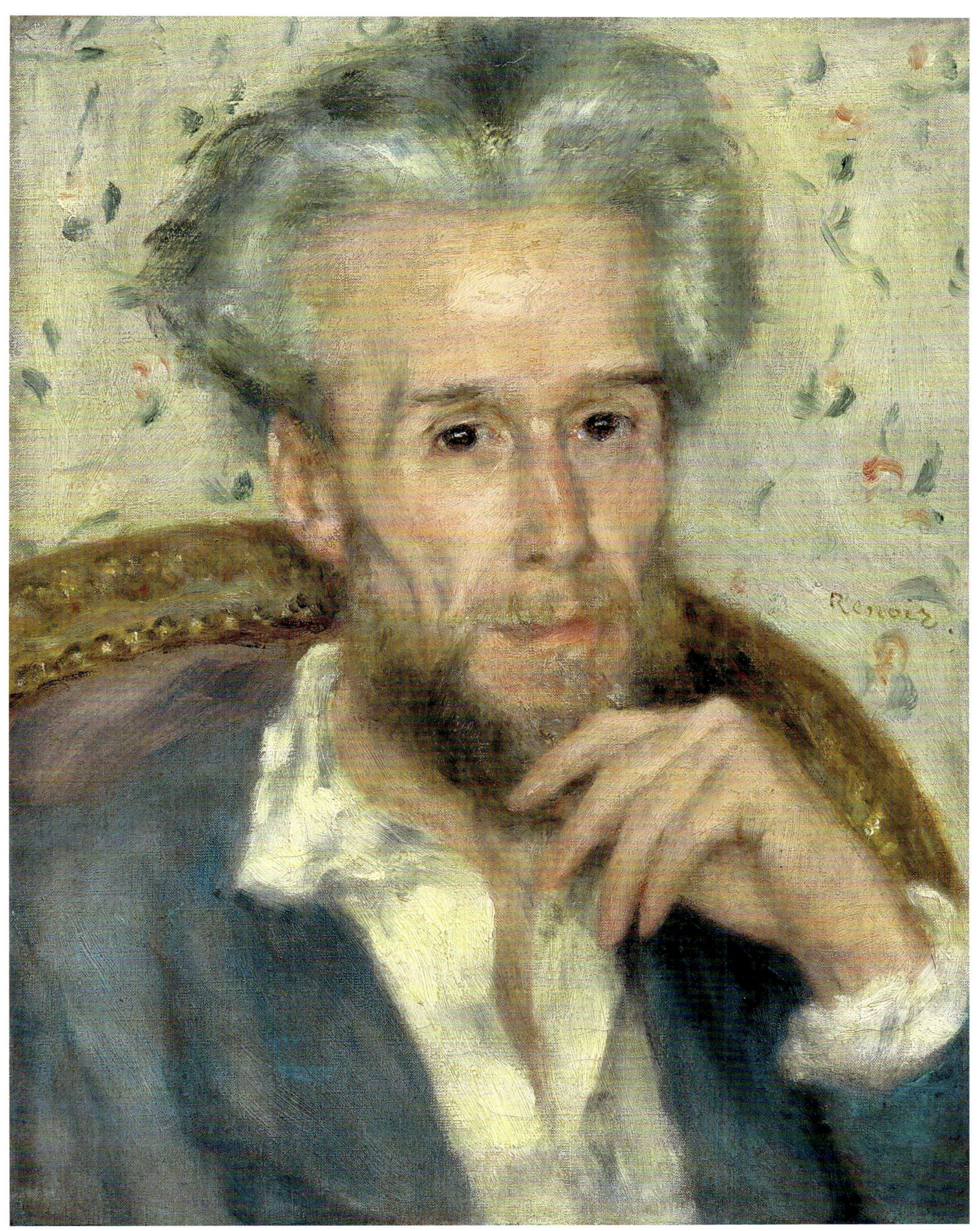

20

PIERRE-AUGUSTE RENOIR
(1841–1919)
Confidences, c. 1876–78

Oil on canvas, 61.5 × 50.5 cm
Inv. 1923.26
The Swiss Confederation, Federal Office of Culture,
Oskar Reinhart Collection 'Am Römerholz',
Winterthur

Provenance Acquired by Oskar Reinhart from
Wilhelm Hansen, Copenhagen, 1923

Although long known by the title of *Confidences*, this painting appears in the 1887 collection catalogue of the pastry chef and Impressionist collector Eugène Murer (1841–1906), its first owner, as *Les Deux Inséparables* (The Inseparable Two). It is unclear whether either title originated with Renoir, but both of them frame the picture as an image of female friendship and shared secrets. Two young women, Renoir's models Eva and Laurenzie 'La Polonaise', seated in dappled shade, are depicted with their heads bowed together in conversation, one with her face turned away from the viewer in lost profile. Her companion smiles at her, lips open and teeth just visible as if caught mid-sentence, as she raises her right hand and displays a plain gold ring. The pose of the woman in the foreground, with her body angled toward her friend and her arm and shoulder partially blocking the view, suggests the intimate nature of the conversation and holds the viewer at a distance, unable to intrude further. Interestingly, the title *Confidences* is also used for another painting, in which Renoir represented a couple reading together in a garden (c. 1873, Portland Museum of Art, Maine).

Renoir painted *Confidences* around the same time as one of his most ambitious works, *The Dance at the Moulin de la Galette* (1876, Musée d'Orsay, Paris). Although the considerably smaller *Confidences* is a much simpler composition, it exhibits similarities with the *Dance* in its light-hearted mood, emphasis on capturing a transient moment and particularly in its treatment of light and colour; one of Renoir's key concerns in both paintings seems to have been how to render the effect of shifting patches of sunlight on colour. Cool blues and greens and rich browns dominate the palette, with two carefully placed passages of warm colour – small dabs of red on the lips of the speaking woman and on what appears to be a flower tucked into her scarf, and the more diffuse rosy pink of both women's cheeks – serving to draw the eye into the composition. The brushwork in the background, especially at left where it seems to denote rustling foliage, is exceptionally loose, blurring the distinction between a sketch and a finished work and heightening the lively atmosphere of the scene.

Oskar Reinhart's interest in Renoir's work is evidenced by the important number of paintings (twelve) by him in his collection, the largest by any artist among those displayed 'Am Römerholz' – the earliest being *Lily and Greenhouse Plants* (cat. 17). His interest in Renoir may have been influenced by Julius Meier-Graefe (1867–1935), who in 1912 authored the first monographic book on the artist, later revised in 1929. Reinhart shared this passion with Winterthur collectors Hedy (née Bühler, 1873–1952) and Arthur Hahnloser (1870–1936), like-minded philanthropists who donated their collection and residence, Villa Flora, to the Swiss Confederation. **RS**

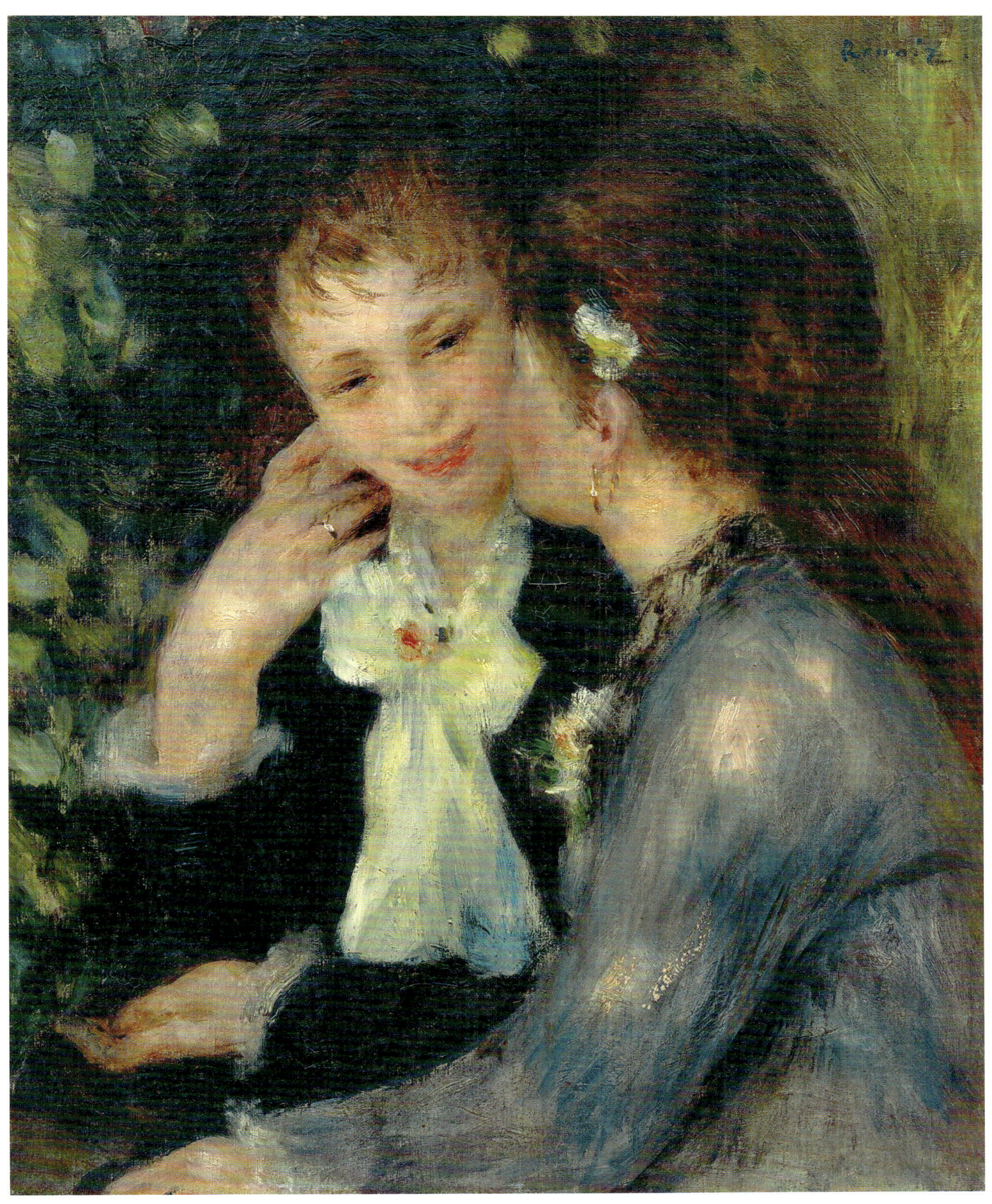

21

PAUL GAUGUIN (1848–1903)
Blue Roofs (Rouen), early 1884

Oil on canvas, 74 × 60 cm
Inv. 1931.6
The Swiss Confederation, Federal Office of Culture,
Oskar Reinhart Collection 'Am Römerholz',
Winterthur

Provenance Acquired by Oskar Reinhart from Alix
Biermann-Ruete, Bremen, through Peter Voigt,
Graphisches Kabinett GmbH, Bremen, 1931

In January 1884, following his decision to give up his career on the Paris stock market and devote himself solely to art, Gauguin moved his family to Rouen. His reasons were twofold: the cost of living was lower there, and he would have the opportunity to work alongside Camille Pissarro (1830–1903), who had served as a mentor to him since his early days as an amateur artist. The time he spent painting with Pissarro in Rouen in the summer of 1883 undoubtedly influenced his decision. He rented a house on the north side of the city. *Blue Roofs*, an elevated view of the cityscape in the vicinity of his house, at first glance shows an artist still discernably under the influence of Pissarro in terms of subject matter, composition and technique; there are notable similarities with landscapes the older artist painted in and around Pontoise in the 1860s and 1870s. Yet a closer look at the painting reveals Gauguin beginning to move beyond Impressionism; this attempt to synthesise contrasting styles and techniques in a composition that hovers on the edge of pastiche shows the artist at a moment of transition.

The state of the vegetation in this painting – trees still bare and hedges and shrubs covered in pale new growth – and the fact that it was deposited with the gallerist Paul Durand-Ruel on 9 April 1884 point to a date of execution in early spring, not long after Gauguin's arrival in Rouen. The sky is rendered in short, curling, nervous brushstrokes reminiscent of Pissarro's handling, and the brushwork used for the trees and fields is also typically Impressionist. In stark contrast, however, the houses form an interlocking series of flat planes of solid, almost unmodulated colour, dominated by the deep blue of the roofs. Even the brushwork has an architectonic quality; parallel strokes of equal length are placed side by side with great deliberation. The compositional structure and treatment of colour point to the influence of Cezanne (1839–1906), whom Gauguin also admired deeply, and whose views of Auvers in the 1870s and early 1880s show striking similarities with *Blue Roofs*. The treatment of the two figures at the lower edge of the painting – the foreground figure sharply cropped at the lower left corner, the other dwarfed by the tree at lower right – disregards the laws of perspective, with the figure in the foreground too large in proportion to both the buildings and the smaller figure. Both the flouting of perspective and the reduction of the houses to blocks of flat colour show Gauguin beginning to turn his back on capturing an optical impression of the world in favour of giving form to an idea of the world created in his mind's eye. This was not a journey on which Oskar Reinhart was prepared to follow Gauguin, and *Blue Roofs* was the only work he ever purchased by the artist. **RS**

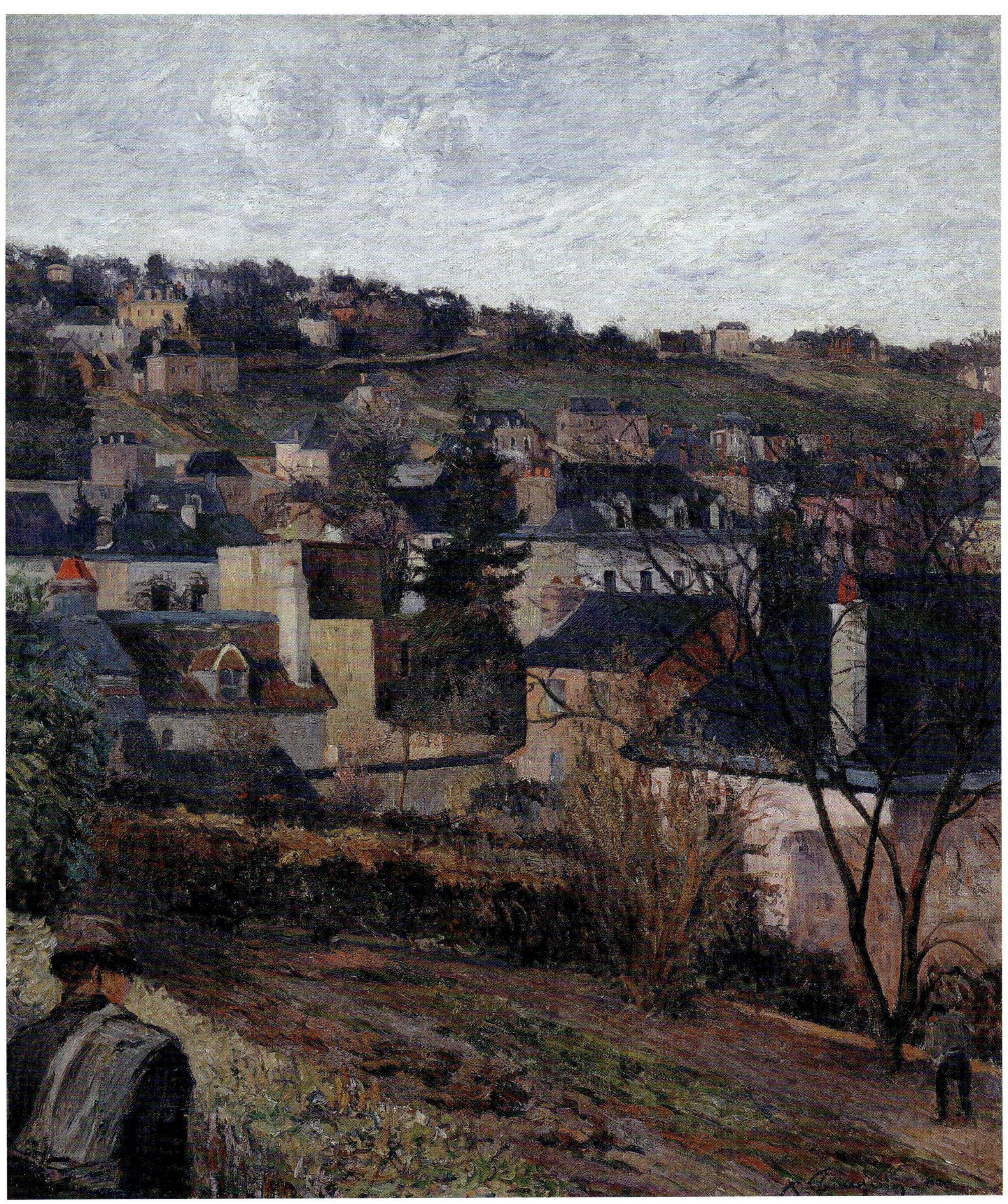

22

VINCENT VAN GOGH (1853–1890)
The Ward in the Hospital at Arles, 1889

Oil on canvas, 72 × 91 cm
Inv. 1925.12
The Swiss Confederation, Federal Office of Culture,
Oskar Reinhart Collection 'Am Römerholz',
Winterthur

Provenance Acquired by Oskar Reinhart from the
Galerie Barbazanges, Paris, 1925

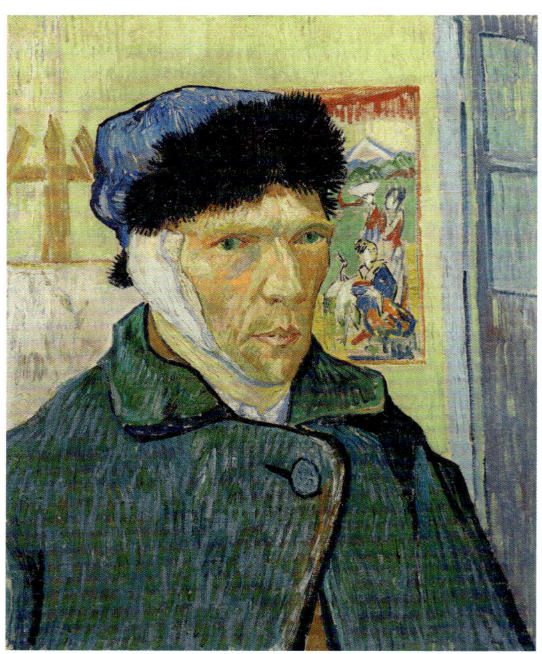

43. Vincent van Gogh, *Self-Portrait with Bandaged
Ear*, 1889, oil on canvas, 60.5 × 50 cm. The Courtauld,
London (Samuel Courtauld Trust)

Vincent van Gogh first set foot in the Hôtel-Dieu Saint-Esprit, which housed the hospital serving the town of Arles, in the south of France, on 24 December 1888. He had been taken there as a medical emergency following a mental health crisis during which he mutilated his ear (fig. 43). After this initial two-week stay, he returned to the hospital for longer periods in winter and spring 1889, as he suffered further breakdowns and became unable to live alone. This depiction of the interior of the men's ward was painted at the end of his time there, in mid to late April 1889. A few weeks later, Van Gogh moved to a psychiatric institution on the outskirts of the town of Saint-Rémy-de-Provence, some 25 kilometres away, taking this work and its pendant, *The Courtyard of the Hospital at Arles* (cat. 23), with him. The pair are the only paintings he made representing the hospital in Arles and it is therefore remarkable that they were only finally reunited when Oskar Reinhart acquired them separately for his collection.

In letters, Van Gogh described the long ward as 'the room of those suffering from fever',[70] which most likely referred to patients suffering from mental illness. Rows of beds, separated by curtains, line the walls as men in the foreground gather around a stove, its long flue pipe cutting through the composition at sharp angles. Nuns from the Order of Saint Augustine, who nursed the patients, are recognisable in their white and black habits in the centre of the room. The length of the ward is accentuated by the perspective lines that converge into a high focal point at the end of the gallery. Van Gogh adopted the same device of tilting the floor upwards in the few other interior views painted during his time in Arles, most notably his *Bedroom* (1888, Van Gogh Museum, Amsterdam) and *The Night Café* (1888, Yale University Art Gallery, New Haven), creating a sense of imbalance and unease.

The Ward in the Hospital at Arles was painted during a difficult period in Van Gogh's life. He had arrived in Arles a little over a year earlier, in February 1888, full of the ambition to forge a life away from Paris, find his artistic path and create a community of like-minded artists. These dreams had been dampened by disputes with his housemate, the artist Paul Gauguin (1848–1903), and severe episodes of mental crisis. In a letter from late April or early May 1889 to his sister Willemien, he confessed that he often worried 'that my life hasn't been calm enough, all these setbacks, vexations, changes mean that I am not developing organically and in full in my artistic career'.[71] Nevertheless, in the same letter, he reported being in excellent physical health and able to paint. Although he still felt 'incapable of having a studio again', he noted that he was

working however & [I] have just done two paintings of the hospital. One is a room, a very long room with rows of beds with white curtains where a few figures of patients are moving around. The walls, the ceiling with large beams, everything is white in a lilac white or in a green white. Here and there a window with a pink or light green curtain. The floor tiled with red bricks. At the far end a door surmounted by a crucifix. It's very, very simple.

A comparison between the letter and the painting, however, reveals some discrepancies. For instance, Van Gogh does not mention the men in

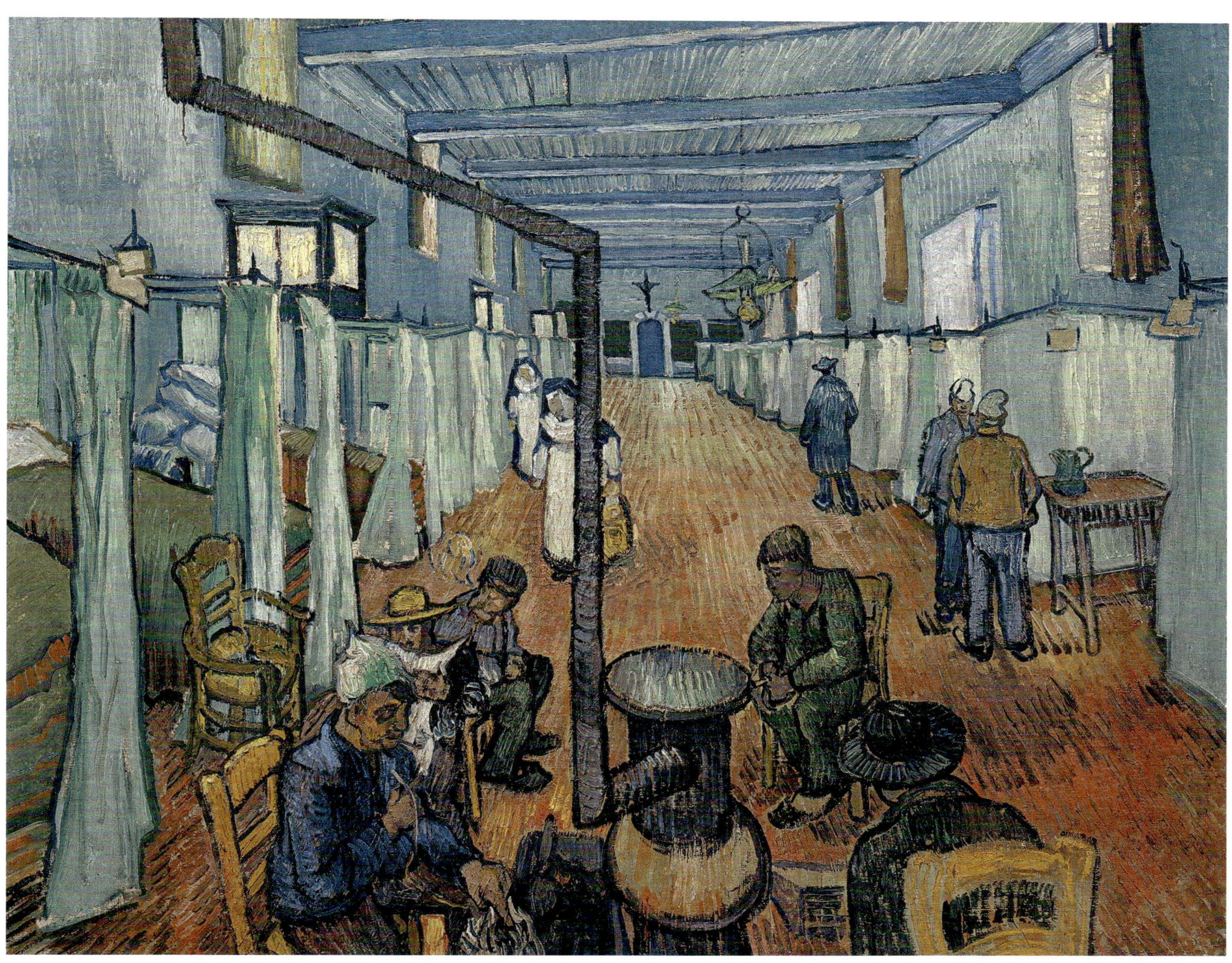

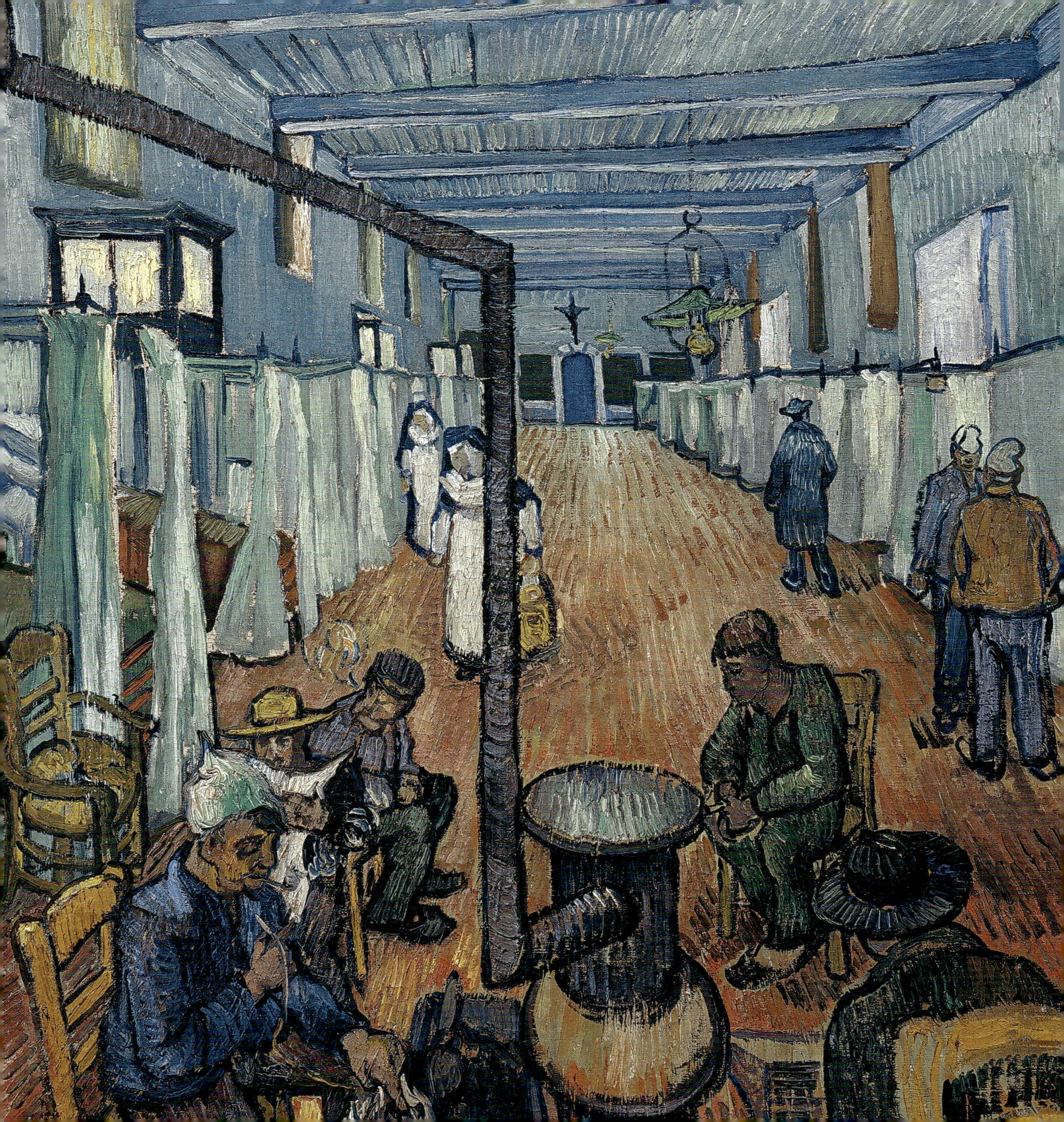

the foreground but speaks only of a 'few figures of patients' moving around. Indeed, the stove and some of the figures were clearly painted over thick, already dry impasto. This can be explained by the fact that Van Gogh heavily reworked this painting six months after its initial conception, when he was no longer in Arles but in the psychiatric hospital in Saint-Rémy. According to another letter to Willemien, dated this time October 1889,[72] the return to the canvas, which Van Gogh now dubbed 'a large study', was prompted by his reading of an article on Fyodor Dostoevsky's *The House of the Dead*, a fictionalised account of the author's time in a Siberian prison camp, which was first published in 1862 and translated into French in 1886. Was Van Gogh prompted to add the men huddling around the stove in the foreground as an echo of Dostoevsky's description of his fellow prisoners? He only stated that he struggled to paint not from life but from memory, as he was far from his initial motif. As he noted in the same letter, 'it is a nuisance to make figures without models'.

Van Gogh had first-hand experience of the men's ward in the hospital in Arles. He had spent time there, although his condition meant that he was later granted his own room. Nevertheless, the chair on the left of the composition takes on a symbolic meaning, inevitably evoking the empty chairs Van Gogh painted in November 1888 to represent himself and his housemate, Paul Gauguin (National Gallery, London, and Van Gogh Museum, Amsterdam). Van Gogh clearly felt a strong affinity with the patients on the ward, writing to his brother Theo at the end of his first hospital stay on 7 January 1889, 'I can assure you that a few days in the hospital were very interesting and one perhaps learns how to live from the sick'.[73] **KS**

23

VINCENT VAN GOGH (1853–1890)

The Courtyard of the Hospital at Arles, 1889

Oil on canvas, 73 × 92 cm
Inv. 1922.11
The Swiss Confederation, Federal Office of Culture,
Oskar Reinhart Collection 'Am Römerholz',
Winterthur

Provenance Acquired by Oskar Reinhart from Theodor
Behrens, Hamburg, through the dealer Alfred Gold,
Berlin, 1922

The Hôtel-Dieu Saint-Esprit in Arles was built from 1573 to house the town's charitable institutions and adopted the architecture of a medieval cloister, with open galleries on two levels surrounding an inner courtyard. By the time Vincent van Gogh became a patient there in December 1888, the courtyard had become a lush garden with mature trees, shrubs and flowerbeds radiating from a central pond. In Van Gogh's depiction, patients and visitors are seen congregating in the galleries – women on the left and men on the right, each in their separate wings – while a nun walks through the garden. Large pots with orange trees and oleanders line the covered corridor on the ground floor. To paint this broad view of the courtyard, Van Gogh positioned himself in the southeast corner on the first floor, which provided him with an elevated view of the vegetation. In a letter to his sister Willemien, he described the painting:

> It is a gallery with arches like in Arabic buildings, whitewashed with lime. In front of those galleries, an ancient garden with a pond in the middle and 8 flowerbeds, with forget-me-nots, Christmas roses. anemones, buttercups, gillyflowers, daisies &c.
> And under the gallery, orange trees and oleanders. It is therefore a painting full of flowers and springtime greenery. Three dark and sad tree trunks however run through it like snakes and in the foreground four large, sad bushes of dark box.[74]

It is interesting that Van Gogh saw the trees as a menacing presence, conveying an unsettling atmosphere also found in *The Ward in the Hospital at Arles* (cat. 22), the only other painting he made of the hospital. One wonders if, by adding the stove and flue pipe to the foreground of his representation of the ward in October 1889, six months after its initial conception, Van Gogh was not echoing the 'dark and sad tree trunks' running through his courtyard composition 'like snakes', as he wrote to Willemien. In the present painting, the marked verticals of the trees balance out the strong diagonal lines of the garden paths and arcaded galleries. The introduction of a solid element in the foreground of a landscape, most often an unanchored tree, was common in Japanese prints and Van Gogh, an avid collector of such works, must have chosen the framing of his composition accordingly. The dark trees and their bare branches act as a counterpoint to the colourful flowerbeds and the vibrant yellow framing the arches of the galleries. The beds themselves look like a painter's palette, with thick daubs of pure colour placed side by side to render the plants.

The Courtyard of the Hospital at Arles was painted at the same time as *The Ward in the Hospital at Arles*, in mid to late April 1889, and is described by Van Gogh as its pendant.[75] Both works are the same size and act as 'opposing pairs'[76] – one a claustrophobic interior with an exaggerated vanishing point, the other a bright and verdant outdoor scene full of criss-crossing lines. The inner courtyard of the hospital was the subject of another work by Van Gogh, this time a large reed-pen drawing made in early May 1889, a few weeks after the painting (fig. 44).[77] It is therefore not preparatory to *The Courtyard of the Hospital at Arles* but created as a completely independent work. In it,

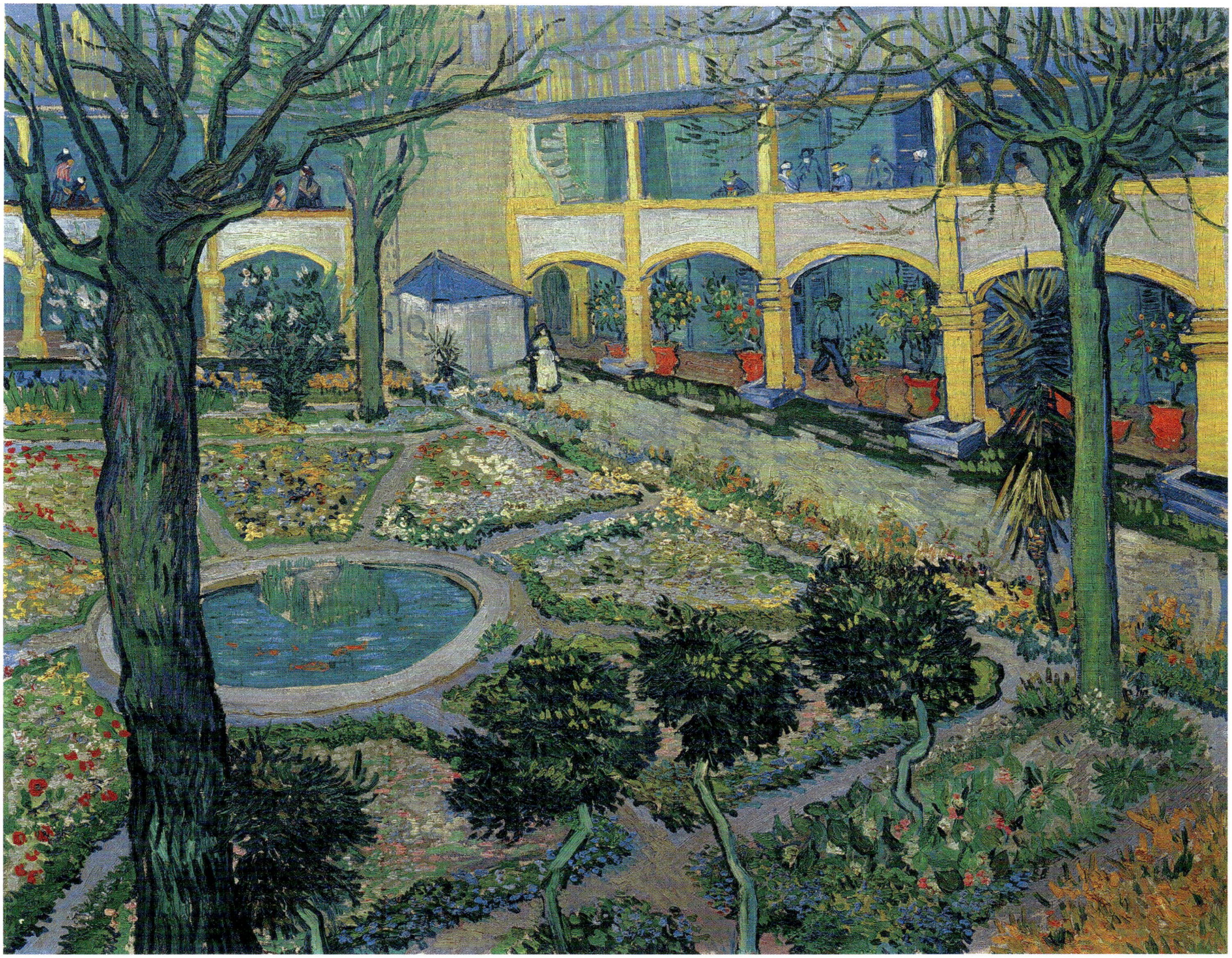

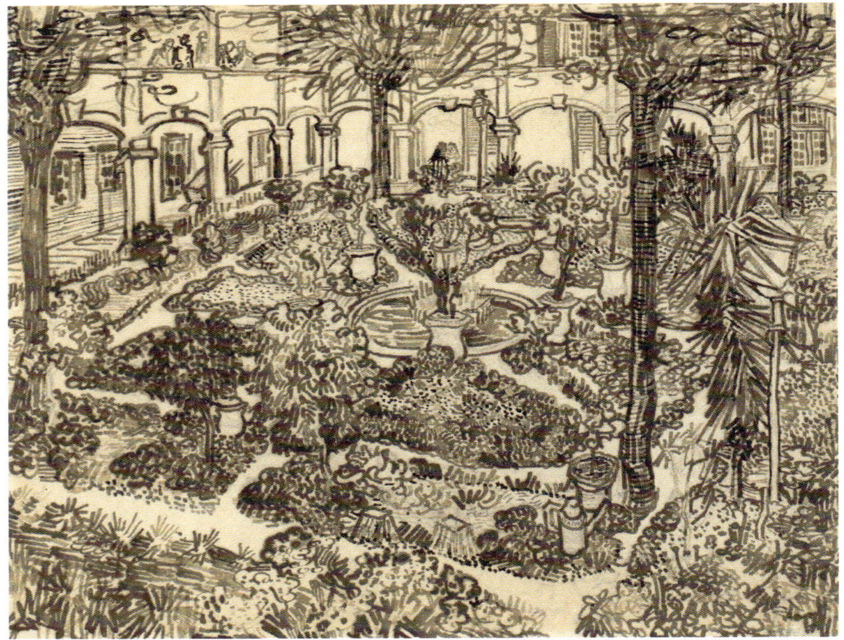

Van Gogh shifted his vantage point while remaining on the first-floor gallery. The vegetation in the garden seems to have grown in the interim. The large pots containing the orange trees and oleanders are no longer confined to the side corridors but dotted around the garden, adding to its profusion.

Van Gogh took the unusual step of not sending *The Courtyard of the Hospital at Arles* nor its pendant to his brother Theo in Paris, who was the recipient of most of his paintings. Instead, he brought the two paintings with him (along with the related drawing) when he moved, on 8 May 1889, to his new home at the psychiatric institution of Saint-Paul-de-Mausole, 25 kilometres northwest of Arles. He may have been keen not only to have a few works to decorate his new room but, crucially, to show the doctors there that he had been allowed to paint at the hospital in Arles, in the hope that the same permission might be granted. The paintings seem to have remained together until May 1894, when Theo's widow, Johanna van Gogh-Bonger, sold *The Courtyard of the Hospital at Arles*. They were reunited by Oskar Reinhart in 1925 when he purchased *The Ward in the Hospital at Arles*, having acquired the present painting three years earlier. **KS**

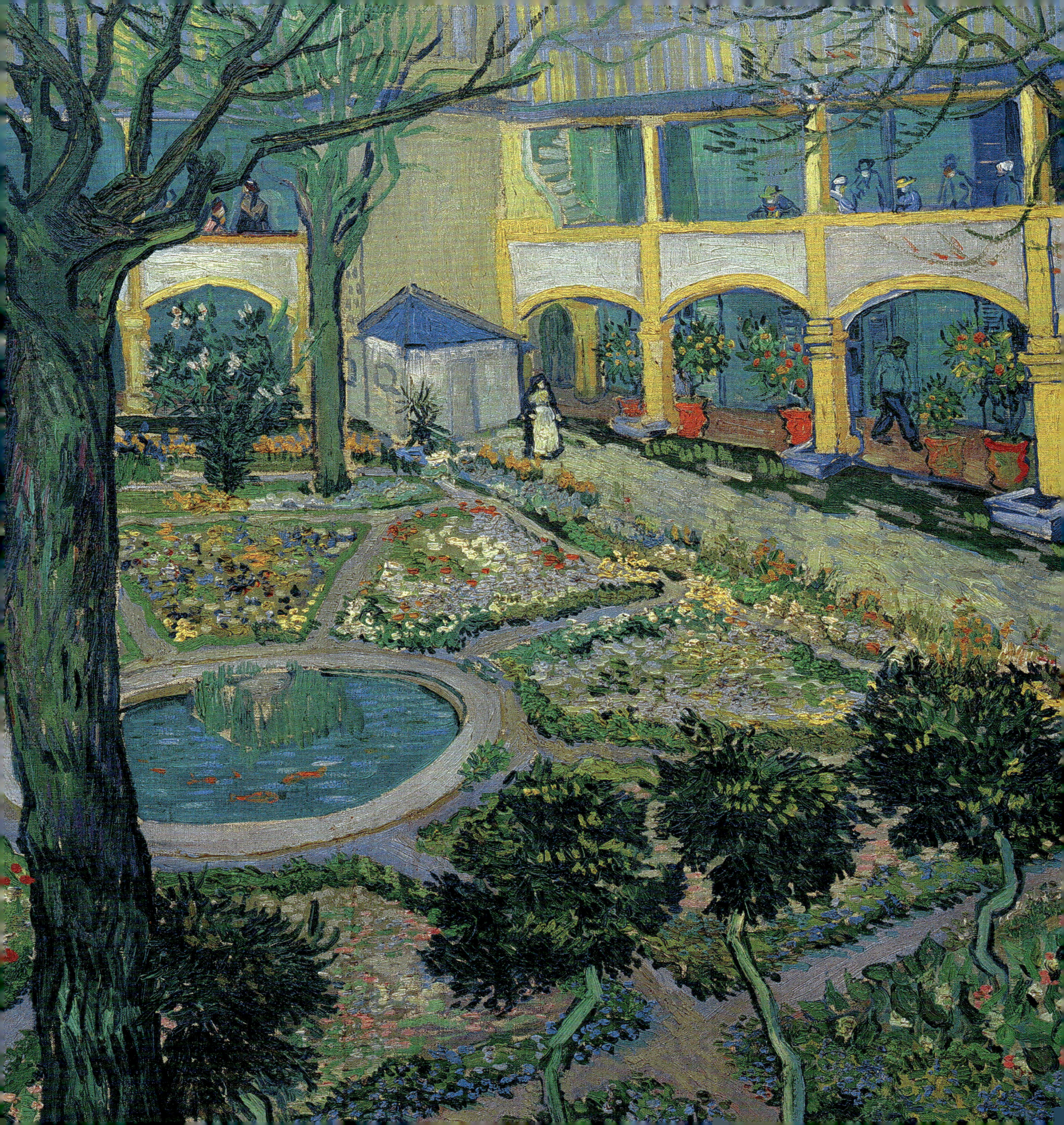

24

HENRI DE TOULOUSE-LAUTREC
(1864–1901)
The Clown Cha-U-Kao, 1895

Oil on canvas, 75 × 55 cm
Inv. 1922.12
The Swiss Confederation, Federal Office of Culture,
Oskar Reinhart Collection 'Am Römerholz',
Winterthur

Provenance Acquired by Oskar Reinhart from the
Galerie Bernheim-Jeune, Paris, 1922

Of all the entertainers Toulouse-Lautrec depicted over the course of his career,
Cha-U-Kao remains the most enigmatic. Neither her real name nor her life dates
have yet been discovered, and only two photographs of her, taken by the artist's
friend Maurice Guibert in 1884, are known (fig. 45). Her Japanese-sounding stage
name is in fact a phonetically spelled portmanteau of *chahut* (the riotous dance,
a forerunner of the cancan, popularised at venues such as the Moulin Rouge)
and *chaos*. Contrary to what the name indicates, however, she was not a dancer;
instead, this former gymnast entered the classically male profession of clowning,
the singularity of which is suggested by the inelegant solution both French and
English arrived at for describing her role: clowness(e). Her name suggests that,
rather than dancing, she might have parodied the *chahut* in the comic tableaux
that were another staple of the Moulin Rouge's offering.

Clad in her trademark costume of greenish-black knickerbockers and
stockings topped with an enormous, flamboyantly flounced yellow ruff, her
hair (or, more likely, a wig) elaborately braided and pulled into a towering
topknot with a matching yellow ribbon, Cha-U-Kao appears to pause as she
crosses the floor of the Moulin Rouge, her gaze captured by something or
someone beyond the picture frame. Her arm is hooked through that of her
partner Gabrielle, a retired dancer, seen in profile. In the background at right,
apparently oblivious to the two women, are two other habitués of the Moulin
Rouge: Toulouse-Lautrec's friend, the writer and editor Tristan Bernard
(1866–1947), in a reddish-brown suit with his bowler hat tilted down over his
forehead, and the Irish singer May Belfort (née Egan, c. 1872–1929), in her
typical stage attire, an outsize Kate Greenaway-style dress and frilly mob cap.

Her legs planted wide apart and her hand thrust into her hip pocket in
a pose that deliberately flouts the conventions of femininity, Cha-U-Kao's

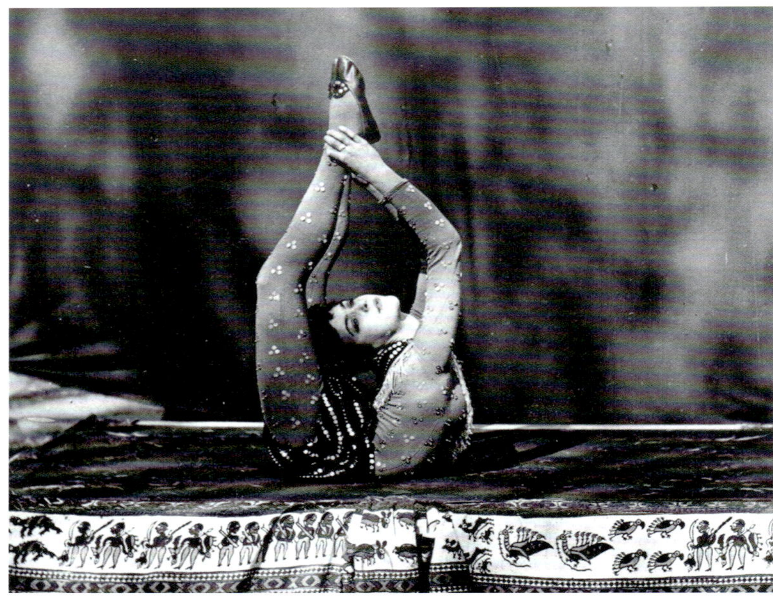

45. Maurice Guibert, photograph of Cha-
U-Kao as a gymnast, 1884, dimensions
and whereabouts unknown

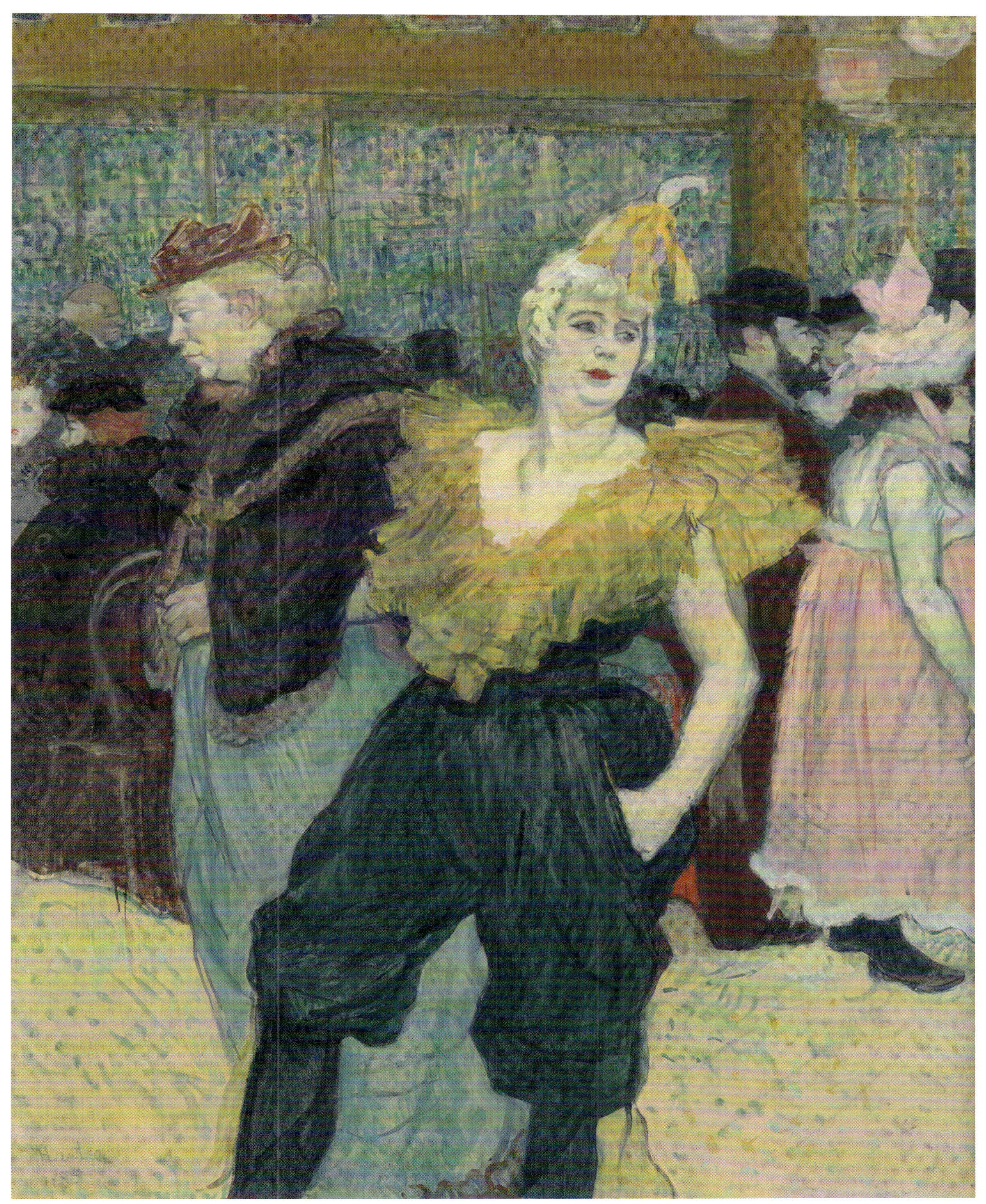

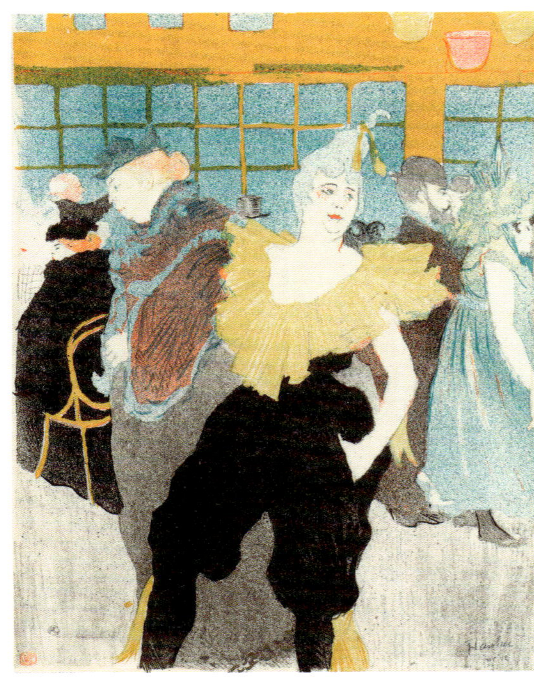

46. Henri de Toulouse-Lautrec, *The Clowness in the Moulin Rouge*, 1897, colour lithograph, 41.1 × 32.3 cm. The Art Institute of Chicago

expression eludes interpretation – it can read as ironic and disillusioned as easily as it can as wistful and distant. The strong diagonals of her pose and that of Gabrielle, as they pivot apart from each other like the hands of a clock, disturb the otherwise regular rhythm of the composition created by the windowpanes and pillar in the background and the verticals of the seated and standing figures, infusing the scene with an unsettling energy – a compositional trope that reflects Toulouse-Lautrec's admiration and close study of Japanese prints. At the same time, skilfully placed touches of colour – notably, the red of Cha-U-Kao's rouged lips – pull together apparently disparate elements of the composition. Gotthard Jedlicka identified this dab of red as 'the perspectival vanishing point of the colour scheme … from them the face is worked back into space'.[78]

Toulouse-Lautrec's unorthodox painterly technique blurs the distinction between drawing and painting; his early biographer François Gauzi described his works in oil as 'drawings highlighted with colour'.[79] Here, crucially, it serves to reinforce the isolation of the couple at the centre of the crowd. Cha-U-Kao herself is rendered in thick, bold, solid strokes of colour that completely cover the canvas, while the other figures – in particular, Gabrielle and May Belfort – are painted in thin, rapidly applied streaks of more diluted paint, allowing the canvas and elements of the underpainting to show through and rendering them strangely insubstantial. The irregular, flickering brushwork used for the floor and the view from the windows (presumably of an artificially illuminated nighttime street) further contribute to this air of unreality. Toulouse-Lautrec would take this a step further in the lithograph *The Clowness in the Moulin Rouge* he made two years later based on the painting, a near-direct translation of the composition that renders the clowness herself as spectral as the other figures, an overexposed ghost in a black-and-yellow costume that seems more tangible than her body (fig. 46).[80]

Although Cha-U-Kao is not the entertainer Toulouse-Lautrec depicted most frequently – that honour belongs indisputably to Jane Avril (1868–1943), who appears in the background at far left in the present painting and in a painting that belonged to Samuel Courtauld, today in the Courtauld Gallery – it is notable that, as he did with Avril, the artist represented Cha-U-Kao both at her place of work (although, interestingly, seldom while performing)[81] and off-duty, as a private individual. Her first appearance in his oeuvre, in fact, is in the 1892 painting *At the Moulin Rouge: Two Women Waltzing* (fig. 47), which depicts her in everyday dress dancing with another woman. Cha-U-Kao was one of a number of queer women who populate Toulouse-Lautrec's work, during a period in which their visibility was on the rise in Paris. Nowhere was this more noticeable than in Montmartre's bars, restaurants, nightclubs and cafés, where they might be workers, customers or, in the case of Le Rat Mort, La Souris and Le Hanneton, owners. Although some of Toulouse-Lautrec's images stress the louche atmosphere of these venues, his depictions of the women who frequented them are distinguished by their empathy and humanity, particularly remarkable in light of the leering disapproval that characterised attitudes in the popular press (the 1899 *Guide des Plaisirs à Paris* invited its readers to visit Le Hanneton 'to see a pathological curiosity').[82] Instead, Toulouse-Lautrec

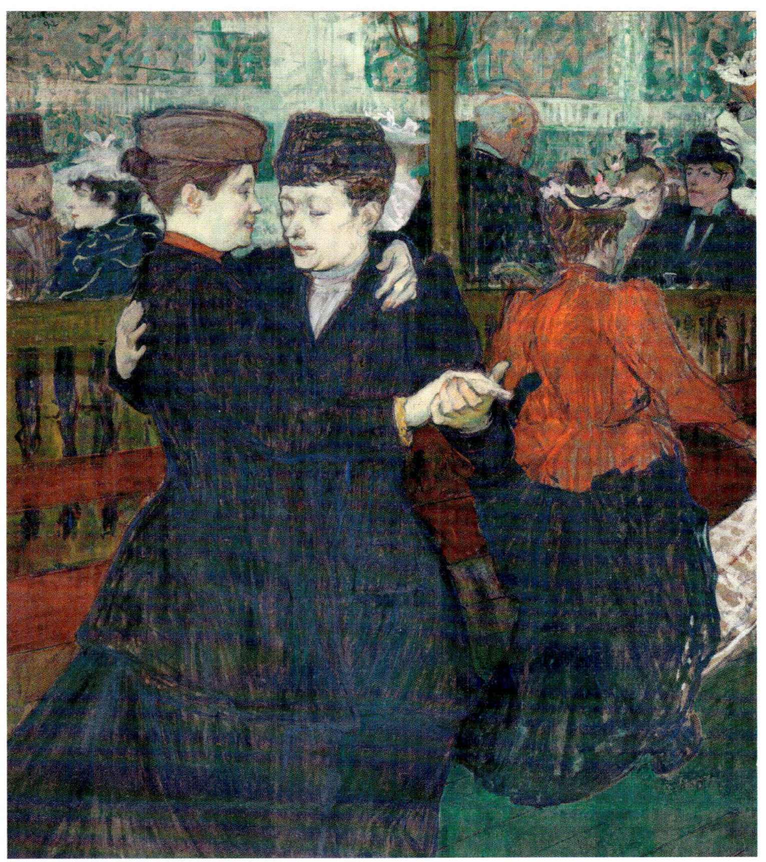

47. Henri de Toulouse-Lautrec, *At the Moulin Rouge: Two Women Waltzing*, 1892, oil tempera on cardboard, 93 × 80 cm. Národní Galerie, Prague

presents Cha-U-Kao as a woman of depth and complexity, and his matter-of-fact treatment of her relationships with her partners stands in stark contrast to most contemporaneous depictions of lesbians by male artists, whose primary aim was to titillate a male audience.

Although Toulouse-Lautrec's name is indelibly associated with the Moulin Rouge, his period of engagement with the nightclub and its denizens was relatively brief and this painting is one of the last he would devote to it. His confidence in the work's quality was soon validated by its purchase early in 1896 by none other than the former King of Serbia, Milan Obrenović (1854–1901), then living in exile in Paris; as he jokingly boasted to his grandmother (with some geographical confusion), 'I could have my cards printed with the words: Painter to the Court of Sofia'.[83] However, the canvas was back in the possession of the artist's dealer Bernheim-Jeune before long, from whom Reinhart acquired it in 1922. Reinhart also later acquired two drawings by Toulouse-Lautrec; moreover, the presence of several paintings, prints and drawings by the artist in the Kunst Museum Winterthur attests to his popularity with Winterthur collectors in the early decades of the twentieth century.[84] **RS**

PABLO PICASSO (1881–1973)

Portrait of Mateu Fernández de Soto, 1901

Oil on canvas, 61.3 × 46.5 cm
Inv. 1935.6
The Swiss Confederation, Federal Office of Culture,
Oskar Reinhart Collection 'Am Römerholz',
Winterthur

Provenance Acquired by Oskar Reinhart from the
gallery Hermann Abels, Cologne, 1935

In May 1901, the nineteen-year-old Pablo Picasso travelled from Barcelona to Paris to prepare for his first exhibition in the city. With not enough work to fill his show, due to open on 25 June at Ambroise Vollard's gallery, Picasso worked fast, painting several canvases in a single day. The bright, energetically painted works he produced were an outpouring of his distinctive version of modern French art, indebted to artists including Henri de Toulouse-Lautrec (1864–1901) and Vincent van Gogh (1853–1890). The result was an exhibition of no less than 64 paintings and many works on paper, which effectively launched Picasso's career in Paris.[85] Several critics recognised that a significant new figure of considerable talent was taking to the stage of modern painting.

Those who saw Picasso's bright, exuberant work in the summer of 1901 would not have imagined the present painting could have been made by the same artist just a few months later. In hues of blue and grey, Picasso evokes an atmosphere of contemplation and introspection in this painting of his friend, the sculptor Mateu Fernández de Soto (1881–1939), gently carving a small object. They had first met in Barcelona in 1899 at the café Els Quatre Gats, a haunt of Bohemian artists and writers. De Soto came to Paris most probably in October 1901 with no money or place to stay, and Picasso let him sleep on the floor of the studio he was renting in Montmartre. Around the same time, another of Picasso's Spanish friends arrived, the poet Jaime Sabartès (1881–1968), whose portrait he also painted in tones of blue (1901; Pushkin State Museum of Fine Arts, Moscow).

Their time together in Paris coincided with Picasso rethinking the character of his art in the aftermath of his exhibition. He became preoccupied with a recent tragedy; the suicide of another close Spanish friend, Carlos Casagemas, in a Paris café earlier that year. Prompted by this and a desire to make art that was more profound than his recent paintings, Picasso began producing works in a sombre palette, with blue becoming dominant. He simplified and outlined his forms, inspired by Van Gogh and Gauguin (1848–1903). His portraits of Sabartès and de Soto, each probably made in October or November 1901, mark the very beginning of what became known as Picasso's 'blue period' – the first of many stylistic periods coined to describe his mercurial artistic practice.

Portrait of Mateu Fernández de Soto was painted in Picasso's Montmartre studio at 130*ter* Boulevard de Clichy. It was, hauntingly enough, the same studio that Casagemas had previously occupied. Pinned to the wall behind de Soto is a version of Picasso's imagined depictions of Casagemas's burial, his prostrate body shrouded in white and attended by mourners. The work on the wall is close to Picasso's two known paintings of Casagemas's burial, *Evocation* (1901; Musée d'Art Moderne de la Ville de Paris) and *The Death of Casagemas* (1901; private collection). The inclusion of the departed Casagemas deepens the mood and resonance of the present work as a friendship portrait. As a depiction of an artist at work, the painting's mournful theme also underscores Picasso's renewed preoccupation with the idea of artistic creativity and melancholy being closely entwined. As he changed artistic direction in the autumn of 1901, Picasso often reused his canvases, painting over his earlier, more colourful compositions. The greens and reds seen, inexplicably, between de Soto's slender figures, might suggest this portrait supplanted a painting Picasso was keen to move beyond. **BW**

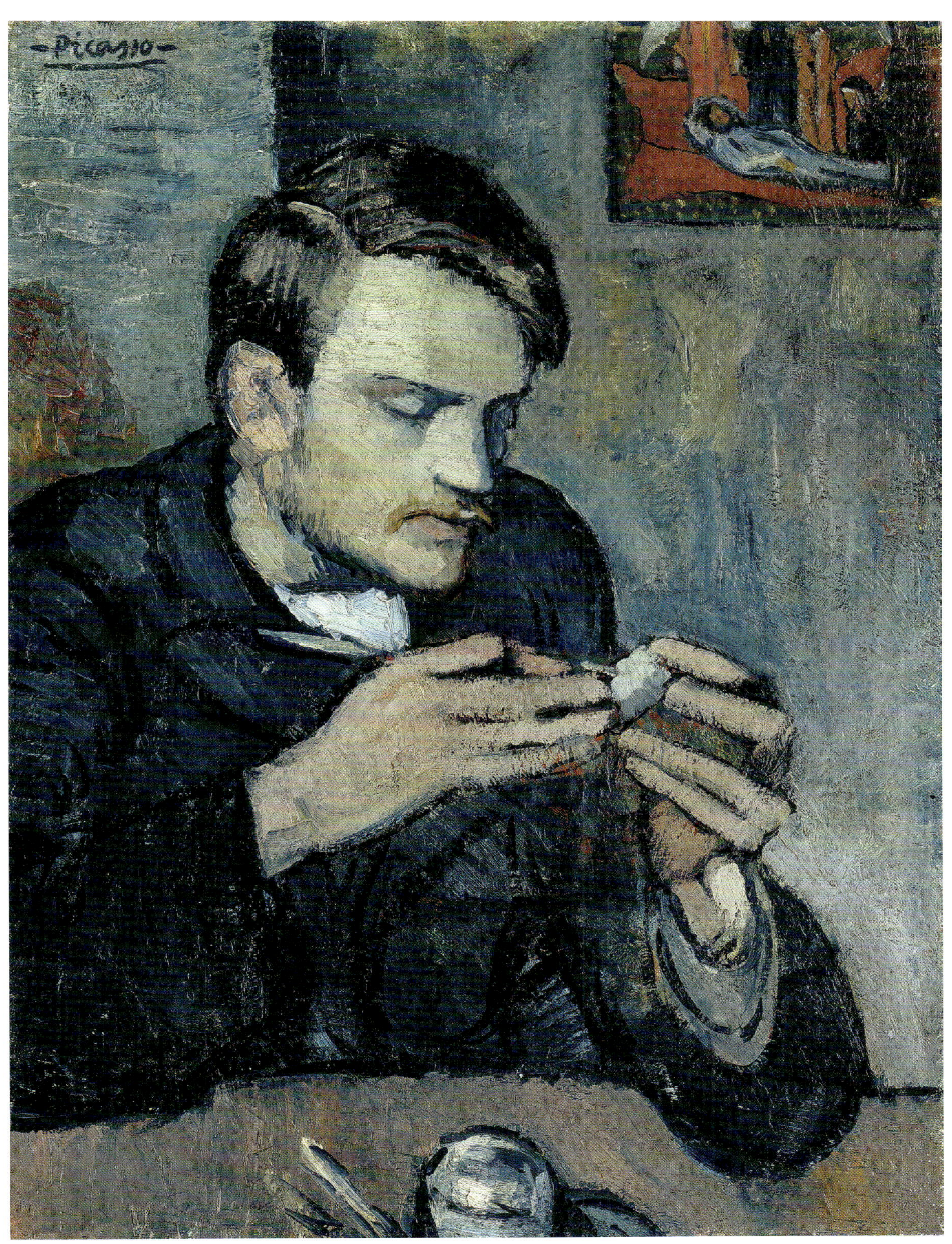

Notes

1   For the full series see Jordan and Cherry in exh. cat. London 1995, pp. 175–202.

2   See De la Mano 2018, p. 111.

3   Charles Sterling defined Goya as 'the first painter of modern anxiety' (1952, pp. 87–88).

4   Jordan and Cherry in exh. cat. London 1995, p. 177.

5   Reinhart's passion for Goya's works is attested by the fact that at the time he already owned two portraits then believed to be by the artist, and later purchased five canvases that were attributed to Goya but are no longer considered to be by him. See Juliet Wilson-Bareau in Reinhard-Felice 2005, cat. nos. 15–19.

6   Respectively Museum of Fine Arts, Springfield, Massachusetts; Museum of Fine Arts, Ghent; Musée du Louvre, Paris; and Musée des Beaux-Arts, Lyon.

7   Viardot 1864, pp. 4–5.

8   See exh. cat. Lyon 2006, pp. 194–95.

9   For a recent summary, see Jubinville 2016, pp. 62–64.; and Wat and Chenique, in exh. cat. Lyon 2006, pp. 37, 194–95.

10 I am grateful to Thierry Herselin for the identification.

11 On Corot's use of costume, particularly Italian-inspired costume such as that worn by the model in the present picture, see Kerstin Richter, 'Vom Reiz des Kostüms. Corot und die italienische Tracht', in exh. cat. Winterthur 2011, pp. 71–82.

12 Paul Foucher, 'L'exposition de Daumier', *Le National*, 19 April 1878, p. 3, quoted and translated in Melot 1988, p. 10. Melot notes that the exhibition provoked comparisons to other artists, including Rubens, Rembrandt and Goya.

13 Daumier is known to have submitted a painting of Don Quixote and Sancho Panza to the Salon of 1850–51. The work was identified by Maison, author of the 1967 catalogue raisonné, as the picture in the Artizon Museum, Chuo, Kyobashi, but this is contested by Bruce Laughton (1996, p. 186, ftn. 15).

14 According to Fragonard's grandson; see Reinhard-Felice 2005, p. 258.

15 These are illustrated in Reinhard-Felice 2005, cat. nos. 47–49. It is possible that Daumier encountered Fragonard's Don Quixote drawings in the original or via engravings by Dominique-Vivant Denon, see Sonnabend 1992, p. 237. It is also notable that paintings depicting scenes from the novel were exhibited at the Salon with some frequency, including in 1849, 1850, 1852, 1857, 1859 and 1867; see exh. cat. Ottawa 1999, p. 516.

16 Sonnabend 1992, p. 238.

17 Maison 1967, p. 165.

18 Ottawa 1999, p. 518. Sonnabend (1992, p. 237) suggests that Daumier's interest in the story lies in part in an association between the knight's idealistic questing and his own pursuit of a 'serious' art beyond his career as a cartoonist.

19 Pothey 1867, unpaginated.

20 An important, yet very different example from later in Courbet's career is *La Source* (1868; Paris, Musée d'Orsay), in which the nymph of the spring is very clearly a modern woman, her pinched waist and broad buttocks shaped by years of wearing a corset.

21 See Courthion 1948–50, vol. 1, p. 78.

22 Reinhard-Felice 2005, p. 422.

23 One of these (*Hunter with Slain Boar*) was found to have a forged signature and is no longer considered an autograph work. In addition to the present work and *The Hammock* (cat. 5), the Courbet paintings acquired by Reinhart include landscapes, figure and genre paintings, a portrait and a still life.

24 Travel diary, 18 June 1938, and invoice from Paul Rosenberg to Oskar Reinhart, 2 July 1938, quoted in Reinhard-Felice 2005, p. 78.

25 Doran 2001, p. 144

26 Marguerite de Conflans sat for Manet for a fifth time in 1876; the resulting portrait is now in the Musée des Augustins, Toulouse.

27 This collective title refers to three paintings of women dressed in white in interiors that Whistler made between 1861–67. Closely associated with the 'art for art's sake' approach of the Aesthetic movement, these works show Whistler experimenting with colour and exploring the correspondences between music and painting.

28 La Touche 1884, p. 2.

29 For a putative reconstruction of the original canvas and a technical examination of its divisions by Malcolm Park, see exh. cat. Winterthur 2005, pp. 69–85.

30 Andrée also modelled for Pierre-Auguste Renoir, as the girl drinking from a glass in *The Luncheon of the Boating Party* (1880–81; Phillips Collection, Washington, D.C.), and for Edgar Degas, as the woman in *In a Café*, also known as *L'Absinthe* (1875–76; Musée d'Orsay, Paris).

31 A woman drinking spirits, as the figures modelled by Andrée in *L'Absinthe* and *Plum Brandy* do, would likely have been read by a contemporary audience as a morally dubious figure, if not potentially a demimondaine.

32 Juliet Wilson-Bareau in Reinhard-Felice 2005, p. 482. According to a notice in *Le Figaro*, the Hanlon-Lees' show began on 24 May, but the *dépôt legal* (copyright) for Chéret's poster was only registered on the 28th.

33 Quoted in Juliet Wilson-Bareau's entry on the present painting in Reinhard-Felice 2005, cat. 138; the whereabouts of the letter are currently unknown.

34 Chasrel 1879, p. 234.

35 See Rewald, Feilchenfeldt and Warmann 1996, vol. I, p. 354.

36 Ambroise Vollard described it in his inventory (I, April 1899–1904, no. 3694) thus: 'in the midst of some trees with almost bare branches some yellow and red houses'; quoted in Reinhard-Felice 2005, p. 498.

37 The term comes from Reff 1962.

38 Letter from Cezanne to Joachim Gasquet, 26 September 1897, in Rewald 1978, p. 26: 'Art is a harmony parallel to nature'.

39 House 2008, p. 35.

40 Letter from Oskar Reinhart to Alfred Gold, 10 December 1921, quoted in Reinhard-Felice 2005, p. 42.

41 Letter from Oskar Reinhart to Georg Reinhart, 26 April 1923, quoted in Reinhard-Felice 2005, p. 47.

42 The quotation is translated in Shiff 2011, p. 76.

43 Louis Le Bail, quoted in Rewald 1948, pp. 201–02.

44 Roger Fry (1952, p. 53) wrote 'not only do the still-lifes give us the clearest insight into his methods of interpreting form, they also help us to grasp those principles of

composition which are characteristic of his work'. More recently, Benedict Leca (in exh. cat. Hamilton 2014, p. 35) has argued that 'the particular attention given by notable artists and collectors to Cezanne's still lifes as works of special significance installed them from very early on as the interpretive touchstones of his production – the revelatory works through which one might arrive at the crux of his enterprise'.

45 'Cézanne', in the *Hannoverscher Kurier: Hannoversches Tageblatt; Morgenzeitung für Niedersachsen*, 14 May 1912, p. 1.

46 'Empfindung und Leidenschaft', in the *Dortmunder Zeitung*, 17 December 1912, p. 2.

47 Reinhard-Felice 2005, p. 42.

48 Ibid., p. 65.

49 The other two versions are at the National Gallery, London; and the Barnes Foundation, Philadelphia. The latter is the closest to the present watercolour, with the exception of the figure at far left.

50 The watercolour's watermark *CHALLET* is very likely a truncation of 'Michallet', a brand of paper Cezanne used throughout his working life. I am grateful to Fabienne Ruppen for this information.

51 The letter is dated 15 April 1904 (inv. MS.1932.SC.1.1); its translation comes from Danchev 2013, p. 334.

52 Vollard 1914, p. 154.

53 Bernard 1904, p. 23.

54 See MaryAnne Stevens in exh. cat. London 1992, p. 100. John House (2004, p. 223, ftn. 25) notes that 'The acceptance of these two paintings [of the Canal Saint-Martin] is the only clear instance when smaller paintings of this type were exhibited at the Salon of 1870 by a member of the Impressionist circle'.

55 Quoted in Goldwater and Treves 1947, p. 309.

56 For Richard Shone (1979, p. 11), such variety of handling 'is as much a direct result of the immediate necessity of feeling, as of conscious surface considerations'.

57 Barr 1966, p. 38.

58 The dates included in Monet's signatures are not always accurate, however, and he sometimes added them at the date of sale, rather than at the date of completion. He sold this painting to Paul Durand-Ruel in February 1881, raising the possibility that it might have been completed earlier – at some point in 1880.

59 See letter from Paul Cassirer to Reinhart, 6 December 1930, and Reinhart, Notebook 51, vol. 3, p. 163, September 1952, quoted in Reinhard-Felice 2005, p. 62.

60 See Petra ten-Doesschate Chu's catalogue entry on Courbet's *Still Life with Flowers* in Reinhard-Felice 2005, p. 418.

61 It is unclear whether the Hamburg version is a study for, or simply a variant of, the Reinhart picture; the handling of the former is slightly sketchier and the composition shows only minor variations.

62 It seems probable that this is the painting Monet sent to the twentieth Exposition municipale des Beaux-Arts at the museum in Rouen in 1864; see Reinhard-Felice 2005, p. 428. Its first owner was the artist's elder brother, Léon Pascal Monet, but it is not clear whether this was a purchase or a gift, or when he acquired it.

63 I am grateful to Leslie Coleman of the New York Botanical Garden for her assistance with the identification of the primula obconica.

64 Exh. cat. Edinburgh 2010, p. 25.

65 Rivière 1921, p. 81.

66 On Degas's interest for the millinery trade, see exh. cat. Saint Louis and San Francisco 2017.

67 Chocquet also sat to Cezanne for no less than three portraits during the same period (1875–77); interestingly, in two of them he adopts a very similar pose to that of the portrait by Renoir now at Harvard. See exh. cat. Winterthur 2015, pp. 151–58.

68 André 1923, p. 7.

69 Leroy 1876, pp. 3, 6–7; Bertall, 'Exposition des impressionalistes, rue Peletier', in *Paris-Journal*, 15 April 1876, pp. 1–2; idem in *Le Soir*, 15 April 1876, p. 3.

70 '*La salle des fièvreux*'; letter 812, Vincent to Willemien van Gogh, Saint-Rémy-de-Provence, c. 21 October 1889 and letter 815, Vincent to Theo van Gogh, Saint-Rémy-de-Provence, c. 25 October 1889: see Jansen, Luijten and Bakker 2009 (full transcriptions and English translations of the letters can also be found online at www.vangoghletters.org, a collaboration between the Van Gogh Museum, Amsterdam, and the Huygens Institute, Royal Netherlands Academy of Arts and Sciences, The Hague).

71 Letter 764, Vincent to Willemien van Gogh, Arles, c. 28 April–2 May 1889.

72 Letter 812, Vincent to Willemien van Gogh, Saint-Rémy-de-Provence, c. 21 October 1889: 'At the moment, I am working on a hospital room. In the foreground a large black stove around which [are] a few grey or black shapes of patients, then behind the very long room tiled in red with two rows of white beds, the white walls (*murailles*) but in a lilac or green white and the windows with pink curtains, with green curtains and in the back two figures of nuns in black and white. The ceiling is purple with wide beams.'

73 Letter 732, Vincent to Theo van Gogh, Arles, 7 January 1889.

74 Letter 764, Vincent to Willemien van Gogh, Arles, c. 28 April–2 May 1889.

75 Ibid.: 'And then as a pendant, the inner courtyard'.

76 Christina Frehner, 'The Courtyard of the Hospital at Arles', in Reinhard-Felice 2005, p. 536.

77 See '350. Garden of the hospital', in Vellekoop and Zwikker 2007, pp. 176–81.

78 Jedlicka 1943, pp. 251–55.

79 Gauzi 1992, p. 26.

80 Delteil 1920, no. 205.

81 A notable exception is an illustration he made for *Le Rire*, *The Entrance of Cha-U-Kao* (1896), which depicts her entering the Moulin Rouge astride a donkey.

82 *Guide des Plaisirs à Paris* 1899, p. 116.

83 Toulouse-Lautrec to his grandmother Mme Gabrielle de Toulouse-Lautrec, January 1896, quoted in Reinhard-Felice 2005, p. 542. The artist evidently confused Serbia with Bulgaria (whose capital is Sofia).

84 Reinhart chose to give the two drawings (*Conversation* and *Study of a Woman*) to the Kunst Museum Winterthur rather than retain them at 'Am Römerholz'; the paintings in the museum's collection were previously owned by the local collectors Arthur and Hedy Hahnloser, and her cousin Richard Bühler.

85 See Wright 2013.

Bibliography

*Paul Cezanne's name appears with an accent,
as Cézanne, when this was used in quotes across
the text or in a publication title.*

LITERATURE

André 1923
Albert André, *Renoir*, Paris: Cres, 1923

Barr 1966
Alfred Barr, *Matisse: His Art and his Public*,
New York: Arno Press, 1966

Bernard 1904
Émile Bernard, 'Paul Cézanne', *L'Occident*,
July 1904, pp. 17–30

Chasrel 1879
T. Chasrel, 'Le Salon d'Anvers', *L'Art*,
vol. XVIII, 7 September 1879, pp. 233–34

Cooper 1954
Douglas Cooper, *The Courtauld Collection:
A Catalogue and Introduction*, London: Athlone
Press for the University of London, 1954

Courthion 1948–50
Pierre Courthion, *Courbet raconté par lui-même et
par ses amis. Sa vie et ses œuvres*, 2 vols., Geneva:
Cailler, 1948–50

Danchev 2013
The Letters of Paul Cézanne, ed. and trans.
Alex Danchev, Los Angeles: The J. Paul Getty
Museum, 2013

Dauberville 1968
Jean Dauberville and Henry Dauberville,
*Bonnard. Catalogue raisonné de l'œuvre peint,
1906–1919*, vol. II, Paris: Bernheim-Jeune & Cie,
1968

De la Mano 2018
José Manuel de la Mano, 'Tradition et
modernité. La nature morte au siècle de Goya',
in *La Nature morte espagnole*, ed. Angel Aterido,
Brussels: Bozar Books, 2018, pp. 100–14

Delteil 1920
Loys Delteil, *Le peintre graveur illustré. Henri de
Toulouse Lautrec*, Paris: Delteil, 1920

Doran 2001
Michael Doran, ed., *Conversations with Cezanne*,
trans. Julie Lawrence Cochran, Berkeley and
London: University of California Press, 2001

Feilchenfeldt, Nash and Warmann
Walter Feilchenfeldt, David Nash and Jayne
Warmann, eds., *The Paintings, Watercolors and
Drawings of Paul Cezanne: An Online Catalogue
Raisonné*, https://www.cezannecatalogue.com/
(accessed 4 December 2024)

Fonsmark 2011
Anne-Birgitte Fonsmark, ed., *Fransk Kunst på
Ordrupgaard, Raesonneret katalog over samlingen
af malerier, skulpturer, pasteller, tegninger og
grafik*, Copenhagen: Hatje Cantz, 2011

Fry 1952
Roger Fry, *Cézanne: A Study of His Development*,
London: Hogarth Press, 1952

Gauzi 1992
François Gauzi, *Lautrec, mon ami*, Paris:
Bibliothèque des arts, 1992

Goldwater and Treves 1947
Robert Goldwater and Marco Treves, *Artists on
Art from the XIV to the XX Century*, London: Paul
Kegan, 1947

Hahnloser-Ingold 2011
Margrit Hahnloser-Ingold, ed., *The Arthur
and Hedy Hahnloser Collection: An Eye for Art
Shared with Artists*, Lausanne: Distributed Art
Publishers, 2011

House 2004
John House, *Impressionism: Paint and Politics*,
London and New Haven: Yale University Press,
2004

House 2008
John House, 'Cezanne's Project: The *Harmony
Parallel to Nature*', in *The Courtauld Cézannes*,
exh. cat. ed. Stephanie Buck, John House, Ernst
Vegelin van Claerbergen and Barnaby Wright,
The Courtauld Gallery, London, 2008, pp. 27–47

Jansen, Luijten and Bakker 2009
Leo Jansen, Hans Luijten and Nienke
Bakker, eds., *Vincent van Gogh: The Letters.
The Complete Illustrated and Annotated
Edition*, Amsterdam, The Hague and Brussels:
Thames & Hudson, in association with the Van
Gogh Museum and the Huygens Institute, 2009

Jedlicka 1943
Gotthard Jedlicka, *Henri de Toulouse-Lautrec*,
Zurich: Eugen Rentsch, Erlenbach-Zürich, 1943

Jubinville 2016
Ginette Jubinville, 'Pour en finir avec les
Monomanes de Géricault: Considérons leur
rôle dans la construction du mythe de l'artiste',
Canadian Art Review, vol. XLI, no. 1, 2016,
pp. 62–75

Krahmer 1996
Catherine Krahmer, 'Tschudi und Meier-Graefe:
der Museumsmann und der Kunstschriftsteller',
in *Manet bis van Gogh: Hugo von Tschudi und der
Kampf um die Moderne*, ed. Peter-Klaus Schuster
and Johann Georg von Hohenzollern, Munich:
Prestel, 1996, pp. 371–76

La Touche 1884
Gaston La Touche, 'Édouard Manet. Souvenirs
intimes', *Le Journal des arts*, 15 January 1884, p. 2

Laughton 1996
Bruce Laughton, *Honoré Daumier*, New Haven
and London: Yale University Press, 1996

Leroy 1876
Louis Leroy, 'Choses et autres', *Le Journal
amusant*, 15 April 1876, pp. 3–7

Maison 1968
Karl Eric Maison, *Honoré Daumier: Catalogue
Raisonné of the Paintings Watercolours and
Drawings. The Paintings*, vol. I, London: Thames
and Hudson, 1968

Melot 1988
Michel Melot, 'Daumier and Art History:
Aesthetic Judgement/Political Judgement',
Oxford Art Journal, vol. XI, no. 1, 1988, pp. 3–24

Pothey 1867
Alexandre Pothey, *L'Album autographique. Peinture, sculpture, architecture: L'Art à Paris en 1867*, Paris: Le Chevalier, 1867

Reff 1962
Theodore Reff, 'Cézanne's Constructive Stroke', *Art Quarterly*, Autumn 1962, pp. 214–27

Reinhard-Felice 2005
Mariantonia Reinhard-Felice, ed., *Oskar Reinhart Collection 'Am Römerholz' Winterthur. Complete Catalogue*, Basel: Schwabe Basel with Paul Holberton, 2005

Reinhard-Felice et al. 2014
Mariantonia Reinhard-Felice et al., eds., *Scripta manent. Schriften zur Sammlung Oskar Reinhart 'Am Römerholz'*, vol. I, Munich: Hirmer, 2014

Reinhard-Felice and Richter 2016
Mariantonia Reinhard-Felice and Kerstin Richter, eds., *Scripta manent. Schriften zur Sammlung Oskar Reinhart 'Am Römerholz'*, vol. II, Munich: Hirmer. 2016

Rewald 1948
John Rewald, *Paul Cézanne: A Biography*, New York 1948

Rewald 1978
Paul Cezanne, *Correspondence*, ed. John Rewald, Paris: Grasset, 1978

Rewald, Feilchenfeldt and Warmann 1996
John Rewald, Walter Feilchenfeldt and Jayne Warmann, *The Paintings of Paul Cézanne: A Catalogue Raisonné*, 2 vols., New York: Harry N. Abrams, 1996

Rivière 1921
Georges Rivière, *Renoir et ses amis*, Paris: H. Floury, 1921

Shiff 2011
Richard Shiff, 'He Painted', in *Cézanne's Card Players*, exh. cat. ed. Nancy Ireson and Barnaby Wright, The Courtauld Gallery, London, 2011, pp. 73–91

Shone 1979
Shone, *Alfred Sisley*, London: Phaidon, 1979

Sonnabend 1992
Martin Sonnabend, 'Don Quixote and Sancho Panza', in *Daumier's Drawings*, exh. cat., The Metropolitan Museum of Art, New York, 1992, pp. 237–51

Sterling 1952
Charles Sterling, *Nature morte de l'Antiquité à nos jours*, Paris: Musées nationaux, 1952

Vellekoop and Zwikker 2007
Marije Vellekoop and Roelie Zwikker, *Vincent van Gogh Drawings. Vol. IV, Part 1: Arles, Saint-Rémy & Auvers-sur-Oise 1888–1890 (Van Gogh Museum)*, Amsterdam, London and Zwolle: Van Gogh Museum, Lund Humphries Publishers, 2007

Viardot 1864
Louis Viardot, 'Cinq études d'aliénés', *La Chronique des arts et de la curiosité: Supplement à la Gazette des beaux-arts*, 1864, pp. 4–5

Volkart 1990
Hans R. Volkart, 'Die Gründer und ihre Nachfolger', in *Volkart. Die Geschichte einer Welthandelsfirma*, ed. Walter H. Rambousek, Armin Vogt and Hans R. Volkart, Frankfurt: Insel, 1990, pp. 39–61

Vollard 1914
Ambroise Vollard, *Paul Cézanne*, Paris: Galerie Vollard, 1914

Wright 2013
Barnaby Wright, 'An Introduction', in *Becoming Picasso: Paris 1901*, exh. cat. Barnaby Wright, ed., The Courtauld Gallery, London, 2013, pp. 12–35

EXHIBITIONS

Edinburgh 2010
Impressionist Gardens, ed. Clare A.P. Willsdon, National Galleries of Scotland, Edinburgh, 2010

Hamilton 2014
The World is an Apple: The Still Lifes of Paul Cézanne, ed. Benedict Leca, Art Gallery of Hamilton, Hamilton, Ontario, 2014

London 1992
Alfred Sisley, ed. MaryAnne Stevens, Royal Academy, London, 1992

London 1995
Spanish Still Life from Velázquez to Goya, ed. William B. Jordan and Peter Cherry, National Gallery, London, 1995

Lyon 2006
Géricault, la folie d'un monde, ed. Bruno Chenique and Sylvie Ramond, Musée des Beaux-Arts de Lyon, Lyon, 2006

Ottawa 1999
Daumier, ed. Sharon Gregory, National Gallery of Canada, Ottawa, 1999

Paris 2019
The Courtauld Collection: A Vision for Impressionism, ed. Karen Serres, The Louis Vuitton Foundation, Paris, 2019

Saint Louis and San Francisco 2017
Degas, Impressionism, and the Paris Millinery Trade, ed. Esther Bell and Simon Kelly, Saint Louis Art Museum, Saint Louis, and Fine Arts Museums-Legion of Honor, San Francisco, 2017

Winterthur 2005
Manet trifft Manet. Geteilt, wiedervereint, ed. Juliet Wilson-Bareau and Malcolm Park, Oskar Reinhart Collection 'Am Römerholz', Winterthur, 2005

Winterthur 2011
Corot, L'Armoire secrète. Eine Lesende im Kontext, ed. Mariantonia Reinhard-Felice, Oskar Reinhart Collection 'Am Römerholz', Winterthur, 2011

Winterthur 2015
Victor Chocquet, Freund und Sammler der Impressionisten. Renoir, Cezanne, Monet, Manet, ed. Mariantonia Reinhard-Felice, Oskar Reinhart Collection 'Am Römerholz', Winterthur, 2015

Photographic Credits

All images of artworks in the Oskar Reinhart Collection 'Am Römerholz': The Swiss Confederation, Federal Office of Culture, Oskar Reinhart Collection 'Am Römerholz', Winterthur.

Pablo Picasso (cat. 25) © Succession Picasso/DACS, London 2024

Other credits: Figs. 1, 2, 3, 4, 5, 6, 8, 15, 18, 22, 23, 24 Archive images courtesy of the Oskar Reinhart Collection 'Am Römerholz', Winterthur; figs. 7, 16, 17 Photo: SIK-ISEA, Zürich, Philipp Hitz; fig. 10 Photo: SIK-ISEA, Zürich, Jean-Pierre Kuhn; fig. 25 Album/Alamy Stock Photo; fig. 27 © Lyon MBA - Photo Alain Basset; fig. 28 Image: Kunsthaus Zürich; figs. 29, 34, 41, 43 Photo © The Courtauld; fig. 30 Flickr CC BY-NC 4.0; fig. 31 © GrandPalaisRmn (Musée d'Orsay) / Michèle Bellot; fig. 32 Flickr CC BY-NC-SA 2.0; fig. 33 BNF; fig. 35 © GrandPalaisRmn (Musée d'Orsay) / Adrien Didierjean; figs. 37, 38 © RMN-Grand Palais (Musée d'Orsay) / Hervé Lewandowski; fig. 39 Image: Cleveland Museum of Art, CC0 1.0; fig. 42 Photo © President and Fellows of Harvard College; fig. 44 Image: Van Gogh Museum, Amsterdam (Vincent van Gogh Foundation); fig. 46 Image: The Art Institute of Chicago (CC0); fig. 47 Image: National Gallery Prague.

Page 2: detail of cat. 11; page 6: detail of cat. 25; page 8: detail of cat. 10; page 10: detail of cat. 17; page 13: detail of cat. 3; page 29: detail of cat. 16; page 32: detail of cat. 24; page 36: detail of cat. 21; page 45: detail of cat. 18; page 49: detail of cat. 7; page 52: detail of cat. 1; page 68: detail of cat. 8; page 104: detail of cat. 22; page 109: detail of cat. 23